LANDMARKS IN GREEK LITERATURE

C. M. BOWRA

LANDMARKS IN GREEK LITERATURE

WEIDENFELD AND NICOLSON

20 NEW BOND STREET LONDON WI

© 1966 by C. M. Bowra
Made and printed in Great Britain by
William Clowes and Sons, Limited, London and Beccles

CONTENTS

v

ILLUSTRATIONS

vii

Acknowledgements

The author and publishers wish to thank the following for supplying photographs for use in this volume: Plates 1–3, 7–9, 13, 14, 16–21, 25, 26, 28, 29, 34, 35, 41–44, 52, Hirmer Fotoarchiv; Plate 4, Antikensammlungen, Munich; Plate 5, National Museum, Copenhagen; Plates 6, 12, 22–24, 32, 50, 51, German Archaeological Institute; Plates 10, 27, 37, 38, Staatliche Museum, Berlin; Plate 11, A.C.L.; Plate 15, Metropolitan Museum of Art, Fletcher Fund, 1932; Plate 30, Museum of Fine Arts, Boston; Plate 31, Metropolitan Museum of Art, Rogers Fund, 1908; Plates 33, 53, 54, British Museum; Plate 36, Archaeological Museum, Florence; Plate 39, Agora Excavations, Athens; Plate 40, Photo Bulloz; Plates 45–48, Ian Graham; Plate 49, Ashmolean Museum, Oxford; Plate 55, NY Carlsberg Glyptotek

I*

PREFACE

A PROPER history of Greek literature would need the co-operation of a band of scholars and run into several large volumes. Such a work does not exist in English, and the present book is in no sense intended to be a substitute for it. As the title indicates, I have chosen to concentrate on certain points in Greek literature and to omit much else. I have said nothing about Isaeus, Timotheus, Corinna, Aratus and others who may have some historical interest, but do not seem to me of primary importance. I have said next to nothing about the pre-Socratic philosophers, or about Middle and New Comedy, not because they are unimportant, but because they call for special treatment of a kind beyond the scope of this book. My greatest regret is my complete omission of the prodigious figure of Aristotle. He has of course a place of highest eminence in the history of thought, but to the history of literature he does not belong, if only because the large mass of his extant works consists not of literary compositions but of notes made for or from his teaching. I have concentrated on the authors who seem really to matter and to call for attention in their own right. I have begun at the earliest date possible, and I have ended with the famous Alexandrians of the third century BC. After this there is indeed much Greek literature, some of it of excellent quality, but it comes from a different world and calls for separate consideration. I have written not for scholars, who will not need my guidance, but for students and lovers of good literature who may find obstacles between themselves and the Greeks. There are no more agreed opinions about Greek than about any other literature, and for what is said here I am responsible. But I do not pretend that I have much original to say, and I am deeply conscious of my debt to the many scholars and critics who have worked in this field and shaped my views for me. I have been much helped by the advice of my colleagues I. M. Crombie, W. G. Forrest, and T. C. W. Stinton, though I would not like to involve them in guilt for my mistakes or to claim their support for my views.

𝕣𝕣𝕣𝕣𝕣𝕣𝕣𝕣𝕣𝕣𝕣𝕣𝕣𝕣𝕣𝕣𝕣𝕣𝕣𝕣𝕣𝕣𝕣𝕣𝕣𝕣𝕣𝕣

I

INTRODUCTION

LITERATURE as a fine art is not an invention of the Greeks. Before they made their first appearance from the north in the Aegean lands which were henceforward to be their own, it was already practised with a conscious distinction in Sumer and Akkad and Egypt, and by the middle of the second millennium BC, when the Greeks were firmly settled and had already begun to show their capacities by absorbing the civilization of Minoan Crete, their Asian neighbours, such as the Hittites of Anatolia and the Semitic people of Ugarit (Ras Shamra) in northern Syria, had their own ripe literatures, from which the Greeks may conceivably have learned, directly or indirectly, some elementary lessons in tales of gods and men, cosmologies and theogonies, prayers and hymns, panegyrics of the living and laments for the dead. They may even have learned that there is such a thing as an art of words, which is different both from common talk and from more specialized discourse. The Greeks did not live in an enchanted isolation from other Mediterranean peoples, and while they conducted military or commercial undertakings in lands outside their own, they may have picked up stories or tricks or techniques, which they could turn profitably to their own purpose. Yet, though Greek literature is unlikely to have burst fully formed and fully armed from the Greek genius, its debts to other peoples are, so far as we can see, few and far less important than the use which it made of them or its own additions to them. What the Greeks took from others, they transformed to match their own visions, to strengthen what was peculiarly their own in taste and outlook. From their first extant verses to the products of expiring Paganism some eleven hundred years later they set on their art of words an unmistakable imprint through their keen and generous notions of what it could and could not do. They gave to it the same respect, attention, and concentration which they gave to their other arts, and in their ardent desire to make the best of it they displayed a bold insight into its possibilities and different ways of realizing them. From the beginning of their known history to the triumph of Christianity, they acted on the belief that words call for every effort to make the most of them, and even when they had lost both their first irresistible impetus and their mature confidence, they still held the art in high honour and clung to it as a living relic of the past which had not lost all power to enchant the ears of men.

Greek literature, in the strict sense of written texts, begins for us, as it began for the classical Greeks, in the second half of the eighth century BC. From this time we have a tiny handful of contemporary documents in short, broken texts, scratched or painted on vases or carved on stone, from places so different as Athens, Ithaca, Perachora on the Gulf of Corinth, and Ischia in the Bay of Naples. Some are concerned with the unfading themes of conviviality such as dancing, wine, friendship, and love; others commemorate the dedication of objects to gods and goddesses. Both kinds are for the most part composed in hexameter verses and are the unconsidered products of what is plainly a thriving art by no means restricted to professional poets. Before these we have nothing, for the simple reason that it was not till the middle of the eighth century that the Greeks had an alphabet which not only, for the first time for some four or five hundred years, enabled them to write words down, but was admirably equipped for this, since it had signs for vowels as well as for consonants and operated not through syllables, like cuneiform, but through single letters. This alphabet, which was an improved version of the Phoenician, assured for literature that permanence which, like all other arts, it demands for its completion. It soon spread over a large part of the Greek world and was used by amateurs to record their thoughts and feelings. These fragments are the scantiest and most casual flotsam and jetsam of what must have been a widespread and highly vigorous art, and they indicate that in this dawn of Greek literature verse had priority over prose. This is natural enough. Prose always serves many useful ends, but the exaltation of it into a fine art comes later when verse begins to reveal its limitations. Yet the Greeks paid to verse a respect which it did not possess on the same scale among the Hittites or Egyptians or Semitic peoples. In concentrating more severely on it they followed that instinct for shapely form which we cannot explain but must recognize as one of their most characteristic qualities.

Even in these casual scraps Greek verse has already a highly polished and complex technique, and its origin is to be found in the existence of something vastly more elaborate and magnificent. More or less contemporary with them, and not wholly divorced from them, are the two long epics, the *Iliad* and the *Odyssey*, which antiquity ascribed to Homer

2

and which may with some assurance be placed in the period between 750 and 700 BC. They have survived, as much of Greek literature has, because, after being committed at an early date to writing, they were through the centuries copied again and again by one scribe after another, and of the innumerable copies once made several hundreds still survive, of which the earliest, a mere fragment, dates from the fourth century BC and the latest from the fifteenth century AD just before the making of manuscripts yielded to printing. To them we owe our knowledge of the Homeric poems, which are for us, as they were for the Greeks of classical times, the first, full expression of the Greek creative spirit. The other early fragments resemble them in language and metre and are by-products of a vigorous, Panhellenic art, of which the *Iliad* and *Odyssey* are mature examples on a large scale. Yet the very character of the hexameter, which provides the metre for all these poems, shows that this poetry is no new invention when it first breaks upon our notice. The metrical unit, upon which so much depends, has been so fashioned to meet every need, so refined and tempered and strengthened, that it cannot be a recent creation or the invention of a single man. Behind the Homeric poems lies a past from which works have not survived because they were, in the absence of any script, not committed to writing, but they indubitably existed and must be reckoned as the first, original, and incalculably formative chapter in the history of Greek literature.

The career of this lost art may with some confidence be traced back to the first great age of Greece when from *c* 1600 to *c* 1200 BC the Greeks, known to later tradition as Achaeans and to modern archaeology as Mycenaeans, ruled Aegean lands as rivals or allies of the neighbouring monarchies in Asia. The visible splendours of their civilization may be seen in the ruins of their Cyclopean fortresses at Mycenae and Tiryns, in their consummate craft in gold-work, ivory, and gems, their lively, painted pots, their frescoed walls, their swords and daggers inlaid with gold and silver and enamel. Though this society was largely organized for war, it cultivated the fine arts and exported its goods to many distant lands. Among its arts poetry surely had a place, if only as a means to praise princes during their lifetime or to commemorate them after their death. The historical Greeks not only looked back to this time as an age of heroes, of men with the blood of gods in their veins, whose achievements could not be rivalled by later generations, but inherited from it tales of noble or fearful doings, which had their roots in history. This age had even its own script and its industrious bureaucrats, who recorded on clay tablets inventories of possessions, titles to land, offerings to the gods, military

operations, and other activities that appeal to officialdom. They used not
an alphabet but a syllabary of some eighty-seven signs for vowels and for
consonants followed by vowels. It was an unusually inefficient system
even by the standards of its time and must have been confined to professional scribes who understood each other's methods almost as a kind of
short-hand. There is, as yet, no sign that the script was used for anything
that might be called literature, and if it was, it would have done its task
abominably. Poetry was not entrusted to writing but performed orally,
as it still is in many half-literate regions of the world, and that is why
nothing of it before Homer survives. Yet it existed, and, when the
Mycenaean script disappeared in the vast cataclysm of the Dorian invasion
c 1200 BC, poetry continued both on the mainland and among the
colonists on the sea-board of Asia Minor, who began to arrive *c* 1100 BC,
bringing with them the art of song which they had learned at home and
treasured all the more because it was a heritage from a tremendous past
now obliterated in destitution and chaos.

This result was due to a living tradition of oral poetry, and such a
tradition is so unfamiliar to us, who are bred on books, that we do not
easily grasp how it works. The art and the technique of poetry are passed
from generation to generation by a strict training in the needs of oral
composition and recitation. The young bard learns from his elders the
main outlines of stories, the names and personalities of characters, the rules
of metre, the appropriate epithets for things and places and people, and,
above all, an enormous mass of formulaic phrases, which are his main
material in composition and his abiding resource to meet almost any need.
Once a phrase has been formed and tested and proved its worth, it com-
mands respect because it is established and comes from the past. It is
expected and even demanded in the appropriate context. Though an oral
tradition must keep up to date in so far as it cannot allow its words or its
themes to become unintelligible, it is concerned with a past that is for
ever receding; and it keeps contact with it by formulaic phrases and passages which embody its habits in war and peace, its arms and armour, its
works of art or craft, its historical or social circumstances. New elements
inevitably break in and are assimilated into an old scheme, but many of
the old elements survive and are more or less understood or credited with
a new meaning when their old is forgotten. Behind Homer lies such a
tradition, which probably goes back for some seven hundred years to
the heyday of Mycenaean Greece. The bards, whose heir he was, treasured
their verbal relics of the heroic past and passed them on, with their own
improvements, to their successors, until Homer learned their craft and

made his own astonishing use of it. Of these bards we know nothing. No name, no legend survives that deserves our credence. Yet it is they who laid the firm foundations of Greek literature. Homer's own school belonged to Ionia and may have come there *c* 1100 BC from the mainland by way of Athens. It cherished ancient memories with all the loving fidelity of colonists living overseas, cut off from the roots of their race and for that reason all the more home-sick for them. But there were other schools, not very different in their methods and sustained by a like descent, outside Ionia. In Boeotia such a school produced Hesiod in a generation not very much later than Homer's; in the middle of the eighth century Eumelus of Corinth told of the past doings of his own people; there may have been similar schools in Crete and Cyprus and elsewhere. In each case the tradition must have worked on the same lines, keeping the past alive through its inherited material and speaking for the present by the new interpretation which it gave to old stories. When Greek literature begins for us, it has already behind it an enormous career which relates the eighth century to the fourteenth by an unbroken succession of bards, each of whom has done something to preserve the living art and to make it relevant to his audience.

Among other bequests which the bards of historical Greece inherited from Mycenaean forebears was the priceless possession of the hexameter. That it was fashioned by them is clear from a number of phrases which betray a Mycenaean origin and are preserved in the Homeric poems. Though often changed to suit new linguistic usage, they are none the less relics of the spacious age which first formed them. If the living tradition had not been equipped from the start with so adaptable a metre, it would hardly have been so strong or so tenacious as it was. Like all Greek metres, the hexameter is based not, as our own are, on accent but on quantity. The balance on which the rhythm of a line depends is determined by the relative positions not of accented and unaccented syllables but of 'long' and 'short'. In accent what counts is the loudness with which a syllable is pronounced; in quantity, the time which it takes to pronounce it. Most modern European poetry is based on accent, but quantity is more likely to have been the original Indo-European practice. It is regular in classical Sanskrit and in Persian, and may elsewhere have preceded accent because accent was formerly less emphatic than now. At first sight the difference between quantity and accent may seem slight or superficial. Accented syllables are often 'long', and unaccented syllables 'short', and, even if they are not really so, they can be manipulated to appear so while in accentual verse quantity may play a subsidiary or accidental part. But such similarities and overlaps prove nothing. Each system is based on quite different assumptions, and, though our own ears, trained to accent, may not always distinguish it from quantity, there is a decisive difference between them. Though rhythm depends on a balance of contrasted syllables, whether accented and unaccented or 'long' and 'short', this balance is obtained by very different means. In accentual versification it is not firm nor always quite obvious, since the accent on a single sound may vary in volume with the whim of the speaker or the requirements of sense, and we cannot always say which syllables are accented and which are not. This gives to accentual verse a freedom of movement which is by no means a disadvantage if skilfully exploited, but may in clumsier hands mean that a line has no very determinate rhythm and lacks structure and balance. On the other hand quantitative verse is based on the assumption that a 'long' syllable takes twice as long to enunciate as a 'short', and this means that the whole system is more regular, firmer, and more disciplined. We always know how it works. Each syllable is taken at its full weight, and both vowels and consonants are reckoned in the whole result. Convention may have a part in settling which syllables are 'long' and which are 'short', while a few others are accepted as doubtful, but once the convention is established, this is an unambiguous system which allows a high degree of exactness in relating one syllable to another and securing between them the balance which is indispensable to any effective rhythm.

The Greek hexameter is based unequivocally on quantity. It consists of six 'feet', each of which is in theory a dactyl, that is a 'long' syllable followed by two 'shorts', but in practice a dactyl can be replaced by a spondee, that is two 'longs', and in the last foot the full dactyl is never used, perhaps to indicate that this is the end of the line. A very faint notion of a hexameter can be gathered from Tennyson's line in which he both attempts to reproduce its movement in English and laments that the result is vastly inferior to the Greek original.

These lame hexameters the strong-wing'd music of Homer!

The Greek line is much more clearly cut than any English approximation to it, and has no wavering syllables or awkward points of transition from one syllable to another. Since the perfection of such a line must have called for much time and trouble, it is possible that the original Mycenaean hexameter was cruder than the Homeric, but in that early age the Greek language enjoyed certain advantages. With its larger number of uncontracted syllables, it had a higher proportion of 'shorts' to 'longs', and this would make composition easier than when 'longs' outnumbered 'shorts'

and contracted syllables hampered an easy flow. We do not know where
the hexameter was invented. There is nothing like it in ancient Semitic or
Hittite verse, both of which move on very different principles and must
come from quite a different origin. It has been thought to be an acquisi-
tion from Minoan Crete, but since we know nothing of that lost language,
we cannot say whether this is so or not. It is perfectly likely to be a Greek
invention, based on the original Indo-European system of quantity and
encouraged by the nature of the Greek language, which is indeed well
suited to it, not because it is easy to compose, which it is not, but because
it suits the genius of Greek by its ability to change its *tempo* and its interior
balance and so to adapt itself to a wide variety of moods. When Tennyson
speaks of the hexameter as 'the stateliest measure ever moulded by the lips
of man', he has in mind not the Greek line but the Roman, and especially
the Virgilian, which is indeed stately but lacks some of the other qualities
of the more versatile Greek, which is at once swift and strong, compact
and sinuous. Its remarkable value as an instrument for poetry is amply
witnessed by its prodigious career from about 1400 BC to the latest, halting
epics of the fifth century AD. Other metres may have had a career equally
long, but very few have kept their ability to adapt themselves to so many
changes in language, thought, and subject without sacrificing something
of their first sprightliness and harmony.

The oral poetry of the dark ages of Greece, before the arrival of the new
alphabet and the emergence of Homer, perished on the air, but it left many
marks on what was to come, and it cannot be dismissed as a mere interlude
between the glories of Mycenae and the dawn of historical Greece. It
fixed, in more than one direction, the path which literature was to take,
and it was responsible for certain predominant characteristics in it. For
instance, a peculiarity of Greek literature throughout its history is a
combination of convention and originality, an ability to remain faithful
to an old form and to adapt it to new purposes. This is abundantly clear in
the epic, which draws its technique and its material from a distant past
and yet sets living, contemporary men and women on its stage; which
keeps ancient themes in their entirety and thinks nothing of mingling
modern themes among them; which centres on 'god-like' kings and
princes but is keenly alive, however incidentally, to many humble folk,
their callings and their destinies. The same attachment to the past and the
same creative use of it may be seen in other parts of Greek literature. Both
tragedy and comedy flourished on primitive conventions which they
inherited from religious rites and which they never thought fit to abandon;
choral song was born of the dance and throve on its religious presupposi-

tions and its wide variety of moods; even history, which found its full scope with Herodotus, kept many allegiances to the ancient art of story-telling as it was practised in the open places of Greek towns and villages; the adroit and subtle dialogue of Plato is not too distantly descended from popular mimes which sometimes discussed matters of scientific or specula-tive interest; the pastoral idylls of Theocritus claim to be new versions of shepherds' songs. Greek literature is not ashamed of betraying its origins at almost every turn and likes to show what rich potentialities lie in the old forms. This saved the Greeks from two dangerous extremes. On the one side, by their respect for the past they did not squander their inventiveness on the pursuit of novelty at all costs. Novelty indeed they sought and found, but within a traditional frame, and not at the cost of breaking it. Even when in the later fifth century they revolutionized the language of choral song in the Dithyramb and tried to make it more luxuriant and ingenious than it could really hope to be, their failure was at least based on past examples, which may have been misunderstood but were at least accepted and established. On the other hand, the Greeks saw that tradition must not be followed too slavishly and should rather be a guide to new work at an agreed level in accord with accepted standards. They knew that it was not enough simply to copy the achievements of the past, that they must always adapt and assimilate them and add something to them and give a new turn to an old tale or a new interpretation of a much-told event. By this they avoided the sterility which has fallen on those peoples who, in admiration for their classics, have stifled their creative gifts and turned themselves into mere imitators, content to say again and again what has been said amply before and may be worth repeating, but not with this degree of conformity and self-suppression.

The quiet adaptation of tradition to new needs accounts for the varied elegance with which the Greeks handled certain techniques of words. The hexameter continued to be used for centuries and was in due course turned from telling of gods and heroes to other, quite unrelated matters such as farming, the nature of being, the vagaries and oddities of religious belief, varieties of good food, oracles of gods, proverbial saws, the habits of fish and snakes and stars, epitaphs and dedications. It might lose some of its limpidity and spacious ease, but it gained in concentration and maintained the old tone by skilfully fashioning phrases which were indeed novel but looked right in their contexts. An even more striking develop-ment is that of choral songs, which began as simple accompaniments to dances. Their words acquired attractive rhythms from the movement of the dance, and in the seventh century Alcman built a firm and varied strophe from metrical units which balance and complete one another by their different rhythms. This art contained almost unlimited possibilities for expansion, and in the fifth century Pindar and the Attic tragedians wrote choral songs which are far more complex both in the nature of the metrical units and in the combination of them into a single metrical plan, but none-the-less conform to the demands of the dance which they accompany and illustrate. In this the Greeks were enormously helped by the quantitative character of their metres, which allowed a variety impossible to the accentual methods of English, French, German, or Russian, but even this was a natural advance from simple beginnings. No matter how elaborate its form became, song remained song and kept the essential character of song, the sprightly or stately movement of words which adds almost a new dimension to their intellectual and emotional impact. Even the elegiac couplet, which lasted as long as the hexameter and is itself derived from it, was at the start a flute-song, and soon established itself as the medium for convivial occasions, when the flute was played, but became normal also in dedications to gods and in epitaphs for the dead. As such it called for an exalted gravity, which it found without difficulty, and continued for centuries to extend the scope of its subjects. The Greeks felt little need to invent new metres or systems of metric, since those which they had were susceptible to many interior mutations of rhythm, and this conservatism impelled them to do something striking in forms which were known to everyone and had to be treated with proper respect.

This combination of conservatism and experiment was closely related to the Greek respect for form. They assumed in all their poetry that words must have a shapely, regular arrangement. Though in choral song this may have been determined by the repeated movements of a dance, this was not the case with the epic, and the explanation seems to lie in the innate desire of the Greeks to impose order on words just as they did on stone or bronze. Once such an ideal was formed, it was likely to last, and the Greeks kept it for centuries. Their notion of such an order was stricter than that of most other peoples. For instance, their rules of metric are far more exact than the parallelism of ancient Semitic poetry or the alliteration of Germanic. Even if they ever thought of using rhyme, and there is no evidence that they did, it would have been superfluous, since a line or a strophe existed in its own melodious strength and needed no such extraneous aid. Even in a single line, such as the hexameter, they observed very strict rules of prosody and placed a caesura, or break, in it. In choral song the metrical correspondence between the several strophes is meticulously precise, and on the few occasions when there are no separate strophes, the shape is kept by the metrical units. This meant that the Greeks did not feel, as some modern peoples have, that a strict form was an encumbrance, to be relaxed or abandoned for a more varied and more instinctive utterance. An established form presented its own difficulties, but they were treated as challenges which a skilful writer was proud to overcome. The result is that Greek poetry has a formal elegance, a discipline which holds the words in check and thereby increases their effectiveness. Nor did this in any way hamper poets from putting their full feelings into verse. On the contrary, it forced them to attend carefully to what they were going to say and to choose their words with discriminating attention. Though in its prehistoric beginnings Greek poetry must have lacked its later balance and control, in its heyday it delighted in making the best of a given form and thereby underlining the difference between poetry and common speech.

Tradition played a special part in the language of Greek poetry. The epic, working through formulas devised to meet the needs of more or less extemporary recitation, possessed a huge repertory of phrases which were hallowed by time and indispensable to all poets before the introduction of writing. The language of the Homeric poems was never spoken by man. It is an artificial creation designed for oral performance, and it draws on many sources and layers of speech. It contains words both new and old, artificial forms made to meet the needs of metre, words drawn from different places and different dialects, words modelled in defiance of philology on old precedents, words of which the original meaning has been forgotten and which are given a new one. Later Greek poetry is not so artificial as this, but artificial it usually is. Even the few lyric poets, Sappho, Alcaeus, and Anacreon, who wrote mainly in their own vernaculars, sometimes admit archaic words, and most poets use a language formed expressly and solely for poetry. The first reason for this is historical. The pioneers of the hexameter had forged for an exacting metre phrases so well fitted to it that it was reckless to cast them aside. That is why they continued to be used long after they had fallen out of common use and attained an obsolete or archaic air. This set a standard which it was natural to follow. What was good enough for the epic was good enough for other kinds of poetry, and poets assumed that, whatever their subject might be, they could not only borrow phrases and words from the epic but imitate to some degree its linguistic methods in spheres which it had not touched, and even when they had no epic precedents in mind, they still sought to give to words a similar distance from common speech. This brought substantial advantages. Since the different districts of Greece were separated from one another by barriers of mountains or sea, they developed from an early date their own dialects. If a poet confined himself to his vernacular, what he wrote might have little appeal for audiences outside his own home and might even be almost unintelligible to them. From this point of view there was much to be said for a language which transcended local boundaries, and, even if it called for some training in its understanding, was yet easily mastered and would be familiar anywhere where poetry was honoured. Since from an early date poets travelled extensively in the pursuit of their profession, it was patently in their interest to use such a language, and we can only admire their prudence in doing so.

Moreover, though the language of Greek poetry is artificial in the sense that it was never actually spoken but fashioned deliberately to meet certain needs, it is not false or pretentious or weary or effete. In the epic new phrases were continually introduced to keep it up to date, and we can still appreciate the skill with which this was done without spoiling the unity of tone, and later, when other forms of poetry were in the ascendant, a poet's choice of words was essentially his own. He could with equal freedom use old-fashioned words, form new words on old models, exploit synonyms and alternative forms, and, when he chose, select from his own vernacular. In this he was deeply beholden to the flexibility of Greek. Just because the Greeks lacked any extensive means of mass-communication such as have prevailed since the invention of printing and are becoming increasingly dominant and intrusive, and because books were until quite a late date rare, language was safe from the assaults and the allurements of standardization. It differed, not merely from place to place but from person to person, but such was its nature that it could without trouble absorb new words or form new combinations with old words. Unlike a modern metropolitan language, it was admirably fitted to sustain a wide spread of vocabulary inside a generous frame. Its main rules were fixed and strict, but within the boundaries imposed by these there was plenty of room for experiment, adaptation, and innovation, and that is why the artificial language of Greek poetry was never artificial in a derogatory sense. It was the product of a linguistic situation which had never been reduced to uniformity and in which words were still savoured and enjoyed for their own sake and welcomed for any novelty in them.

There is no call for regret or embarrassment that much of Greek poetry was written in a language of this kind. Poetry has always to purify itself from the wearied commonplaces of practical speech, and it can do this in more than one way. The Elizabethans extended the scope of their language by absorbing any words that came their way and by reinforcing them with others of their own invention; Racine went to the other extreme and by his highly selective and choice vocabulary secured an effect of dignity and distance through a deceptive simplicity; to-day reaction against the book-ish, overworked language of the last century has encouraged the cult of the colloquial and the unpretentious. But never does the language of serious poetry coincide with actual speech, and, through its very nature, it cannot. It may not matter by what means it seeks to make itself different, but it must somehow do so if it is to assert its proper rights and fulfil its first duty of making words more forceful than anywhere else. So when the Greeks followed a method which is, after all, not very different from that of the Elizabethans, their aim was to exalt language above the common level in abundance and expressiveness, and this did not put too great a strain either on them or on it, because Greek is so adaptable and so rich in unexploited resources that it can be fitted to poetry of many kinds and still keep its vitality and its dignity unimpaired.

Tradition also provided the Greeks with a huge mass of stories about gods and men, which were the staple of early poetry and remained of the utmost relevance and utility in later times. Those which confine them-selves to the gods may be the older, and what they were like in the lost centuries may to some degree be inferred from the passages about the gods in the Homeric poems and the Homeric Hymns, which are later than Homer but belong to his tradition and relate with much grace and gaiety the enterprises of the Olympians. They are told for their own sake and reflect an age which liked to hear of actions which men would like to perform if only they had the power to do so. But any people conscious of its own human qualities cannot expect to be satisfied with tales of the gods alone, and from a very early date, probably in the Mycenaean age, stories of the gods must have been supplemented by stories about men. Such stories could be refashioned, enriched, extended and reinterpreted, but behind them usually lies some element of belief or myth or folk-lore or history. Myths about the gods were often derived from rites which had lost their first meaning and called for a new explanation, and this took the form of a fanciful or fearful story. Myths about men may be derived from history, like the cycle of tales which centres around the indubitably historical Trojan War, but they may also, like some of the adventures of Odysseus, be folk-tales which have an immemorial past and float over many parts of the world. All these elements may be detected in Homer, and, though the *Iliad* has its roots in history and the *Odyssey* in folk-tale, both introduce men and gods, even if their main attention is paid to men.

Yet, though such stories come from very different sources, they are all merged in a single body of myth, which belongs to an undated past and presents an inexhaustible quarry for poets who wish to delight or instruct their audiences.

The antiquity of such stories may account for the strong contrast which they present between gods and men. While tales of the gods are light-hearted and graceful and charming, tales of men are often dark with horror and violence. Incest, cannibalism, parricide, matricide, human sacrifice, bloodthirsty vendettas, and hideous deaths abound in Greek heroic legend. This may be a legacy from the Mycenaeans who undoubtedly delighted in war and whose kings were in later times associated with a dark array of disaster and doom. Certainly they reflect a world which found a fierce delight in such stories, if only because its own existence did not lack savage thrills and agonizing anxieties. When these tales were taken up in later times, it was in a new, more probing and more serious spirit. Through their very violence they provided opportunities for the imaginative consideration of the state of man, his ambitions, his passions, and his fate. The Greeks were trained in a hard school not only of life but of literature. By making use of their own legends, they had at their disposal a dramatic means for clarifying their own thoughts through the startling, disturbing character of what their ancestors had done and suffered. The brutality of many stories provided a starting point from which later generations could, even while they felt their extraordinary fascination, react and recoil. Just because such tales were related to a remote past, they could be judged in the light of a riper experience and turned to illustrate other events which might be less dramatic but still had something in common with them.

This mythical material, in all its breadth and richness, was an incalculable asset. Through its long career Greek poetry had at its disposal a mass of stories remarkable for their superb variety, their dramatic tension, their delicate fancy, their unbridled passion, their human widsom and pathos and charm, and could use them as points of departure for many developments. Other peoples have had something of the same kind organized in a like way in the doings of a heroic age, and we have only to look at the mediaeval cycles of stories which revolved round Sigurth or Arthur or Charlemagne to see how they stimulated imaginative creation. But with the Greeks the possession of such material was even more influential. Because it centred not on a single, dominating figure but on a whole age, it had a wider scope and offered more openings for enterprise; because it ruled literary tradition and had no serious rival in the present, it encouraged concentration within its own field, and this gave to the poetical impulses of the Greeks a continuity with the past and an insight into the potentialities which a new treatment might disclose. This deeply affected the character of their literature. A knowledge of most myths could be taken for granted, and a poet could embark on his story without explanation or preliminaries. Both Greek epic and Greek drama assume that the audience knows more or less what is going to happen, and the poet can from the start impose his own pattern on the familiar material. Provided that he keeps the main outline of a story, he can do very much what he likes with the rest – give his own interpretation, add new episodes and new characters, bring old characters into new relations, lead to an unforeseen finale. His liberty is greater than that of the mediaeval painter or sculptor who deals with biblical themes; for, since the Bible is a sacred book, the actual outline of its events cannot be changed. But in principle the parallel is apt enough. Just as mediaeval artists found their individual vision of biblical events and not only added many new touches to them but in many small respects transformed their tone and temper, so the Greeks used the traditional material freely and were in no way inhibited or discouraged by its limitations. On the contrary, knowing that their art sprang from a thriving and abundant tradition, they had confidence in themselves and were able to pursue their aims without spending too much time in looking for a suitable vehicle for their expression or being hindered by uncertainty whether the conditions of epic or drama really allowed them to say what they wished. The Greek combination of tradition and experiment is nowhere so clear or so decisive as in the art of words.

Much of Greek literature is concerned, directly or indirectly, with problems that have always troubled man – his place in the scheme of things, his relations with the gods, the worth of his actions, the meaning of his successes and his failures, his claims on society and society's claims on him. In due course such matters were to be debated at the loftiest level by philosophers in a language which moved easily among abstractions and made its meaning clear through its masterly command of them. But abstractions, especially of this kind, are not intimately related to the living scene and have little immediate appeal to those who move in it; they set forth its problems in too schematic and too disembodied a form to win everyone's interest; and they are liable to float off into an empyrean of undisturbed thought, which has indeed an impressive majesty but does not touch everyone in his essentially human self. To bring large ideas into the range of daily experience is a hard task for imaginative literature and one of the most satisfactory ways of doing so is to present them through concrete examples or images or symbols and to make these display their significance in individual instances for individual men. Greek myths provide a fruitful means of doing this. They belong to a world in which abstractions have as yet found only a subordinate place, and the issues which they embody can more easily and more effectively be presented in solid, compelling forms. In their imaginative thought the Greeks made an abundant use of symbols derived from myths, and though this may sometimes have blunted the sharp edge of their thinking, it made up for this by giving an immediate, striking relevance. Such symbols concentrate in themselves a mass of associations which are instinctively apprehended, and are therefore more urgent, more vivid, more intimate, more charged with personal emotion than the usual run of abstractions. What a familiar hero does or suffers stands for much that happens to other men and throws a fresh light on it, while many stories, no matter how remote on the surface from common life, gain a new significance because they illustrate other situations by some essential similarity. The mind moves as easily and as lightly among images of this kind as among any neat abstractions since imagery gives pattern and contour to the most tangled states of mind and turns them, in all their complexity, into words, without the impoverishing simplification which comes from moving on too abstract a plane. Though the Greeks enjoyed abstract notions and excelled in the creation of striking maxims and the reduction of disparate instances to a single rule, they saw that to make their lessons cogent to a large audience they must give them an individual shape, and for this they had an excellent instrument in their myths about the multifarious doings of gods and men.

Relying as they did upon tradition, the Greeks were fully conscious of what they owed to the past. When they said that Memory was the Mother of the Muses, they meant it, since in their oral poetry Memory was indeed indispensable, but in later times the doctrine was still true, even if it had changed its meaning. Poets must be masters not only of technical devices but of a whole mass of inherited stories. These set them to work, and on them they relied for their basic material. Even their manner of work was founded on ancient notions. When Homer opens his epic with a summons to the Muse to sing of the wrath of Achilles or tell of the man of many wiles, he may follow common form but his words are by no means meaningless. They present what the Greeks thought about poetry, and especially one important side of their approach to it. When they claimed that the Muse spoke to them or through them, they affirmed the existence of inspiration, in the sense that a poet cannot do his best and perhaps cannot do anything unless a divine spirit is at work in him and tells him what to say. At the least this means that he stretches himself to the utmost; at the most, that he is almost carried away by the force of the words which surge up in him and pass through his lips. The Greeks accepted the fact of inspiration and attributed it to the celestial presence of the Muse. They did not claim to understand the process by which words came with so unusual an urgency and force, but they recognized that this happened and was indispensable to the whole task of creation. What we ascribe, vaguely and hesitantly, to the unconscious self, the Greeks, with more conviction, ascribed to an external, celestial power, and their explanation is as good as ours. The process exists, and it is wise to admit that it does without trying too carefully to explain it. Many modern writers know of such an experience and admit that, when it comes, their work is at its best and differs almost in kind from anything that they write by a mere act of will. The Greeks were more candid. They welcomed the fact of inspiration and assumed that only by divine aid could a poet pass beyond the limitations of everyday speech.

At the same time they knew that this was only one side of the creative process. The words that come, as it were from nowhere, may still call for patient care and hard work and ruthless discrimination before they are set in a satisfying order and harmony. The Greeks, who put their first trust in the Muse, recognized that they themselves had their own task to perform in treating her gifts as seriously as they possibly could. However strong their inspiration might be, they were none-the-less craftsmen, and they compared themselves variously with builders and sculptors, workers in gold and ivory, planters of gardens, weavers of garlands, drivers of chariots, helmsmen of ships. In each case the given, inexplicable impulse must be mastered and made the most of, and from the alliance of inspiration and craftsmanship comes the work of art. This is, after all, to be expected from the Greeks with their extraordinary taste and talent for making objects to delight the senses, and it is natural that they should exert themselves to delight the mind through the ears. But it was not merely delight at which they aimed. The nearest word which they had for art is *sophiâ*, which quite simply means 'wisdom'. The good poet, like the good painter, is a wise man, whose wisdom lies in understanding the ways of the gods and in knowing how to use their gifts. We may regard his task as a form of craftsmanship, but it is more exalted and more dignified than most other forms and, though other crafts have their presiding and inspiring deities, the art of words depends more closely and less explicably on them. In it the artist certainly creates, and it is largely by his own will and his own effort, but what he creates would have little worth if he were not prompted and sustained by something beyond himself. It is this which gives an honoured place to poetry and earns respect not merely for the skill with which it is fashioned but for the importance of what it has to say. In Greek life it had almost a religious significance and was indeed closely related to religion, not merely in some of the uses to which it was put but in the lofty spirit in which it was composed and heard and remembered. In the dark centuries when the Greeks had almost no other arts, poetry throve and grew, and, much though they thought later of their music and painting and sculpture, poetry was their most ancient art, and perhaps their fullest and finest means of expressing certain matters which touched or troubled them.

The Greeks looked at poetry in this religious light, not merely because it came from the gods, for, after all, in their view that was true of almost anything, but because it was deeply concerned with them and through it men formed a special relation with them. It might tell tales of them for their own sake, or be the vehicle of prayers and hymns, or examine with imaginative insight their relations with men, but they were seldom far from it, and often powerfully present in it. This was a natural consequence of what the Greeks thought divine nature to be. The gods were sources of life and energy and power, and the poet's task was to reveal their ways and their works as he, with his favoured insight, saw them. He was vividly conscious of their mystery, and it was this that he tried to pierce, to explain, to make intelligible through striking myth and illuminating symbol. Moreover, it was this that gave special seriousness to his work. By human standards the gods might not always behave seriously, and there was much in their behaviour that called for admiring laughter, but they were none the less the disposers of human fortune, and a man was unwise indeed if he did not pay proper attention to their ever-present power. In Homer's laughter at the carefree enjoyments of the gods there is a deep respect for them, if only because they are in the last resort inexplicable and must therefore be watched with awe and fear. Greek poetry and much of Greek prose gain a special depth by their consciousness of the gods and of what is due to them. The doings of men are set against a background which is sometimes radiant with divine light, sometimes dark with menace and doom, but always to be reckoned with, because it alone puts human affairs in a right perspective and forbids man to see himself as the centre of the universe. Behind and around and above him are the gods, and his thoughts and actions, which are pursued largely for their own sake in the familiar world, must be judged against what the gods think about them and do to further or to hinder them. Against the omnipotence of the gods the struggles of men are shown in their prodigious exertions and their all too frequent futility, in their essentially human worth, which is different from divine worth and in its own sphere at least as impressive and worthy of pursuit.

The Greeks regarded intelligence as one of the highest gifts bestowed by the gods and insisted that it must be used in trying to understand their ways. For them faith, in the precise Pauline sense, had little meaning, and, though of course their belief in the gods was a boundless act of faith, it did not discourage them from trying to clarify it with persistent, candid and at times ruthless enquiry. In their literature they relied much on the emotions and appealed frankly to them, but it was their emotions that set their intelligence to work with an unusual force and sharpness. Just because literature did something which neither music nor the visual arts could do, it had its own eminence in a society which liked to think out its problems in a firm, lucid way and saw that without treating words with the utmost respect this could not be done. Without this means of stating, analysing, and explaining their problems the Greeks would have found it far more difficult to face them in a purposeful spirit, and if Greek literature mirrors Greek curiosity, it does so at a level at which curiosity is an ardent, searching, unrelaxing passion to know the truth. This means that literature is always close to the intellectual endeavours of the Greek people and reflects its struggles and its changes, its secured positions and its irking uncertainties. At whatever level and in whatever sphere it operates, it gives a full scope to the active intelligence. Because it deals with questions which excite hard thought and stimulate it by their very recalcitrance, it appeals to the whole being of a man with his intelligence, his imagination, and his emotions. In this alliance we seldom feel that any one of the three partners gains at the expense of the other two. The intelligence is always at work – probing, questioning, suggesting, answering, but it is prompted and enriched by a whole range of emotions to which it pays proper respect as the sources and springs of its driving activity; the imagination is firm and confident and clear but is not allowed to run riot or to create worlds which exist only for their alluring charm without regard to their relevance to the actual human state; the emotions are indeed rampant and sometimes formidable, but their control in art is as severe as the intellectual content which they inform and set to work. This combination of faculties reflects the Greek temperament as we see it alike in the vigour of their practical life and in their visual arts. Just as a Greek sculptor portrays a mythical scene with an unerring fidelity to his shaping vision and puts into it his strongest emotions without allowing them to disturb its overriding harmony and order, so Greek poets and historians and philosophers are indeed inspired by an obsessing concern for their subjects but keep them in hand not only by reducing them to an economical and shapely form but by never saying too much and by always saying as much as possible in the fewest possible words.

The Greeks regarded writers as public teachers, not in any pompous or arid sense but with a lively conviction that the highest lessons about men are best conveyed in a noble and satisfying form. The writers responded to this confidence and thought that they owed to their people the best that they could give. For this reason Greek literature is always to some degree a public art. The size of its actual audience might vary from select aristo-cratic circles, like those to whom Alcaeus and Sappho sang, to the whole sovereign people of Athens, which watched tragedies and comedies in the theatre of Dionysus, but a writer's public was always larger than any clique or coterie and concerned with very much more than the niceties of literary accomplishment, and any fine display of it soon passed into general circulation. Writers were keenly aware of their responsibilities, and this saved them from becoming cranks or from pursuing private whims into finicky refinements. This does not mean that they did not speak fully and freely for themselves, but it certainly means that, in speaking for them-selves, they addressed their words closely and candidly to their compatriots. They had the uplifting strength which comes from knowing that they belonged to an attentive, appreciative, and critical society, which expected them to strain to the limit of their powers and to put every ounce of them-selves into their work. This enhanced their sense of public duty, since they knew that with such an audience anything false or feeble would soon be detected and derided. They could always draw support from the knowledge that they were at once the interpreters and the instructors of a national consciousness. Such a situation was possible, not because the Greek states were democratic, since many of them were not, but because, even when there were notable inequalities of rights and riches, the population of a city-state was far more homogeneous than any modern society with its advanced differentiation of upbringing and work and manners. Most Greeks were brought up to much the same pursuits, as befitted men who lived from labouring on the land or exploiting the sea, and this provided a basic culture which intellectual leaders could take for granted and through it have some assurance that, if they had something serious to say, it would be taken seriously by a circle far wider than that of their intimate friends.

Greek literature embodies over a wide range what the Greeks felt and thought. There must of course be aspects of their life upon which its extant remains do not touch or even in its heyday it never touched; it is unlikely that it ever spoke at all effectively or intimately for isolated communities in remote regions, or for the large class of slaves upon whom Greek economy depended, though even these get an honourable share of attention both from Homer and from Euripides. But it speaks fully and finely for large numbers of the Greek people between its emergence from its Dark Age to the decline of Hellenism. It is conscious of their local idiosyncrasies, their political differences, their social barriers, but it manages to transcend these through its knowledge of what they have in common and its unquestioning assumption that they are all Greeks, who in the final analysis follow a common pattern of life. It is closely related to what men were and did, and it speaks for a people which indeed loved fine words but was not totally occupied with them, and saw in literature a means for forging new instruments for action and enterprise, for understanding what opportunities beckoned to adventure, and what was necessary to win success. It made the Greeks think about themselves seriously and carefully and come to closer grips with their personal and their national predicaments. It would not have had so great an influence if it had not been governed by very exacting standards of artistic achievement, and, just because it is so governed, it has weathered the centuries and remains as lively and fresh to-day as it was in its prime. Through it we see the Greeks from within as they really were, and appreciate the vast efforts which they made to grasp their place in the scheme of things and to establish on firm foundations their unique vision of the world.

HEROIC SONG

THE Greeks gave to literature an unqualified seriousness because they treated it as a means for the understanding of human life, especially in their struggles to explain the place of man in a world which is at once both natural and supernatural, both imposes its own multifarious claims on him and turns his curiosity to probe what lies behind its appearances. Greek literature is much more than a criticism of life, since criticism suggests an impartial judge watching and deciding from above the battle; rather, it is deeply committed to the elucidation of what man is and what he is worth, why he behaves as he does, and what his behaviour means in some embracing scheme of comprehension. It carries out this task in many ways, but this is normally its inherent purpose, and that is why so much of it is focussed, not merely on gods or merely on men, but on both together as they are interrelated in a single world. Though some of it is specifically sacred, and some secular, it is usually both, and each gains from the other. Unlike some characteristically Christian literature, it is not other-worldly in the sense that it is more concerned with a supernatural 'beyond' than with the here and now. Even when it deals mainly with the gods, their actions are often on the earth, and their behaviour is what we might expect from beings who differ from men only in their vastly superior powers and their unassailable security. A Greek writer keeps his feet firmly planted on the ground because he knows that it is the meeting-place of gods and men, and he is not interested in other regions known to mystics and metaphysicians. In this the Homeric epic sets an example. It is concerned with the doings of men, and, rather less, of gods, but it presents both at work in a common world and makes each class display its determining qualities from so many angles that we soon get a clear picture of what they are, and from this, under the poet's almost unnoticed guidance, we look at the whole living scene and grasp what questions it raises for any embracing notion of the human state.

For some two centuries the *Iliad* and the *Odyssey* have been the victims of technical controversy on their composition and authorship. The Greeks themselves thought that the poems were the work of a single man called Homer, who lived in Chios and whose poems were preserved and recited after his death by a guild of bards who called themselves the Sons of Homer. At the other extreme some modern critics have argued that the poems are collections of separate lays from many hands put together at Athens in the sixth century BC. Many of the arguments for this case have been discredited by recent investigations into oral traditions and their ways of working and by our realization that a poet who composes in his head for recitation constructs his tale quite differently from a poet who relies upon writing, that an audience which listens to a recited poem must have events put to it differently from a public which reads books. In our present state of knowledge we may say that the *Iliad* and the *Odyssey* may fairly be regarded as the work both of many poets and of a single poet. Behind them lies a long tradition of poets who told tales like theirs and certainly invented a large number of phrases and devices and episodes and characters which appear again in them. They are more directly dependent on this tradition than Shakespeare, for instance, is on North or Holinshed, and their debt is far more general and pervasive. More than this, they are composed in a certain way because this had been evolved and established through many generations for heroic poems. This means that in many respects they are highly conventional, but this in no ways reflects on their worth, for it is in his new use of conventions that a poet shows his strength. Nor can we doubt that behind these long epics lies a large number of short lays, whose technique can be discerned in both poems at many points and suggests that individual episodes in them were retold in a manner appropriate to a short song. To this extent the authorship of the *Iliad* and *Odyssey* is multiple, but we can in no way assess how many poets have contributed to them in the centuries when their stories and story-telling were fashioned. On the other hand the Greeks believed in a man called Homer, and we must respect their belief. It is true that they attributed to him poems which he is unlikely to have composed if he composed the *Iliad* and *Odyssey*. It is also true that we know next to nothing about him, and such attempts as were made in antiquity to write lives of him are flights of fancy compiled from the poets themselves. Yet both the *Iliad* and the *Odyssey* are single works of art, each composed on a recognizable pattern, with clearly discernible main movements in a commanding scheme, with a sustained tone and temper to be found in no other oral poetry, with a consistent and elevated style which could hardly have been maintained at such a level if some very uncommon poet had not been in control of it. There are indeed substantial differences of temper and outlook and vocabulary between the two poems, and these have led some scholars to assume the existence of two separate poets, each of whom was responsible for a complete work of art. This is by no means impossible, but the difference may just as well be explained by the hypothesis of a single author who first composed the *Iliad* and then in his riper years, when some of his first, fiery impetus had abated and he had mastered some new linguistic devices and matured some of his ideas, composed the *Odyssey*. We shall probably never know the right answer. But in the last resort it does not matter. What matter are the poems, which are works of art based on a long tradition and themselves composed in the latter part of the eighth century BC, and it is not improper to speak of Homer and by him to mean the poet or poets who composed the *Iliad* and the *Odyssey*.

Because the poems are both derived from the ancient tradition and permeated by the outlook of their own time, they are guided throughout by the need to keep the first alive by relating it to the second and to enhance the dignity of the second by relating it to the first. In solving this problem Homer took advantage of his own circumstances and found a right balance and fusion of the two elements. On the one hand convention laid down that he must sing about the great doings of the past, and we may assume that his audiences would include Ionian princes and nobles who prided themselves on being descended from legendary heroes and inheriting some of their prowess. The essential superiority of the past must be maintained. We know too little of the Ionian Greeks in the eighth century to be able to say what their social conditions were, but we may suspect that rule still belonged to petty kings who had not yet had their powers taken from them and divided by land-owning aristocrats. In such a society the poet was not himself likely to be of noble birth. It is true that Homer makes Achilles, sitting in his tent with Patroclus, sing to the lyre of 'the glorious doings of men',[1] but his own position is more likely to have resembled that which he gives to bards in the *Odyssey*. In Phemius at the court of Odysseus in Ithaca and in Demodocus at the court of Alcinous in Phaeacia Homer presents bards as he must have known them and as he himself must have been. They are neither nobles nor slaves, but hold a midway position as craftsmen, comparable to physicians, seers, and workers in wood. They are free men, respected for their skill in song but dependent for their living on the patronage of princes, and that is why Phemius collaborates with the Suitors who devour Odysseus' substance in his absence. It is likely that Homer at least began his career in such a position, and, if he did, it would account for an important element in his art, its complete absence of personal references and even personal judgments. He hides himself from us as completely as Shakespeare, and though heroic song is in its very nature objective and dramatic, it is seldom so stern on its author or so rigorous in its repression of his comments as are the Homeric poems. The reason for this is that the poems were composed for patrons who wished to hear about the glorious past, with which they somehow associated themselves, but not to hear the judgments of a social inferior on it. This kept Homer to a highly objective art in which he had to create the past as he knew it from tradition and as he himself imagined it. He was free to do this as he pleased, provided that he maintained its dignity and gave it a new reality which did not interfere with its legendary prestige. What he saw around him he used indirectly and almost casually, but it was this which gave life and immediacy to his presentation. Just because he could not speak too directly of the present, it made his evocation of the past firmer and clearer, and compelled him to think out for himself what its episodes meant before he put them into poetical shape.

Both the *Iliad* and the *Odyssey* are tales of lively and vigorous action, and our first response is to their thrills. The story in both is of first importance, and it is through the story that we get to know the characters and learn what we can of the poet's creative personality. The *Iliad* tells first and foremost of war, of the last year in the ten years of the siege of Troy by the Achaeans, and the *Odyssey* of the adventures of Odysseus on his long voyage home after the sack of Troy. There is a gap between the contents of the two poems, but it is covered by incidental references in the *Odyssey* which make the second poem a kind of sequel to the first. Each is composed on a generous scale, which allows for the full description of actions and ample reporting of speeches. The original audience was expected to enjoy the story, and then they could think what they liked about it; it was not the poet's task to point explicit lessons. This means that their strength is primarily that of narrative, with its anticipations, its detailed moments of crisis, its unforeseen developments. Episodes may hang loosely together, but each moves with its own effortless rapidity and wastes no time on divagations and diversions. The central point of the *Iliad* is the wrath of Achilles, which leads first to the defeat of the Achaeans, and then to the death of his friend Patroclus, and his vengeance on Hector, who has killed him. But this provides a structure on which many other episodes are built, especially when Achilles is absent from battle, and his work has to be done by others less gifted than himself. The *Odyssey* turns

on the return of Odysseus to his home, but the first four books are concerned with the sad state of that home in his absence, and provide a prelude
to what comes later, and before he gets home he tells in the first person of
his marvellous adventures on the edges of the world. In both poems the
action becomes simpler and more concentrated in the later books, as the
various threads are brought together towards the dramatic finale. On this
simple structure Homer builds his rich, imaginative stories and gives to
them all that he can both from tradition and from his own love of life.

Tradition and contemporary circumstances alike insisted that a bard
who told about the past must confine his attention to characters who were
royal or noble. When Homer commonly calls them 'godlike' or 'peers
of gods', he both pays a tribute to a generation of heroes and shows how
select his list of *dramatis personae* is. Among his characters very few are of
humble origin. Even Odysseus' swineherd, Eumaeus, who has been kidnapped by Phoenicians in childhood and sold into slavery, turns out to
be a prince by birth. On the other hand characters who are not of high
lineage are sometimes presented in a derisory or ludicrous light. Thersites,
who rails at the Achaean kings in the council at Troy, is not only offensive
but ugly, and nobody complains when Odysseus strikes him with a staff
and leaves an ugly weal on his back. Dolon, who foolishly attempts to
behave like a hero, is not noble but rich and slightly absurd in being an only
son with five sisters, nor do we much mind when he is caught in night-
operations and has his head cut off by Diomedes. In the household of
Odysseus the goat-herd Melanthius works for the Suitors and reveals his
brutality and his base opportunism in his contemptuous treatment of the
unrecognized Odysseus, while some of the slave-women, who sleep with
the Suitors, are duly strung up, like thrushes, on a rope by Odysseus.
Slaves have their place in heroic society, but their worth is judged by
their loyalty to their masters, and against those who have betrayed
Odysseus Homer sets the admirable Eumaeus, who stands faithfully first
by his master's son and then by his master, and the old nurse Eurycleia, who
through all the troubles has remained with her mistress Penelope and,
when by accident she recognizes her returned lord, keeps her head and
does not give him away. The world of Homer is more royal than aristocratic. The centre of society is the king, and if in the *Iliad* all other kings
are subordinate to Agamemnon as commander-in-chief, that is after all a
necessity of war, and his subordinates are none the less kings in their own
right. Homer's first concern was with kings and princes because tradition
demanded it, but the tradition was no doubt much to the taste of his
patrons, and he saw no reason to forsake it.

Heroes of this calibre must be presented in all their strength and prowess and be worthy of the legends which clustered round their names. They were indeed regarded as superior to later generations, and Homer is well aware of this and accepts it. In the first place their manhood is tried in battle, which is not only the main field of heroic endeavour but the ordeal which tests the full range of a man's abilities, physical, moral, and intellectual. Homer's heroes perform prodigious feats of strength in war, and in his audience, which knew all about fighting and would appreciate the finer points of conflict, his careful account of individual duels between well matched heroes would excite a professional interest and appreciation. In the *Iliad* the leading heroes, Achilles, Hector, Ajax, Patroclus, and the rest, are also the most adventurous and most skilful fighters. In battle they realize the full scope of their gifts, whether it be in strength of arm, or fleetness of foot, rapidity of decision, or ingenuity in stratagem, unyielding endurance, or irresistible impetus in attack. Though the *Odyssey* is not concerned with actual war, the slaughter of the Suitors by Odysseus in his own hall is a combination of reckless audacity and far-sighted cunning. The qualities displayed in battle are matched by others, which belong of right to the great man, who must be generous, courteous, and loyal, and is fully entitled to his fair share of appetites, whether for women or food or the display of arms and armour. The heroic ideal finds physical gifts indispensable, but sets hardly less value on gifts of mind and character, which ennoble them and make them more effective. The world in which such men live is worthy of them in its wealth and its state. At home they have large establishments glittering with gold, where they are served by slaves of both sexes and keep herds of cattle and swine for their prolonged and abundant feasts; at war they take pride in their accoutrements, made of bronze, but often studded with gold or silver or inlaid with enamel, in their horses, upon whom their mobility in fight depends, and whom they treat as intimate friends, appealing to their loyalty to do their best in times of crisis; in council they must display not only wisdom but eloquence, and even in their dealings with one another they speak with a weighty decorum and a considerate courtesy. They provide hospitality to all strangers and send them on their way with handsome gifts. Their sacrifices and feasts are conducted with a reckless expenditure of oxen and pigs. Homer depicts a world which in its main outlines was much richer and more magnificent than anything which he himself knew, and into this he had to fit his human story. The heroic frame set a standard which he must observe. He might easily have used the past as an escape from reality, a first excursion into romance, a flight of fancy into the unfamiliar and the incredible. Instead he finds in it a challenge to refine and strengthen his picture of the human state.

At the start this appears in his treatment of his characters. His heroes have indeed pre-eminent qualities and much that is beyond the capacity of men 'such as they now are',[2] but they are not, like so many figures of heroic song elsewhere, vast phantoms looming in a fog. They may lack subtlety of delineation, but this is because an oral art hardly allows it, and they certainly stand foursquare, and are emphatically themselves. We know them less by what they think, which is seldom revealed, than by what they say and do, and their actions follow naturally from their personalities. If the wrath of Achilles starts the *Iliad* and leads to the defeat of the Achaeans and the death of his friend Patroclus, it is closely related to the mainspring of his being, to the high, proud spirit which makes him fiercer and more formidable than other men. If the cunning of Odysseus is mentioned more than his courage, it is his courage which gets him into the scrapes from which his cunning has to deliver him. If Hector is both a ruthless fighter and a loving husband and father, it is because he has indeed something to fight for in his family and his city. If Agamemnon is both courageous and anxious, both kingly and arrogant, it is because he has heavier responsibilities than his fellows, and is heavily burdened by them. If Telemachus is at first unable to stand up to the Suitors, it is because he is still a boy without experience or self-confidence, but when he meets his father and learns from him what to do, he does it without faltering or fear. The clue to Homer's male characters is that they reveal and prove themselves in action. In the quality and strength of their responses to its challenges we see how they work and what they are. No doubt Homer learned something about them from tradition and may even have had to conform to it in their main outlines, but he makes them live in their own right as men of action. His sense of the abiding qualities of human nature is stronger than his respect for the ancient past, and he does not allow all its lure and splendour to prevent him from depicting men in their essential humanity.

In presenting women Homer was faced by a different problem. Some of them must have had important parts in old tales; others may have been his own creations, fashioned to meet the needs of his story. Indispensable to the tradition are Penelope and Helen, the long-suffering wife, who in her husband's absence finds her household devoured by brutal suitors who covet her money and her position, and the woman of incredible beauty who is the cause of the Trojan War. Penelope might all too easily have been depicted as no more than a victim of oppression, and relied upon her pathos to win our sympathy, but Homer gives her traits which counter the tedium of such a method. The slyness with which she unravels a web at night to put off her final answer to the Suitors is never quite absent from her actions. She is cautious and wary, slow even to recognize her husband even when he has produced unanswerable evidence of his identity. Nor is she without courage. Though she laments the brutal behaviour of the Suitors, and feels that she is at their mercy, she has enough presence to cow them when she appears among them. She is much more than a mere victim of oppression, and though she often weeps at her own sad state, we do not take her entirely at her own assessment, but appreciate her adroitness in handling an impossible situation. Helen presented a far more difficult task. She might easily have been depicted, as Attic tragedians were later to depict her, as not only the source of evil, but evil in herself. Homer goes to the opposite extreme and shows that it was almost impossible not to fight for such a woman; for, as the old men say on the wall of Troy: 'she is terribly like the immortal goddesses to look on'.[3] More than this, Homer goes out of his way to make us feel for her and with her. When she is unwilling to sleep with Paris, who has abducted her, she is forced to do so by Aphrodite, who stands implacably over her, and when Hector dies, she laments for him quite as pathetically as his wife and mother, and recalls with gratitude the kindness which he has always showed to her. Even ten years later, when she is back with her first husband at Sparta, she is much the same woman, guiltily conscious of all the harm that has come from her, and yet more eager to look after others than herself. Homer's characters belong to their situations and their circumstances, but they are far richer and more alive than this alone would require. He takes advantage of their positions to make them more human and more attractive.

If Homer brings his heroic figures into a human orbit, he still keeps them at a level of high distinction. They may have their human failures, but they are not feeble or trivial. Even the Suitors, who come to a deservedly bloody end, keep a certain style at least in their dealings with Penelope, and do not lack courage when they are trapped to death by Odysseus. From whatever ultimate source a character comes, from heroic legend, or folk-lore, or the poet's own invention, he is made to fit into the general pattern of the Homeric world, where simplicity, directness, vitality, and style are indispensable. For instance, when Odysseus crawls out naked and battered from the sea on Phaeacia, he is tended and helped by the king's daughter, Nausicaa. This is the age-old yarn of the shipwrecked mariner who is saved by a princess, and yet Homer gives very much his own version of her. Nausicaa is a girl on the verge of womanhood, and when she is faced by a naked figure emerging from a copse and looking like a lion, she keeps her head, speaks to him with a quiet dignity, sees that he is washed and clothed, and tells him how to get into the palace of her parents without being observed. It is all delightfully straightforward and natural and easy, and yet Nausicaa shows her fine breeding and her royal touch. She is a worthy princess to rescue such a hero. So too in the *Iliad*, though the captive girl Briseis is necessary to the plot because Agamemnon's arrogant seizure of her from Achilles leads to the fatal wrath, at the time of this she plays almost no part, since it might distract attention from the chief antagonists. Yet later, when the dead body of Patroclus has been laid out in the tent of Achilles, she comes back and finds it there and bursts into bitter grief as she recalls his gentleness to her. So too Hector has a wife and a mother, and each has not only her own reality, but her own tragic pathos. Andromache, the young wife, relies for everything on her husband, and in her very love for him knows that he will be killed. When suddenly she comes out from heating the water for his bath, and sees his dead body being dragged by Achilles behind his chariot, she knows that the end is near for her and her small child, and she becomes the type of every stricken and widowed woman. Hector's mother, Hecuba, is an old woman, who, after losing many of her sons in the war, has an old woman's fears and furies. She begs Hector not to fight Achilles, and her husband Priam not to take the risk of ransoming her son's body, but in her frailty she yields on both points, and, though in her hatred of Achilles she wishes to drink his blood, she ends by accepting her doom with resignation, as if she could not fight against it. She fulfils the part of the old mother of a mighty champion, but she has also her individual being, her sudden passions, and no less sudden surrenders. Homer's characters have indeed the dramatic interest of their situations, but they have more than this: they are so firmly conceived that their situations reveal new facets of their selves, and they become integral parts of a drama of human destinies.

A different question was posed by those traditional characters who were less tractable because they were not human beings but monsters. Greek fancy played with these odious or uncouth creatures and had many tales of them. Except for a passing mention of the chimaera, they are not to be found in the *Iliad*, but in the *Odyssey* they play a large part in the adventures of Odysseus once he has passed out of the known world into that of fable. They may be treated in one or the other of two ways. The first is to make them as monstrous as possible, to stress their difference from all other creatures, and to give a frightening picture of them in all their unique odiousness. This is what Homer does with Scylla when he gives her six heads, each with three rows of teeth, twelve legs, and the bark of a dog. She is unquestionably horrific, and we sigh with relief when Odysseus escapes from her. But she is almost alone in her detailed portraiture. Homer tends to bring his monsters closer to the human range by not overdoing their monstrosity. For instance, the queen of the Laestrygonians is indeed a formidable figure, but all that Homer says is 'they found a woman as big as a mountain, and they loathed her'.[4] When she takes one of Odysseus' men for her supper, the picture is complete, and anything else might spoil her vast horror. Conversely, the Cyclops Polyphemus provides an extended tale, in which he is portrayed from all sides until we see him solidly in the round. He is a gross brute, as he lies in his enormous bulk like a peak among mountains, or receives strangers with a most un-Greek offensiveness, grabs them, and cracks their heads on the floor, like puppies, before he eats them, bones and all, then falls into a drunken sleep and vomits gobbets of flesh. Yet there is something touching when, after he has been blinded, he speaks to his ram, and tells him how he has been tricked by 'No-man'. Polyphemus is a hideous figure of life at its most bestial, and that is why he convinces us of his reality. Homer indeed tends to reduce such figures to human proportions. For instance, both Circe and Calypso must once have been witches, the one, 'the Hawk', who turns men into beasts, the other, 'the Concealer', who hides her victims in a cave. Homer keeps Circe as a witch, and she turns Odysseus' companions into animals with a light-hearted indifference, but once he has subdued her, she becomes his loyal friend and helper. Calypso is given an entirely unexpected role. She is a goddess who lives alone on a beautiful island at the end of the world, and there she saves Odysseus when his ship is wrecked and his companions drowned. She falls in love with him and looks after him with tender solicitude, hoping that he will always stay with her and trying to make him immortal, and when at last she gets an order from the gods to send him away, she obeys with a quiet dignity and does all that she can to help him, even though he tells her that he prefers Penelope to her. So different are Circe and Calypso that we never suspect that once they must have had much in common, and yet, though they are highly differentiated, they are both much more human than we should expect any witch to be.

By such means Homer centred his world on man and reduced even monsters to some approximation to his image. It is his way of lessening the horror of the unknown and especially of the frightening creatures of imagination which had haunted the Mycenaean Greeks and still held their own on the earliest vases of the seventh century. Homer saw these uncouth aberrations through human eyes, and so brought them into an intelligible system. For somewhat similar reasons he seems to have shrunk from crediting his characters with those marvellous powers which play so large a part in much heroic song. He eschews magicians, and when something marvellous happens, it is the work of the gods, as when Aphrodite spirits Paris away from a duel with Menelaus before he can be seriously hurt, or Athene twice changes the appearance of Odysseus into that of a broken-down old beggar that he may not be recognized, or Hera makes Achilles' horse speak and foretell his death. The speaking horse is a very common theme of heroic tale and is usually not thought to be at all odd, but Homer's grip on reality leads him to excuse it by the intervention of a goddess. If he can make his events move by natural agencies he does so, and for him this means that he must keep close to the workings of men. A notable case of this is when Odysseus, coming home at last and made to look like a poor beggar, sees on a midden his old dog, Argos, covered with ticks. The dog wags his tail and drops his ears, but is too old to be able to move. Odysseus notices him, and speaks of his former strength, and as he goes on his way, the dog dies, having seen his master again after twenty years. The dog is presented and treated in human terms, and yet remains the eternal type of the faithful dog. It is all true to experience, and any hint of the supernatural is strictly excluded. Homer relates the varied inhabitants of earth to one another through what they have in common. This gives a unity to his creation and holds it together in all its richness and variety.

Yet this is no more than the central point from which Homer works. Once he has found the main pattern for his story, he has still many other problems to solve. At the start tradition limited his art by insisting that his main narrative should be confined to the great ones of the earth, and to this he obediently conformed. But it does not mean that he was unaware of its humbler inhabitants, or that he despised them for their lack of heroic magnificence. They must be excluded from the main action, but they could still be brought into the poem, and Homer found a subordinate place for them, which reveals the width and the warmth of his sympathies. First, when he describes the wonderful shield which the divine smith, Hephaestus, makes for Achilles, he tells that on it were fashioned many scenes, which can come only from the contemporary world. The main design is a contrast between a city at war and a city at peace. In the city at war he marks the sudden intrusion of violence into a land at peace, where herdsmen drive their flocks, not knowing that enemies are

31

ambushed in a river-bed, and waiting to steal their cattle. The enemy attack and kill the herdsmen, and make off with the booty, and then comes the battle proper as the army of the attacked comes out to fight. It is the kind of raid in which Achilles himself has taken part, but it is also something that Homer himself could have known in Ionia, and though Ares and Athene lead the attackers, the men who suffer are the humble herdsmen, caught as they play their pipes. In the city at peace a gay marriage-procession moves to a loud song and the antics of tumblers, while women watch from their doorways; two men quarrel in the market-place over the amends for a man's death, while old men wait to give judgment for them. These are supplemented by other scenes of the most habitual and ancient activities of men – ploughing, reaping, and gathering the vintage, oxen drinking at a river, lions attacking bulls, sheep in a rich valley, and finally a dance of young men and young women on a dancing-floor like that which Daedalus made long ago in Cnossus for Ariadne. The description of works of art was no doubt traditional, and metal-work of the kind that Homer describes, in gold and silver and enamel, was a Mycenaean accomplishment, but Homer's treatment of the subjects so depicted is modern and up to date. These are the activities which he knew in his own life, and brought into his poem to provide a contrast with the high heroic thrills of his main narrative.

Homer has a second means of portraying humble life, in the traditional art of the simile. A simile illustrates the character of an action by comparing it with something else which is on the surface quite different. It relieves the tension of violent events by turning our minds for a moment to another order of things, and this order is often of a quieter, less exalted kind. The simile, no doubt, goes back to a very distant past, but many of Homer's similes, especially those which are long and more elaborate, are his own invention and depict what he saw around him. In them he often touches on the ordinary life of men and women. A woman wards flies off from her child; another woman stains a piece of ivory to make a bridle for horses; men reap barley; boys beat an ass that has broken into a field of corn; a child builds a sand-castle; workmen fell a tree to make planks for a ship; a woman works at her wool to save her children from poverty; herdsmen beat off a lion at night with torches from a steading; children feel a sudden relief when their father begins to recover from a dangerous sickness; a man turns a haggis over a fire, waiting for it to be cooked; a traveller pauses in his journey uncertain which way to go; an audience waits eagerly for a singer to begin his song; a diver fishes for oysters; a potter shapes a pot on a wheel; a man starts back at the sudden appearance of a snake; a father weeps at the funeral-pyre of his young son. Each of these similes, and they are but a selection from a large number, has its own poetry of a humble situation. Homer often leaves the exact point of comparison to elaborate his scene with some additional detail, which is not always to the immediate point and may even be at variance with it, but shows how deeply he feels what he describes, and how clearly he has marked its essential character. The similes complement his main story by suggesting in an unobtrusive way that the heroic world is not everything, and that there are times when it can be seen at its true worth by comparison with something perfectly familiar and even undignified. Homer's high actions still hold the stage in a brilliant light, but he hints that they are not the only things that matter, and gives to them a new perspective by his brief incursions into another level of being.

In treating his main characters Homer shows a far greater percipience than we expect in a heroic poem, and a keener sense of what is expected from them. It is this which sometimes leads him to change the events of a traditional story, and we can see why he does so. In earlier versions we can hardly doubt that Achilles, having killed Hector in vengeance for the death of Patroclus, mutilated his body as a sign of his victory. This would be well fitted to primitive ideas of pride and vengeance, but it is not what happens in the *Iliad*. We are indeed led to expect that this is what Achilles will do, and there are times when Homer suggests that he intends to cut off Hector's head and throw his body to the dogs. Yet Homer shrinks from making him do this, no doubt because it is too barbarous. Instead, Achilles keeps the body in his tent with the intention of dealing with it after the funeral of Patroclus, but the gods preserve it from decay, and in the end Achilles is moved by the entreaties of Hector's old father, Priam, to give it back that it may be burned with the proper rites by Hector's own family and people. So the poem ends on a note of grave generosity in the finest heroic temper, and nobody would wish it otherwise. And more than this, the story which began with the outburst of Achilles' wrath, ends with its healing. In giving back the body of Hector to Priam, Achilles ceases to feel the wrath which has driven him first to forsake his comrades in battle, and then to pursue Hector to death. By this means Homer changes the whole spirit of the *Iliad*. Achilles, who despite all his gifts, might otherwise seem to be no more than a magnificent barbarian, achieves in his moment of compassion a different grandeur from before, and reveals the full scope of his heroic nature.

In the *Odyssey* Homer faced a similar problem of adjustment. Behind it lie countless tales of the Wanderer's Return. Odysseus, who has been away from home for twenty years, comes back unrecognized and finds his wife beset by greedy Suitors, who want to marry her for her wealth and position. While they court her, they devour her substance with a reckless callousness. In earlier versions this alone would justify their destruction. No decent hero can allow his home to be ruined in this way, and violence is the only means of saving it. If Odysseus is to regain his wife and his position, he must destroy the Suitors, and, no doubt, the climax always came in the great hall when Odysseus first traps the Suitors, and then kills them with the bow which he alone is able to string. The Suitors have, by any standards, behaved abominably, and nobody is expected to like them, but Homer feels that their destruction must be more than a matter of Odysseus getting his own back on them, and makes them deserve their end. They are presented as low fellows, a loud and coarse generation which has grown up at home while all the best men have been at the war of Troy. As such they lack heroic stature and have few redeeming points. It is true that they maintain an outward semblance of respect for Penelope, and are superficially courteous to her, but that is because each one of them wishes to marry her, and with her lies the decision which it is to be. Otherwise they show a brutal disregard for the house of Odysseus, waste his wealth, bully and insult his son, treat with odious presumption his few faithful servants, and sleep with his slave-women. Nor is there anything to choose between them. The braggart Antinous is as nasty as the smooth Eurymachus. Homer's presentation of the Suitors prepares the way for his audience to approve and welcome their deaths. They have taken advantage of the hero's absence to ruin his home, and this is the beginning of their doom, but what finally clinches it is when, in their fear that Telemachus has gone away to seek help against them, they decide to kill him on his return by lying in ambush for him behind a small island by his home. Fortunately, he evades them by taking another route, but their decision has been made, and through it they forfeit any small compassion that we may still feel for them. In the end we can only rejoice when Odysseus catches them unarmed and kills them. In the fight he is helped by Athene, and this shows where Homer's own feelings lie, but even without this he so plans his finale, that we take the side of Odysseus at every point. As in his handling of Achilles, Homer almost imperceptibly moves away from a more brutal story to something that embodies his own notion of what a hero ought to be. Odysseus' honour has been deeply wounded by the behaviour of the Suitors, but, when he kills them, more than honour is at stake. It is the triumph of a truly heroic standard of manhood over a base corruption of it. The Suitors have fallen into foul criminality, and for this reason they deserve to perish.

In presenting his characters with such understanding and insight, Homer also balances and arranges them in a striking pattern. In the *Odyssey* the contrast is between Odysseus and his few faithful supporters, who include Athene, on the one hand, and the whole mass of the Suitors on the other, and this provides a simple and neat scheme. In the *Iliad* the arrangement is more subtle. It combines two worlds, the almost exclusively male society of the Achaean camp and the city of Troy with its own warriors, but also with its old men and old women, its wives and its children. Such a contrast gives a view of war and its meaning from more than one side, and greatly enriches what might otherwise be no more than a series of battles. Homer uses it specially to display two kinds of heroic manhood. The absolute hero, like Gilgamish or Sigurth, fights for his own glory. He may sometimes attach himself to a cause, as Roland does against the Saracens, but that is simply because it gives him opportunities to display his prowess and win honour. This is the enlargement of existence which he seeks, and in most countries the heroic ideal is of this exclusive, self-centred kind. Of this type Achilles is a splendid example. He has indeed his human affections, especially for his friend Patroclus whom he allows to go to battle and death, and it is this which makes him hate Hector, who kills Patroclus. Achilles has also warm feelings of comradeship for other warriors like Odysseus and Diomedes and old Nestor. But despite these ties he remains solitary and self-sufficient. His old father is still alive, but far away across the sea; his mother may comfort him in his troubles, but she is a goddess and outside the human bonds between mother and son. Though Homer presents his motives as well as his achievements, and thus gives him a humanity which few absolute heroes possess, he remains a hero, tied to his ideal of prowess and glory and ready to suffer and die for it. The other Achaeans resemble him in one respect or another, but far more than they he imposes himself by an innate force which surpasses that of any other man. In a sense he represents others, but only because he does far better what they all do well. Against him stands Hector, who is cast in an utterly different mould. He too is a bold and enterprising soldier, but his significance is that he embodies not only the spirit of Troy but its actual existence. He has his touchingly human side, when he comforts his wife or plays with his small boy; he is deeply considerate to his old mother and courteous to Helen. It is he who rallies the Trojans to sterner efforts, who leads the attack on the Achaean ships, who chides Paris with a timely rebuke. He knows that he must fight Achilles, and that he will certainly be killed by him. He steels himself to his resolve, and dies, and with his death it seems as if Troy itself were falling. If Achilles stands for the pure ideal of personal heroism, Hector stands for a new adaptation of it in which it is closely tied to a man's duty to his city and his family. In this Homer shows how well aware he is of the change in Greek life between Mycenaean times and his own. Mycenae itself and other places like it were not strictly cities but fortresses, the homes of soldier-kings and their armies, but by the eighth century the city-state had come into existence and claimed the loyalty that in the old days a man would give to his own pride. Almost unconsciously Homer presents this momentous change in the contrasted figures of Achilles and Hector. In practice the harsh ordeal of the battlefield may make the two ideals look similar, but there is a real, historical difference between them, and we see how the living tradition of the past has been turned to suit the new conditions of the present.

The consistent seriousness with which Homer presents his human beings has no counterpart in his treatment of the gods, to whom his attitude shows remarkable variations. They too come from tradition, and tales of them may be even older than tales of heroes. Custom decreed that they should have a part in heroic tale, perhaps because the first of such tales were confined to them and the doings of men were a later addition. In Homer's treatment of the gods there is more than one strand, and there is no reason to think that all are not very ancient. In fact the main contradiction arises from the peculiar nature of the Greek belief in the gods. They are all anthropomorphic, and their behaviour is very like that of men, but of men who do not grow old or die and have an immeasurably greater degree of power than any man can ever have. Such a view leads to different views of them. On the one hand there is no doubt of their power, and Homer is well aware of it, and uses it with impressive majesty. When Zeus nods, he shakes Olympus; when Poseidon comes from Samothrace to Aegae, the mountains and the woods shake under him, and he does the journey in three steps; when he or Ares cries aloud, the cry is like that of nine or ten thousand men; when Poseidon knows that Odysseus is at sea on a raft, he raises such a storm that within a few moments Odysseus is wrecked. The gods have indeed almost unbounded power, but on the other hand, just because they live for ever, they pass much of their time as men would if they were free from danger and death. Because they lack the limitations of men, they enjoy such relaxations as men do in their hard-won leisure. Hence on Olympus they form an argumentative and quarrelsome family, which even Zeus has difficulty in controlling. When he forbids them to take part in the battle, Hera deceives him by making love to him, and he is handsomely gulled. The gods are not omniscient, and sometimes they are even ignorant of the latest news of the war, as when Ares, wrapped in a golden cloud on Olympus, does not know that his son, Ascalaphus, has been killed. This is part of the likeness between gods and men but when they really begin to display their human side, it tends to deprive them of their dignity and make them figures of comedy. At the court of Alcinous, Phemius tells how Ares makes love to Aphrodite, and is caught at it by her husband Hephaestus, who encloses them in an invisible net so that all the gods watch them and make fun of them. The means by which Hera decks herself to seduce her husband and turn his attention away from the battle is hardly less decorous, especially when Zeus, overcome by her charms, gives her a list of his triumphs in love and tells her that her beauty surpasses that of any of his mistresses. Both gods and goddesses take part in battle, but despite the incalculable advantage of being free from death, their behaviour is far below the standard expected of men. When the war-god, Ares, is wounded by Diomedes, he screams in pain, and in a like case Aphrodite weeps with her mother, and begs to be comforted.

Such scenes make an impression almost of comic relief, and this is not wrong. But the comedy does not come from any disrespect for the gods or incipient scepticism about them. It has rather the unquestioning assurance of complete belief, somewhat as mediaeval artists and playwrights made fun of Joseph or Noah, about whose reality they had no possible doubts. Yet, even so, it calls for some explanation, and the answer is that the gods behave much as men would if they were free of old age and death, and did not have heavy duties and responsibilities. The comedy comes from the absolute security of divine life. The gods run no real risks by going to battle, and not only spend much time in feasting and making love, but in laughing at one another, as men also do when they are free from cares. If the gods laugh at one another, it is not disrespectful for men also to laugh at them; for such laughter is simply an enjoyment of their doings as they themselves understand it. These episodes may reflect myths, which once had a very different significance, but they were rationalized, and given a new interpretation, and they passed into a realm of fable and fancy, even of pure art, in which men delight just because of its irresponsibility and paradox and gaiety. Because these stories have a long history behind them, they have developed peculiar characteristics and add an unexpected element to the poems. They have indeed an important place in them, and Homer seems to have felt no awkwardness in treating the gods from several, not always consistent positions.

Though tales of the gods are often highly enjoyable, the gods themselves are not for that reason to be underrated; for in the end everything depends on their will and their whims. In this Homer illustrates a time when the Greeks were changing their views about them, and beginning to assign to them a more responsible and more serious interest in the doings of men. In the *Iliad* the gods constantly interfere in the affairs of men, but their motives for so doing are not usually exalted or ethical by human standards, and no doubt this reflects an ancient point of view. So far as the Trojan War is concerned, they follow their own preferences and support whichever side their fancy favours, and it is characteristic that Athene and Hera are implacably hostile to Troy, while Aphrodite supports it, because it is to her that Paris has given the prize for beauty. In this the goddesses act as human women would in like circumstances, and conform to the demands of injured pride as it was understood in the heroic world. Artemis kills Niobe because she has boasted of the beauty of her children, and in the same spirit, Poseidon harries Odysseus because he has blinded Poseidon's son, Polyphemus. Conversely, the gods often favour men who have been generous in their sacrifices to them, and for this very reason appeal to their past services when in their prayers they wish to get something from the gods. When the old priest, Chryses, wishes to get his daughter back from Agamemnon, he prays to Apollo and reminds him of their old ties, with the result that Apollo descends 'like the night' and spreads plague in the Achaean army. Apollo shares his servant's injury and takes up his cause for him. In this the gods, like men, act from considerations of honour, and it has its impressive side. When Achilles debates with himself whether to draw his sword and kill Agamemnon for insulting him, Athene, appearing to him alone, stops him from doing so. Her motives are not stated, but must be that, since she supports Achilles, she does not want him to do something which would both be below his heroic honour and do irreparable harm to the Achaean cause, of which he is the champion. Again, when the gods in concert see that Achilles intends to mutilate the body of Hector, they stop him by getting Priam to ransom the body. Here too the honour of Achilles is involved in that of the gods who support him, and they must restrain him from going too far. By slight, almost imperceptible changes the cult of honour, displayed alike in gods and men, moves from the lower levels of injured pride to a higher conception of what is owed to a man both by his friends and by himself. Honour is a tricky and rather incalculable system, but it has its grand occasions, and of these Homer is fully conscious both in gods and in men.

Yet behind the parade of honour and its fundamental importance to both poems, there is something else, as yet only emergent and tentative, but tending towards a belief that the gods are in some sense guardians of human morality. This is less obvious in the *Iliad* than in the *Odyssey*, but it is certainly present in both poems and plays a formative part. Towards the end of the *Iliad* the poet, speaking in his own voice for himself, says that the Trojan War began because of the 'lustfulness' of Paris when he accepted the bribe of Helen's beauty in his judgment between the three goddesses. Now, whatever we may think of the goddesses themselves, Homer here makes a human failing the cause of a vast disaster, which is a punishment sent by the gods. The quiet way in which this is inserted and its relegation to the last book of the *Iliad* suggest that the poet did not wish to put too much emphasis on it, but at least he mentions it, and it looks as if he were shyly asserting a personal view, which might run counter to the traditional and even the contemporary view of the real cause of the Trojan War as seen from the point of view of the gods. In attributing guilt to Paris, Homer moves away from this outlook, and the action of Paris both attacks the honour of the gods and is discreditable for its own sake and condemned as such.

In the *Odyssey* this new spirit is more apparent and plays a more decisive role. The poem begins with a council of the gods on Olympus in which they discuss first the murder of Agamemnon by Aegisthus and point out that he deserved his vengeance from Orestes since he did not listen to the warning which the gods had sent him. This is a simple statement of principle, and it recurs later in the poem. Its purpose is to suggest that the Suitors are in a like case, that they have gone too far in their treatment of Penelope and deserve and must get their doom. The gods condemn their behaviour, and then set the machinery in action by which Odysseus is to return, and take his vengeance from them. Once this begins, the cause of the gods is conducted mainly by Athene, who keeps a watchful eye upon Odysseus in his adventures and helps him out of his worst perils. She encourages him to kill the Suitors, and plainly regards it as right. Yet this moral spirit is fused with heroic notions. Athene stands by Odysseus as a loyal and candid friend, and he is as outspoken to her as she is to him. Such a friendship imposes obligations, and since Odysseus is in grave trouble, Athene behaves according to the highest standards of friendship by doing all that she can for him. Yet this sense of honour is strengthened, and made more purposeful by the conception that the Suitors deserve their doom, and must therefore get it, and in this the gods must help. Homer makes no attempt to show that the gods always act in this spirit, and many of their actions are wilful and even in the last resort inexplicable. They have no clear system of rewards and punishments, but sometimes at least they punish the wicked just because they are wicked. Such adumbrations of ethics arise out of the cult of honour, but have their own place in a new world of speculation. Men are set against an order of divine beings, who may indeed be incalculable, but at times judge human actions, and deliver appropriate punishments for them. A man's duty to himself has begun to approximate to a man's duty to the gods.

The omnipotence and the omnipresence of the gods does not prevent men from trying to shape their own destinies, or to make the most of their specifically human powers. So far from being discouraged by the contrast presented by the gods, or acquiescing in defeat and depression, they find in it a challenge to do the best that they can by their own means with their own resources. The gods allow them to go their own way within generous limits, but the ends to which men direct their efforts are not in the least like those of the gods. Since the gods are ageless and deathless, it is quite proper for them to spend eternity in enjoyment, but for men, with their short term of existence, this would be ignoble. Since human life is set within close bounds, the utmost must be made of it, and there is no hint that men should seek to resemble the gods. Indeed, though Calypso wishes to make Odysseus ageless and deathless by feeding him on nectar and ambrosia, he takes no pleasure in the prospect and gladly takes the chance of getting back to his home and his wife and his human circumstances. The Homeric heroes assume that their task is to exert their human faculties to the utmost in action; if they do this, they will live up to the full demands of their responsibility and show that they are fully and truly men. The gods go their own way because they are gods, but men must find a different way suited to their mortality and their talents. Their assumption is that just because life is short, they must crowd it with achievements, and it is in this conviction that Hector and Sarpedon summon their troops to an utmost effort, in which the prospect of death counts as nothing against the exertion of courage. Personal prowess is the end of man, and Glaucus proudly tells Sarpedon of his father's counsel:

Ever to seek to be best and surpass all others in action.[5]

This aim is realized in war, and that is why the hero knows that his life is fated to be short. Achilles may indeed for a moment feel that the game is not worth the prize but it is only a passing mood, and it is not long before he reverts to his true self and returns to battle, knowing that his death is not far away. In this mood his courage flames with all its power, and he crowds all that he can into the fleeting moments as he pursues his irresistible course on the battlefield. His sense of his own impending doom makes him merciless to others, even to Priam's young son, Lycaon, whose appeal to be spared Achilles dismisses with terrible and magnificent words:

> See what a man I am also, both strong and comely to look on.
> Great was the father that bred me, a goddess the mother who bore me;
> Yet over me stand death and fate's overmastering power.
> To me a dawn shall come, or a noon-tide hour, or an evening,
> When some man shall deprive me of life in the heat of the battle,
> Shooting at me with a spear or an arrow sped from a bow-string.[6]

The urgency to pack his life with achievement is the heroic answer to any doubts about the littleness of man in comparison with gods. In his own world and in his own way man can do what the gods cannot. By risking his life he shows his attachment to something beyond it, to an ideal of manhood which the gods can never possess, and from a human point of view this has a nobility, which the feasting and the pleasantries of Olympus must for ever lack.

This obligation to dangerous action offers no reward beyond itself. It is true that a man who displays his prowess may be remembered after his death, but there is little hint that he will be conscious of any such memory, or that it will do anything for him personally. Nor does Homer anticipate later ideas that preeminent heroes find an after-life of splendour and happiness. In his view all men come to a like end. When the dead body is burned, there survives indeed a spirit, but it is faint and feeble. When Achilles tries to embrace the ghost of Patroclus, it disappears under the earth like smoke and Achilles laments:

> O woe is me, for truly abides in the mansion of Hades
> Nought but a phantom and breath, and from it all wits have departed.[7]

The spirits of the dead are compared with bats twittering in a cave, and when Odysseus calls up ghosts at the end of the world, he is able to give them consciousness and speech only by letting them drink the blood of a slain ox, which for a moment restores something of their old memory. When they speak to him, they tell of their miserable state, and Achilles sums up what it means:

> Rather would I be on earth and work as the serf of another,
> Someone without possession, a man without any substance,
> Than be a king over all the ghosts of men who have perished.[8]

Not merely do Greek heroes have no reward or consolation after death; they are in exactly the same case as men who have made no efforts to win honour, and the darkness in which they move over the asphodel meadow offers no substitute for the sunlit world which they have lost. In this sense Homer's outlook is indeed pessimistic, almost tragic. When Patroclus asks Achilles that their ashes may be buried together, he knows that it will mean almost nothing to either of them and count for no more than the merest sign of their devoted love. Homer is rigorously insistent that heroic action is nothing but its own reward and must be pursued for its own sake. He hardly even troubles to explain this, so deeply is it ingrained in his out-look and so supported by what his heroes say in moments of decision and danger.

The paradox of the Homeric outlook is that, though human life is seen as short and unrewarded, it is for this very reason desirable. The lust of living flames through the poems and is all the brighter because of the dark prospects which lie beyond it. In both poems the lure of action is always at work, summoning men to new adventures and efforts and excitements. In the *Iliad* these are mostly to be found on the battlefield, and Homer conveys their savage thrills by his comparisons of heroes in action with natural forces such as fire or wind or waves, with fierce animals like wolves and lions, with birds of prey and shooting stars. He sees at work in them some formidable natural force, which makes them akin to physical phenomena and drives them onward, not indeed in spite of themselves, but certainly with an impetus, which is almost beyond their control. This makes them feel that they are doing a man's work and showing their full worth. It is the same spirit that brings Odysseus into deadly situations, whose perils he savours with an expert taste as when he has himself tied to the mast of his ship that he may hear the deadly song of the Sirens without coming to harm from it, or ventures into the cave of the Cyclops. Still more it carries him through his vengeance on the Suitors who outnumber and outmatch him. He is a truly Homeric hero in his command of himself in the face of danger, which brings out all that is most resolute in him, and sets all his faculties to work together. In struggles of this kind Homer finds the right realization of manhood. He inherited tales from a far past, which had gloried in its conquests and its victories, and he extracts from these his opportunities for showing what action means for men, and since it means so much, it must be of the most dangerous kind; for anything less would mean some effort not fully made, some risk avoided, some thrill unfelt.

Homer is well aware what this costs. Against the 'delight of battle' he sets its sorrows and its bitternesses. The clearest case of this is his treatment of Hector's wife and family, who are unable to share his glories, and depend upon him entirely for their safety and survival. His wife, Andromache, knows that he will be killed, and he himself does not dispute it, and both of them know that it means misery for their small son. Though Homer closes the *Iliad* before the capture and the sack of Troy, it is not far away, and the menace of it hangs over the Trojans and especially over those who do not enjoy the enthralling antidote of battle. Nor is Troy the only city to suffer. Andromache's home at Thebes has been sacked by Achilles, and in the sack her father and her seven brothers were killed; the captive Briseis has seen her husband and her three brothers killed on a single day. Homer knows that there is an irreconcilable conflict between the glory of war and the price which has to be paid for it, and he makes no attempt to reconcile them. The highest excitement known to man is won at the expense of the blackest misery, and between these poles his doom oscillates. Perhaps the last word on it is said by Achilles when he tells Priam that on the threshold of Olympus are two jars, of which one contains evil dooms and one good, both given by Zeus. At the best a man's life may be a mixture of both; more commonly it contains evil only. War, which brings glory, brings also death and doom to both sides, and in the end Achilles will die as surely as Hector. Such an outlook may depend upon the whims of the gods, and to some degree Homer suggests that it does. But he does not blame them for it. If after all they have given man chances to find his own unique glory, he must be prepared to pay the full price.

A life given to action and the pursuit of honour calls in the first place for outstanding personal gifts, but almost no hero can exist on these alone. He lives after all among other men, and for the fulfilment of his nature and a sense of security in his daily perils he needs the affections and relies greatly upon them. Such an affection may exist between heroes, and in Achilles and Patroclus it is a noble love. When Patroclus is killed, Achilles is overwhelmed with grief, and even when he has sated his fury of vengeance by killing Hector, he is still heart-broken, and it is almost a comfort to know that he himself has not much longer to live. The very uncertainty of the heroic life makes such affections necessary, and when they are broken by death, the loss is almost irreparable. Achilles' love for Patroclus is based on a complete identity of ambitions and pursuits; each understands the other and is perfectly at home with him. Such a friendship calls for sacrifice, and Patroclus sacrifices himself for the honour of Achilles, which is smirched by his refusal to fight and which Patroclus feels that he must put right for him. In a lesser degree a like friendship exists between two heroes on the Trojan side, Glaucus and Sarpedon, and when Sarpedon is mortally wounded, he calls on Glaucus to rally the troops around him and tells him that, if he fails, he will be reproached and ashamed henceforward. Friendship imposes the strongest duties, and a man must not fail in them, but in fact he carries them out gladly because his being is deeply identified with that of his friend. It would not occur to him to act otherwise, and, if he did, he would be no true hero.

Love of this kind provides a stabilizing and comforting influence in the hazards of heroic life, and just because Homer feels this strongly, he regards passionate love as a dangerous and disrupting force. Though he never condemns Helen, he makes her lament the doom by which she has brought so much suffering into the world, and he has little liking for Paris, who is chidden by Hector for lagging and plays no gallant part in the fighting. On a lesser scale the disastrous love of Clytaemnestra and Aegisthus, which leads to the murder of Agamemnon, receives nothing but condemnation from men and gods. Passion on such a scale was far too likely to upset the precarious balance of human relations and could not be approved. On the other hand Homer depicts with deep sympathy the warmth of domestic affections. His Hector and Andromache are completely in love with one another, and how strongly Andromache depends on Hector is revealed in her words to him:

> Hector to me you are father, and you my beautiful mother,
> And you are also my brother, and you my powerful husband.[9]

Though honour insists that Hector must risk his life for Troy, he tells his wife that neither Troy nor his father and mother mean so much to him as she does, and indeed in their love we see how Homeric heroes need something to counter and assuage the violence of their active lives. The love of Penelope and Odysseus is less absorbing than this, but after all they are much older and have been separated for twenty years. Yet even after this long absence Odysseus prefers the thought of his wife to the living presence of the goddess Calypso, who wishes to keep him with her for ever. It is to regain his wife and all that she means to him that Odysseus fights the Suitors, and when at last he is united to her, order again reigns in Ithaca. Of course women depend on men more than men on women, and for this reason women's affections have a special depth and constancy. Nor is their love moved by any considerations of advantage. When Odysseus speaks with the ghost of his mother, he asks her about the manner of her death, and her answer is final in its pathos and truth.

For it was not that she, the keen-eyed archer of Heaven,
Stole on me unperceived and painlessly smote with her arrows,
Nor did a fever attack me, and with its wasting consumption,
Such as is common with men, drain out the life from my body,
But it was longing and care for you, my noble Odysseus,
And your kindness of heart that robbed me of life and its sweetness.[10]

Just because the affections provide a stable element in a world incessantly
on the move, the loss of them in death is all the more pitiful and painful.
Like heroic prowess, they too are doomed to a short career, and for this
reason shine all the more brightly against the darkness that will soon cover
them.

From this central outlook Homer builds up his scenes of action. Though
he is limited by his traditional themes, he succeeds in making the utmost of
them and creating almost every kind of effect that a narrative poem allows.
His art is in one way extremely simple. In describing an event he aims at
one main effect, and to this he gives all his power. He has no hesitations or
afterthoughts or qualifications. What he tells stands up firmly and clearly
in its own nature. Moreover, he covers a whole gamut of effects, and draws
from each its most human quality. Since he was concerned with glorious
doings, he rises with apparently effortless ease to the fierce, dramatic
moments of crisis. When Achilles, having decided to go back to battle,
shows himself to the enemy at the trench, a bright light shines on his
head, and the mere sight of him so terrifies the Trojans that twelve chariot-
eers die. When Odysseus has strung the bow, he flings off his rags and
leaps upon the platform in his hall, ready to kill the Suitors. The same
firmness of touch is manifest in all Homer's scenes of violent action, but it
is only one of his effects. His feeling for human events is Shakespearean in
its breadth of sympathy and imaginative understanding. He is in his quiet
way a master of pathos, as when old Priam kisses the hands of Achilles, the
terrible man-slaying hands, which have killed many of his sons, or when
Hector's small child, Astyanax, shrinks back in tears from his father's
plumed helmet, and Hector laughs and takes it off, or when Calypso, who
wishes to keep Odysseus with her, lets him go, and wishes him good
fortune, or when the ghost of Achilles rejoices to hear of his son's prowess
on earth, or when Odysseus finds his old father firming a plant on a small
plot of land. Though Homer's heroes in their moments of decisive crisis
seem to be carried away by some more than mortal force, they are pro-
foundly human in their susceptibility to ordinary feelings, and it is this
which makes them different from the mass of heroes in other literatures.
Their moments of power and irresistible impetus in no way detract from

their essentially human natures, and these natures are themselves of a candid simplicity and instinctive straightforwardness.

If Homer's moments of crisis and excitement are to get their full worth, they must stand in contrast to less exciting events before and after, and Homer is master of a quiet poetry, which deals with the commonest events and yet makes them catch and hold our attention. He gives an unexpected charm to a young man folding his clothes before he goes to bed, or a ship scudding through the waters with a following wind at dusk, or the felling of trees to make a raft, or the washing of dirty clothes in a river by Nausicaa and her maidens, or piling a cart with gifts for Achilles, or fetching wood from the hills for the funeral-pyre of Hector, or old Laertes wearing gloves to keep off the thorns as he works in the fields, or the otherwise unknown Axylus, who welcomes all who pass on the road, or Dresus, whom a nymph bore on the mountains, or the priestess Theano, who nurses her husband's bastard son. These are the merest background to the main plot, and yet they have their own poetry and life. The give-and-take of blows in battle may seem monotonous to us, but there is in them a variety far beyond the range of such a poem of battle as the *Chanson de Roland*, and, if we pay attention to them, we see what a Greek audience would enjoy in their expert and detailed presentation. Homer is not unaware of the grotesque side of war, as when a stricken man falls from his chariot on his head and stays stuck in the deep sand, or when another man is struck with a stone and his eyes fall out on the dust before his feet. Though there is horror in such cases, it is not pathetic but grotesque. Homer marks many unnoticed aspects in the human scene and finds for each its own special poetry. That is why his mood is always changing, why he does not make events conform to any preconceived pattern, but finds in each something special and significant and illuminating.

Homer's first concern is with human beings, and just for this reason he has a discriminating eye for the stage upon which an action is played. He does not go out of his way to describe it but tells enough to make it real. For instance, he is fully aware that Troy and the Trojan plain must be intelligible if his story is to make its full effect. In this he was helped by the ancient epithets for Troy, such as 'windy', 'high-gated', 'broad-wayed', 'steep', 'beetling', and these he may have learned in his training. But it is likely that he saw the site and the ruins of Troy with his own eyes; for he knows the landscape with the rivers Simois and Scamander, the trees and shrubs on their banks, the mounds from which the gods watch the battle, the batter of the walls of the city which makes it possible for Patroclus to climb as far as the battlements and then to be thrust down by Apollo, the distance from Troy to the Achaean camp, the plan of the walls, which means that Andromache is suddenly confronted with the sight of her dead husband. The details are unobtrusive but they give a sense of reality. So too in Ithaca, on which Homer is less well informed, and combines certain authentic details with others less accurate or even invented, he gives a picture of a real island, with its small town, its harbours, its cave to hide Odysseus' treasure, its plots of ground where old Laertes works, its ferry-service to the mainland, its hills for goats and swine, its lack of oxen and horses. Again he is, like all Greeks, intimately acquainted with the sea in all its moods, and makes his Odysseus set off from Calypso with a fair, following wind, which is in due course succeeded by a sudden storm which wrecks him. His swim to land is recounted with a lively apprehension of the dangers of a rough sea and a rocky coast, and Odysseus is more than once near death, but is saved at last by reaching the estuary of a river, where there are no rocks, and there is a shelter from the wind, and he finds a deep thicket in which to hide his naked body. When the physical scene is necessary to the story, Homer makes it clear and visible and fit aptly into the action.

At times he goes beyond this and describes a scene for its own sake, notably the cave of Calypso on the remote island of Ortygia and the gardens of Alcinous on Phaecia. Both are outside the limits of the known world, but in neither is there anything very magical or suggestive of fairy-land. Calypso's cave is surrounded by trees, covered with a vine, and by it are four streams of water and meadows of violets and parsley. That Homer loves the thought of it is clear from his comment that even an immortal would wonder at it in delight. In contrast with this wild scene is the cultivated garden of Alcinous, surrounded by a wall and amply planted with fruit-trees of every kind. Yet for all its appearance of ordered normality, it has the special gift that its trees bear fruit in succession all the year round. In neither case does Homer allow himself to pass beyond a strictly factual description, and the poetry is all the firmer for it. From these cases, we might conclude that he liked natural scenes and gardens, but it is clear that he also liked much more. His similes abound in scenes of wild nature, and cover almost every aspect of the Greek scene – a poppy broken by the rain, waves breaking on a rocky headland, the stars around the moon on a windless night, snow coming with the north wind, a cow standing over her first calf, winds shaking a wood, flies gathering round pails of milk, fish scattering before a dolphin, wolves stealing lambs from a herd, vultures crying on a lofty rock, a lion leaping on a bull, a hawk frightening jackdaws and starlings, a rainbow appearing in the sky, fire driven by a

wind. He is fully at home with nature from her humblest to her fiercest
and most impressive manifestations, and gives to her what is indeed a subordinate part but none the less deeply felt and absorbed and mastered. He
lacks not only any trace of the 'pathetic fallacy' but even any hint that the
gods are at work in the workings of nature. He sees them just as they are,
and presents them briefly with an unerring eye for what is dramatic and
telling in them. The natural scene is far from being his first interest, but he
is acutely aware of it and uses it to complete his story and to show the
kinship between it and the doings of men, which so often recall it. In his
single universe birds and beasts, waves and winds, have a place along with
men.

Homer's creation is a microcosm of the world around him, and though
he is tied to the past for his stories, he succeeds in including somehow
almost every aspect of life as he knew it. He is the first universal poet in
that he saw the living scene as a whole and marked all its significant aspects.
With some of course he deals all too briefly, but his world remains complete and true both to legend and to what he saw about him. His duty to
the past does not in any way hamper him. Indeed in so far as it forces him
to create characters larger than ordinary men it gives him just that element
of distance which a work of the imagination requires, and at the same time
he never allows it to fade away, as heroic songs often do, into vagueness
and vastness without character or contour. In minor matters, such as arms,
and clothing, and the use of horses and chariots, he may combine ancient
and contemporary elements, but in all that matters, in his vision of the
place of man in the natural scene, in the relations of gods and men, in the
portrayal of passions and affections, he fuses the past and the present into
an indissoluble, harmonious whole. He sees men and women from within
and presents them in their full human appeal for their own sakes, almost
without comment or criticism. If he has something to say about them, it
is said through the action, through the enterprises which they initiate or
the dooms which they bring upon themselves. He does not feel the same
sympathy towards all of them any more than Shakespeare does, and he
makes his own fine discriminations on their worth. But his world lives in
its own strength because his characters are not puppets whom he manipu-
lates to illustrate a lesson but recognizable and understandable specimens
of humanity, with all its greatness and its weakness, its essential magnificence, and its sudden failures. What touches him most deeply is the way in
which men give themselves to a cause, especially to honour, and fling all
their powers into its pursuit. It is this which brings out their separate
individualities and their common humanity, which emphasizes their pre-

carious, menaced, and yet noble condition, which gathers all the varieties of human endeavour into a single pattern and makes them intelligible in it.

Homer's identification of the past with the present in his stories is matched by his technique of narrative, which is both traditional and intended for contemporary use. He composed for recitation, and, though his poems were in due course written down, he is unlikely to have used writing in their composition, and we may with some confidence assume that, like many other poets in many parts of the world, he composed his poems in his head, and did not so much learn them by heart as know so well what he wished to say, that he found no difficulty in saying it. To be able to do this he mastered a very large number of formulaic phrases and even passages, and that is why his poems contain a striking amount of repeated, conventional matter. For us this creates a difficulty. We may feel not entirely at home with a technique which operates so freely with formulaic elements, and we may complain that even the famous Homeric epithets soon cease to touch us, and are even at times inappropriate, as when the sky by day is called 'starry' or beached ships 'swift'. The epithets are indissolubly wedded to their nouns and necessary for oral composition in that they meet the needs of grammar, and sense, and metre, and their original audiences would probably pay as little attention to them as we do. But our uneasiness may be deeper than this. We are brought up to expect every word to do a special task, and in the Homeric style they do not quite do this. We may even feel that this kind of composition lacks the individual touch which we regard as indispensable to the highest art. Yet this is to state the problem wrongly. Homer operates, not so much with individual words, as with phrases, and each phrase is chosen with the same care as literary poets give to each word. The phrase, and not the word, is his unit, and his poetry is none the less lively for this reason. Homer's skill lies in choosing the right phrase, and, if we compare his art with that of other oral poets working on his methods, we see at once his transcendent ability. A poet must be judged by the skill with which he uses the language which he inherits, and of Homer's skill there is no doubt. He was fortunate in succeeding to a rich legacy, but he made the fullest use of it, and, in keeping its rules, showed that it could be used with a high degree of freedom, and ease, and adaptability.

The Homeric poems were composed not for a reading public, but for a listening audience, and this accounts for some of their differences from modern books. The reciting bard must hold his listeners' attention, dispense with much that a reading public thinks necessary, and act on the principle of 'one thing at a time'. He must make each episode as clear and dramatic as possible and not confuse his hearers with other considerations which may be relevant, but are not quite on the immediate point. This leads to various features in the Homeric manner which have been mis-understood in the past, and may be misunderstood again. First, an action may be described in some detail because it is necessary at this point of the story, but as the interest shifts, nothing more is said about it. Achilles lays his spear against a tamarisk, presumably that he may use his sword more easily; later he has his spear in his hand, though we are not told that he has picked it up. When Athene, disguised as Mentes, arrives in the palace of Odysseus, she puts her spear in a spear-stand, but later she flies away as a bird and presumably leaves it behind, though Homer does not trouble to say so. These are the merest trivialities, but they illustrate the need to concentrate on what really matters and to keep the main thread of the story clear. Secondly, once a theme has served its purpose for a special effect, it may be abandoned and forgotten, and we are wrong to recall it when the action takes a new direction. So Diomedes, who first attacks the gods vigorously, later says that he would not think of doing so. In the new context he is presented in a different light, and his earlier activities are ir-relevant. Athene twice transforms Odysseus into an old beggar, that he may not be recognized in his home, and though we hear that after his first transformation he is for a short period restored to his usual shape, nothing is said about this after the second. It follows from his behaviour and the general movement of the action, and to mention it would interfere with his new adventures. This neglect of what is not immediately relevant to the context leads sometimes to what we might regard as real contradic-tions in the story. In Book 9 of the *Iliad* the Achaean leaders beg Achilles to go back to battle, and he refuses, but in Book 16 he behaves as if nothing of the sort has happened, simply because he has now his own powerful reason for fighting in his desire to avenge Patroclus. When Achilles lends his armour to Patroclus, it is on the assumption that this will deceive the Trojans into thinking that he is Achilles, and so spread panic among them. For a time the trick works, and then suddenly the Trojans see through it, the spell is broken, and we hear no more of it. In the *Odyssey* Odysseus and Telemachus concoct a plan for the destruction of the Suitors, but events overtake them, and they have to carry out their design by quite different means. In such cases we may feel that Homer could have secured a new effect without abandoning what he has already told, but he cannot allow any backward looks to interfere with the dramatic completeness and clarity of a given moment. Thirdly, Homer has to arrange his scenes so that they do not trespass upon one another. Quite early in the *Iliad* comes what is really a scene of farewell between Hector and Andromache, and they are never presented again together. But if we read between the lines we may deduce that, though nothing is said of it, they spend the night together when the Trojans retire from the battlefield into their city. The farewell is necessary for the full delineation of Hector, but it must not interfere with his later actions, and by placing it where he does Homer shows what he means to Troy and its people and what sort of man he is away from the fight. In the same way, when Odysseus has to leave Calypso, there is a touching farewell between them, but in fact he does not leave her for four days. The farewell comes at this place because it must not distract attention from Odysseus' construction of the raft which is to take him on his journey and is now more important than Calypso. These are not the methods of the modern novelist, who can afford to write complex chapters which combine different themes, but in oral performance they are indispensable. We notice their incongruities because we read the poems instead of listening to them, but when we see them in their proper setting, we appreciate how skilfully they are managed.

Through means such as these Homer keeps his separate scenes remarkably vivid before our eyes, and the ease of his narrative matches the simplicity of his outlook and his unfaltering conception of his characters. If he were to elaborate his episodes with less immediately relevant details or peripheral considerations, something essential would be lost. Both the *Iliad* and the *Odyssey* are built up largely from self-contained episodes, which may be enjoyed for their own sake, and to this extent reflect an art of short lays behind them, but each poem has also its grand design and its main movements. The *Iliad* begins with the wrath of Achilles and ends with its healing, but between these are the main movements first of the defeat of the Achaeans without Achilles, then of even worse disasters culminating in the death of Patroclus, and finally of Achilles' own career on the battlefield which ends with the killing of Hector. In the *Odyssey* Books 1–4 set out the situation on Ithaca before Odysseus returns, and show into what a state it has fallen, and how Telemachus sails off to get advice and help. In Books 5–12 the emphasis is turned to the hero and we hear, largely through his own lips, of his adventures between the sack of Troy and his arrival on Ithaca. Books 13–24 tell of the series of events which culminate in the destruction of the Suitors, and the recognition of Odysseus by Penelope. The *Odyssey* has a more complex plan than the *Iliad* but fundamentally follows the same rule of presenting each episode for its full worth as it comes and making it part of an overmastering design. The Greek sense of order is fully at work in both poems, but as yet it feels no need for elegant complexities. What matters is to tell the story in its variety and richness, and make every theme stand out as self-sufficient in its own worth.

We may presume that Homer told these tales for patrons who were accustomed to this kind of art, but, of course, this did not prevent him from having his own notion of their significance, or indeed from thinking that the aim of his art might be more than mere enjoyment. In so far as he presents his own vision of human life, he is always more than a mere entertainer, and it is impossible to read even a few lines from him without seeing that he has pondered deeply and seriously on what these ancient stories mean for his own day. He succeeds, as we have seen, in presenting a full picture of human society, but he has also his own idea of what poetry is and what place it has in the generations of men. In each poem he lets fall a hint of his artistic intention and what lies behind it and, though it is only a hint and he puts it forward casually and shyly, it cannot be disregarded. When Helen, who is largely responsible for all the horror of the Trojan War, thinks of what disasters she has caused, she has an explanation of it:

> Zeus set an evil doom upon us, that we may for the future
> Give unto men unborn a theme of song to be told them.[11]

This might pass as Helen's own notion, but it is remarkable that in the *Odyssey*, Alcinous, king of Phaeacia and host of the castaway Odysseus, speaks of the sufferings of Achaeans and Trojans in not dissimilar words:

> Gods fashioned it for them, and wove a thread of destruction
> For mankind, that it might be a song for men in the future.[12]

At first sight this looks rather a heartless explanation of what was, by any standard, a gruesome catastrophe, but in fact Homer has something much more serious in mind. The strains and the sufferings of the Trojan War have won an immortality through song, and though this may mean little or nothing to those who perished in it, and now live a shadowy and faint existence in death, yet something remains for mankind as it changes from generation to generation, and this is a memory to be treasured and cherished and honoured, a link with the stupendous past, a chapter of history rich in tales of prowess and sacrifice, a lasting source of life and humanity and understanding. Through poetry the horrors of the present are transcended and transferred to a sphere, where in the telling of them they enrich and expand experience. This is the lasting monument which Homer erected from his knowledge of the dark and violent past, spending on it all the wealth of his imagination and his understanding. Man perishes, and leaves little but a name behind him, but this name and the legends which sometimes cluster round it inflame and inspire men who come later, and remain to give comfort and assurance in the shifting scenes of mortality.

3

THE EMERGENCE OF
PERSONALITY

IN the seventh century and later, the Homeric poems were performed at public festivals, like that of Apollo on Delos, by professional bards, some of whom claimed to be descended from Homer and to have a special knowledge of his works. Before reciting the actual poems, which they must have learned by heart from written texts, they sometimes recited shorter works of their own composition as preludes to what was coming. A collection of such poems has survived and is known as the Homeric Hymns, since each of them is addressed to a god or a goddess, at whose festival the recitation is to take place and about whom they tell stories. The authorship and the dates of these poems range from the early seventh century to the fifth and later, but their manner is a prolongation of the epic tradition, and they use the hexameter as Homer used it with many of his themes and phrases. Yet they differ from him in the far greater attention which they pay to the gods. This is their first concern, and, though they come from different times and places, they reflect almost a uniform spirit. In them the gods are presented, neither as incalculable incarnations of power, nor as overseers of the doings of men. Though to some degree they recall tales in the *Iliad* and the *Odyssey*, in which the gods relax themselves in pleasure or pursue their wilful whims and fancies, they lack the violence and the irresponsibility which appear in Homer, and move in a more decorous and more graceful order of being. They have some- times a touch of playfulness, notably in the Hymn to Hermes, when the child Hermes, who has just been born, tricks Apollo of his cattle, or in the Hymn to Dionysus, when Dionysus, kidnapped by Tyrrhenian pirates and taken on board their ship, becomes a lion on the prow, makes the mast burst into vine-leaves, and turns the captain and his crew into dolphins when they jump in terror overboard. Even when the Hymns touch on more serious matters, this gracefulness does not forsake them. When

Aphrodite falls in love with the young Trojan prince Anchises as he pastures cattle on Mount Ida, and makes him return her love, the relation is tender and natural, and hints at no nasty risks or grim consequences. When Demeter, having lost her daughter Persephone, who has been carried off by Hades, the god of death, to the underworld, seeks her through the earth, she comes to a household, where, disguised as an old woman, she looks after the child of the house with a touching affection, and tries to strengthen him every night by putting him among the ashes, until she is caught by the parents, and forced to go away. The gods dance on Olympus, and the Graces and the Hours, Harmony and Youth take part holding one another by the wrist; Ares and Hermes join in, but none lifts so lofty a foot as Apollo playing his lyre. The old brutal or uproarious tales of the gods have been softened and refined, without making concessions to any new conceptions of them that may trouble the consciences of men. From the first part of the Hymn to Apollo, composed in the early years of the seventh century, to the Hymn to Pan, composed probably soon after 490 BC, the tradition continues unbroken and unperturbed. The epic objectivity is applied to the gods, and awkward elements in the old stories are skilfully avoided or tempered into a more genial form. This art helped to maintain a vision of the gods which lacked alike the crudity of primitive beliefs and the forbidding abstractions of new speculations. In a way the writers of the Hymns are Homer's most accomplished successors. They do not attempt to rival him in his own field, but in a small region, which is incidentally his, they make happy innovations. Theirs is a delightful world of divine beings, who have their own gaiety and resplendence, but are none-the-less sufficiently close to humanity for it to understand, and admire them.

The Homeric Hymns are still to a large degree objective and impersonal. They are composed for special festivals and deities, and address themselves to their claims, but their main task is to tell a story in the epic way. Yet their bards do not hide themselves so modestly as Homer does. More than once the singer, on coming to the end of his song, prays to the gods that in return for it he may be given a livelihood to his heart's content, and in this we see how the wandering bard, no longer kept by the bounty of some prince at his court, has to make his living as best he can and hints at his need with becoming tact. He has abandoned his old anonymity, and begun to assert himself and make claims on his audience. At one place the bard goes far beyond these delicate hints and speaks out boldly about his work. In the first part of the Hymn to Apollo, which was performed at Delos, the bard, after telling of the gay company which has gathered on Apollo's island, begs the audience to remember him and his song:

> Mercy upon me, Apollo, and Artemis, show me thy kindness;
> Then good-bye to you all. Keep me henceforth in remembrance,
> Maidens, whenever there comes in after days to you hither
> One of the labouring sons of the earth who asks you a question:
> 'Maidens, tell me what man is truly the sweetest of singers,
> Coming hither to you, and by whom are you chiefly delighted?'
> Then do you, each one of you, make answer together, replying:
> 'There is a man who is blind, and in rocky Chios he dwelleth:
> Finest of all are his songs, both now and in time that is coming.'
> Your good fame shall I carry with me wherever I wander
> Over the earth thro' the cities of men unto all who are in them;
> And all men shall believe, for the truth will be what I tell them.[1]

This revealing passage is the work of a professional, who commends his own wares by promising to commend the young women of Delos, who have danced at the festival, where he performs. He makes proud claims for himself, and yet he is clearly a poor man. Here, in the impersonal context of a tale about Apollo, he introduces something about his profession, his powers, and his claims. In antiquity the lines were thought to have been written by Homer, and they are probably the source of the legend that Homer was blind. This ascription of authorship was accepted even by the critical Thucydides, and yet it is hard to believe it. The language of the poem is not quite Homer's and lacks his precision and firmness. Yet it is possible that the bard, who is about to recite the Homeric poems, somehow identifies himself with Homer and claims the reward that is due to so august a poet. It is his way of asserting himself, of bringing his work to the notice of a large, mixed audience, of claiming pride of place for the art which he practises. The anonymity of the epic is broken, and the poet, despite his humble station, claims a special authority. Personal poetry is already on its way even within the bounds of a strict tradition, which usually rejects any manifestation of individual idiosyncrasies.

The Homeric Hymns belong to a time when the composition of the epic was in decline. Having reached its zenith with Homer, it began to lose its preeminence and its unique prestige. Poems were still composed in the old manner, filled the gaps between the *Iliad* and the *Odyssey*, and extended the cycle of Troy both forwards and backwards. Only scanty fragments of them remain, and though the epic style is still strong enough to give them an air of distinction, they were condemned by Aristotle for their poverty of construction, and we may doubt whether their authors were able to compose on Homer's generous scale or with his eye for a commanding design. They marked the beginning of a long decline in epic. It was still composed even in the fifth and fourth centuries, but it had lost its old ardour and sweep. The introduction of writing meant that poets little by little abandoned the oral style with its formulas and composed in a more deliberate, premeditated, self-conscious manner, choosing words for their own sake, and trying to speak in a distinctively individual tone. This had to happen, but, so far as the epic was concerned, it seems to have brought almost no advantages. Homer's precedents were too powerful to be easily avoided, and attempts to find substitutes for his time-hallowed phrases tended to look factitious and pretentious, as when Antimachus of Colophon, writing his *Thebaid* towards the end of the fifth century, tried to find variations on the stock theme of drinking wine. Nine such attempts survive, but none has the dignity or the polish of Homer's standard treatment of the same subject. As new forms of poetry emerged in response to new outlook, the epic waned. Homer indeed was increasingly known and honoured, but his manner belonged to a vanishing world and could no longer be profitably followed. The oral tradition, which had come from Mycenaean times, broke down with the introduction of the alphabet, but the break was gradual, and there was still enough strength in the old style to encourage some remarkable moves in other directions.

This purely literary revolution was accompanied by a social revolution which had no less influence on literary matters. In the eighth century the old system of local kings still prevailed in most parts of the Greek world, and it was they who patronized and encouraged the epic. But in the seventh century kings gave place in many districts to small classes of nobles, who divided among themselves the royal powers and privileges. Full of the pride of success, and eager to draw attention to themselves, they turned from the past to the present, from the old heroic ideal to a new sense of personality and individual worth. So, far from expecting poetry to be objective and anonymous, they wished it to tell of themselves, to enrich their lives by recording even quite unimportant events in it, to have their own doings so set down in words that later generations should know of them. With this aristocratic pride came a new understanding of human worth, not perhaps so splendid as the Homeric cult of honour, but interested in many matters of which Homer was indeed conscious, but thought inappropriate to his heroes. What he had kept for his similes, poets now made matters of central interest as they wrote about the contemporary world with a keen sense of its significance. All this meant that poetry was free to advance in new directions and to reflect the actual scene directly without having to shape it into images of the past.

The most striking feature of immediately post-Homeric poetry is its departure from anonymity and its desire to put the self into prominence. Despite the living appeal of the epic an art was needed for contemporary issues and individual utterances, and various efforts were made to provide this. Towards the dominating Homeric presence poets stood in an ambiguous attitude. On the one hand they could not escape from it; its metre, its manner, much of its temper, and many of its devices were bred into their consciousness and indispensable to them. They could make innovations and variations and approach new subjects, but they still remained in thrall. On the other hand the impersonal objectivity of the epic was alien to the new needs. That personal poetry existed before Homer is more than likely, but it must have occupied a very humble position in comparison with the epic and been very much under its influence. As the epic declined, this much humbler art came to the fore and strove to extend its sphere and its influence. In this development there is no single line of progress, and more than one means of self-expression was devised. Poetry was brought down from its majestic detachment to play a fuller part in common life, and for the first time we are able to know the Greeks not through their dramatization of ancient legends, but as they saw themselves in their own surroundings.

The first surviving signs of this change come almost from Homer's lifetime in two small pieces of evidence revealed by archaeology. The first is a wine-jug from Athens painted with geometrical patterns, and on it is an inscription which fades into illegibility but begins quite clearly:

> He who of all in the dance does now most tenderly frolic.[2]

The jug comes from about 720 BC. It looks as if it were a prize or a present given to a dancer, whose performance, however fine, was not very decorous and seems to have won the admiration of some spectator at a convivial gathering. The line concerns a present social occasion, and is composed in a good hexameter, whose choice of words certainly owes something to epic, if not necessarily Homeric, precedent. It comes from a higher social level than the Homeric Hymn to Apollo and may have been inscribed by the actual donor. Even by this early date writing had become an accomplishment, and was fully capable of recording a verse. Our second example consists of two lines written on a geometric cup, found at Pithecussae on the island of Ischia off the Bay of Naples and dating from just before 700 BC. After a mysterious introduction, which says: 'I am the cup of

Nestor', and seems not to be in verse, come two lines which indicate that the cup works as a love-charm:

> Whosoever shall drink from this man's cup shall be straightway
> Seized by desire for her of the beautiful crown, Aphrodite.[3]

Here too the hexameter is used and the language is drawn from an epic supply, though not actually from Homer. We may conclude that, when in the latter part of the eighth century, men wished to speak about their present occasions or feelings, they resorted for aid to the language of the epic, that is of the whole oral tradition spread through many parts of Greece. This tradition must have had many local variations, but its central character remained constant, and in these stray lines we can see how this art of words was turned by ingenious amateurs to new, personal ends.

Parallel to these gay, convivial hexameters are others of a more formal and more serious kind, inscribed not on cups or jugs but cut on stone or bronze to mark something worth remembering. These fall into two classes, dedicatory and commemorative, the first being inscribed on offerings made to the gods, the second on memorials to the dead. The first class goes back to at least 700 BC, when a single line records the offering of a handful of spits – an early form of currency – in the temple of Hera at Perachora on the Corinthian gulf, and in the next century this is followed by a thin stream of other such dedications. At very much the same date Thebes provides a bronze statuette of Apollo, on which it is recorded that the offering is made by Manticlus 'to Apollo, the far-darter, lord of the silver bow',[4] and he asks the gods for a kind return for it. The middle of the seventh century provides a female statue from Delos, archaic in its stiff formality and the lack of treatment in the clothing, which has an inscription in three lines, saying that it is an offering made by Nicandrê 'to the far-darter, who delights in arrows', gives the names of her father and her husband, and describes her as 'surpassing other women'.[5] Against these we may set a series of early pieces inscribed as memorials to the dead. These begin about 620 BC, but there is no reason to think that the type is not earlier. One example from Corinth states that it is the grave of Dveinias, 'whom the shameless sea destroyed';[6] another from Corcyra is more adventurous and has its own vaulting splendour:

> Arniadas lies here. Ares, with his eyes flashing, killed him
> Fighting beside the ships on the banks of the flowing Aratthus,
> Proving himself far best in the groans and the clamour of battle.[7]

This little group of inscriptions whether dedicatory or commemorative, marks a notable advance in personal poetry. In each case the name of the donor or of the dead is given with some brief detail to distinguish him from other men, and in each case the hexameter is used, with small, stylish touches, which have an epic colouring, and not only give titles to the gods, but make some telling point for the men and women concerned, who were of some consequence and able to make dedications to the gods or had relatives rich enough to set up fine memorials to them. In origin they are not far removed from the inscriptions from Athens and Ischia and, like them, they show how the traditional art of epic was used for short pieces of verse concerned with personal and contemporary themes.

These scattered pieces show what was happening in different places, but they reveal their full significance when we set them against the most substantial literary remains of the late Homeric or immediately post-Homeric age, the two poems ascribed to Hesiod, the *Theogony* and the *Works and Days*. There is no doubt that the poems are the work of a single man, who gives his name as Hesiod and lived in Boeotia. Behind him lies an epic tradition not unlike that behind Homer, but perhaps less rich and accomplished, and certainly manipulated with a genius much inferior to Homer's. Neither poem is in the pure epic tradition of heroic tale. The *Theogony* may have its roots in an even remoter age which told of gods rather than of men, but Hesiod speaks more in the spirit of instruction than of re-creation, and seems to wish to set in order conflicting and chaotic tales, and to make some sense of them in a cosmological scheme. He does not sing of them for delight, but because he thinks that men ought to know about them, and to versify their origins and relations is the best way of getting this done. The *Works and Days* is a personal, even a private work, addressed by the poet to his feckless brother, Perses, and concerned with various aspects of the struggle for existence in a hard land. Nor is Hesiod merely different from Homer; he almost sets himself against the heroic tradition and outlook. He does not accept its assumptions or its admirations, and his view of life is not that of a king or a noble, but of a struggling farmer, who is bitterly occupied with the hard present. If Homer presents a radiant and dramatic past, Hesiod sets out with unflinching realism the laborious and unrewarding present. He may have known Homer's actual poems or other poems from the same school, and legend tells that once the two poets competed for a prize. This may be no more than a mythical way of expressing their differences, and that at least it does neatly; for it tells that the judge, king Paneides, gave the prize to Hesiod, who had been defeated throughout the contest of passage for passage, because the crown ought to go to the poet who incited to agriculture and peace, not to him who told of wars. The story presents Hesiod as he himself would like to be known and sets him appropriately in his historical place.

Hesiod was not, like Homer's Demodocus and Phemius, a professional bard, but a farmer, who took to composing poetry because of a remarkable experience, which he had when still a young man. Tending his sheep under Mount Helicon, he had a vision of the Muses, who said to him:

> Shepherds abiding in fields, poor brutes, who are nothing but bellies,
> Many indeed are the lies that we speak that appear to be truthful,
> But when we wish, we can also reveal in words what the truth is.[8]

They then gave him a staff of olive-wood and breathed into him a divine voice that he might celebrate the things that were to come and that had been. This vivid revelation made Hesiod a poet without ceasing to be a farmer. That he believed in its authoritative authenticity we cannot doubt, and the result was his *Theogony*. Homer is content to summon the Muse to his aid, but Hesiod goes to some lengths to explain the source of his inspiration and insists that he has been specially chosen for his task of song. He claims for himself an authority far greater than Homer claims, and yet he is not quite sure of it. He seems to go back to a distant past when poets were prophets, and spoke with the tongues of gods, but such a claim was apt enough in his own time when the old art of the epic was losing its supremacy, and yet poetry still had a part to play in social life and needed all the authority that it could summon. From the start Hesiod's honesty compels attention, and we can understand why he made such an impression upon the Greeks and was held in high honour for many hundreds of years. He speaks for the common man, for the small farmer, who has never crossed the sea except over the narrow strait from Aulis to Euboea, where he won a prize at Chalcis, and later dedicated it to the Muses of Helicon. To them he was himself dedicated, but his range of poetry was very much of his own gifts and his own making.

It was the *Theogony* which Hesiod wrote at the prompting of the Muses, and it is a comparatively early work, which attempts to sort out a confused jumble of myths into a more or less coherent system. He may well have been the first to attempt such a task, and in that case his influence was enormous; for his account of the beginning of things and the genealogies of the gods was accepted for many centuries as a classical work of reference. His approach to this tangled subject is that of a man who has had a revelation, and speaks without hesitancy or fear that he may be wrong. Much of the *Theogony* has rather a mechanical air, as befits a versified record of multifarious marriages and begettings, but it is not without a guiding plan or incidental splendours. Hesiod sees the growth of the world and of the gods who rule it, as a slow and painful movement from chaos to order. Just as in the beginning Chaos and Erebos and Night produce the bright sky and the day, so, as the process continues, the gods defeat and displace other elements of disorder. Cronus comes to power by castrating and deposing his father Uranus (Sky), and is himself displaced by his son Zeus. Violent breeds like the Giants and the Titans, who threaten the Olympian theocracy, are defeated and driven down into darkness. Even when all this is done, there are still other sources of evil, like Might, who bears Doom and Death, and Strife, who bears a whole hideous progeny of destruction. Yet against them the powers of order and beauty emerge, creatures whose names echo the Greek gift for giving shape and character to abstract things, whether the children of Themis (Right), who are Lawfulness and Justice and Peace, or the nymphs of the sea, whose musical names echo its magical allurements. Hesiod is well aware that he is dealing with abstract powers, but they are none the less powerful and none the less divine. If he anticipates the first beginnings of Greek science by his sense of a cosmic order established by a struggle for survival, he is true to Greek belief in seeing divine forces at work everywhere and attributing to them all that matters in the physical world or in the hearts of men. This was the inner meaning of his vision, and though it did not turn him into a great poet or save some of his verses from halting, it gave him an embracing conception of the world which he knew, and in which he saw some kind of harmony holding it together.

The *Works and Days* looks like a work of Hesiod's middle years, when prolonged and often unsuccessful effort had taught him the hardness of the human condition. He speaks for the class of free poor, whom Homer mentions only incidentally and who play no large part in Greek literature. His own village of Ascra, isolated and difficult of access, had no great appeal for him, being, as he said, bad in winter and hard in summer, but he took no steps to leave it. His chief enemies are the local kings, for whom he has nothing but hard words, accusing them of taking bribes to pervert justice. If Homer's pessimism is countered by his belief in prowess and glory, Hesiod's is bitter and naked. For him the state of mankind has got steadily worse. Beginning with a Golden Age, when men lived in peace and enjoyment and died as if overcome by sleep, and a Silver Age, when they passed their lives in a childhood of a hundred years, but neglected the gods, he passes to a Bronze Age, which formed a taste for violence and war, and worst of all to an Iron Age, in which he himself lives, when children despise their parents and nobody attends to good or bad, or thinks of shame or righteous indignation. Homer has no knowledge of this historical notion, which may have come from the East or from a remote Indo-European past, but Hesiod pays an unexpected tribute to Homer's imaginary world when between the Bronze and Iron Ages he sets an Age of Heroes in which men were demi-gods and performed great feats at Thebes and Troy and were rewarded by being moved by Zeus to the Islands of the Blest by the deep eddies of the Ocean. Hesiod respects this age, but has no hankering for it. His concern is with life as he knows it, and this allows no place for glory. He sees himself and his kind as tied to the daily hardships of scraping a livelihood from the niggardly soil, and though he knows that seafaring might perhaps provide an escape from his troubles, he is not prepared to face it. At a time when many Greeks were risking long voyages to found colonies overseas, Hesiod stayed at home, complaining about his lot, but unwilling to change it. It is just this which gives a special power to his poetry. Faced by the age-old challenges of his native land, he found his answers to them, and presents in his adaptation of the epic style his personal problems and anxieties, and the solutions and consolations which helped him to master them.

Hesiod's dark view of life is shown by his myth of Pandora, the beautiful creature fashioned by the gods to torment men. She brings a jar and from it scatters sorrows among them. At its bottom is hope, which might have helped to redeem their misery, but she puts the lid back on the jar before hope can come out, and keeps it hidden. The result is that ten thousand evils wander among man, and the earth and the sea are alike full of them, and just because hope is locked up, the condition of men is literally hopeless. Yet from this Hesiod draws positive conclusions. If man is to survive, he must work, and Hesiod preaches his gospel of toil as the only antidote that makes life tolerable, or even possible, and by work he means farming, which alone averts starvation. Though he speaks with authority on the technicalities of farming and tells in detail how to make a plough, he does not find much pleasure in them. He may enjoy certain moments of relaxation, as when in summer he lies under the shadow of a rock and drinks wine and milk, and eats bread and the flesh of a young cow, but such occasions are rare, and his real approach to farming is described in language that approaches myth:

> But on the way to virtue the gods undying have stationed
> Sweat, and long and steep is the upward journey towards her,
> And at first it is rough, but when you come to the summit
> Easy then it becomes, tho' before it was hard to pursue it.[9]

Such an expense of effort not only keeps a man alive, but has its own dignity and grandeur. Hesiod rejects the Homeric notion of greatness and glory, but he offers a realistic and feasible alternative to it. For him hard work is the truest kind of prowess and the industrious farmer is a good man.

Because he believes this and because he bitterly resents the injustices against which he himself and others like him struggle in a corrupt social system, Hesiod passes beyond his private quarrel with his brother and his own injuries and speaks for a whole class of toiling and maltreated men. Homer once refers to the 'crooked dooms'[10] given by judges, and means the verbal decisions which take the place of law before written codes come into existence and are for that reason all too easily perverted, but Hesiod is full of the subject, and speaks of it with outspoken courage. Addressing himself directly to the kings, he warns them that they make a great mistake in ignoring the anger of the gods; for thrice ten thousand Immortals move on the earth and, clad in mist, keep watch over men. He proclaims, as Homer never would with a like assurance, that in the end Zeus punishes the wicked. Yet he knows that this is hard to foresee and that men act in full despite of it. Just as Homer contrasts two cities on the shield of Achilles, the one at war and the other at peace, so Hesiod contrasts another two, in one of which justice reigns, and in the other outrage; and, though he puts his trust in the justice of Zeus, he knows that the temptation to injustice is indeed formidable because in an unjust world it pays. How keenly he feels the brutality of such a struggle for existence may be seen from a fable which he makes for it. A hawk carries off a nightingale in its claws, and tells it that all its singing will be of no avail against the hawk's power, and strength of will to do what it chooses:

> Foolish is he who wishes to battle with those who are stronger;
> Victory soon he loses, and with disgrace he has anguish.[10]

Yet though he knows the weakness of justice, Hesiod clings to it, and in him the voice of Greek morality speaks fully and firmly for the first time known to us. On the positive side a man must work; on the negative side he must not steal, not wrong the suppliant or the stranger or the fatherless, not enter into his brother's bed. He must honour his parents in their old age, and, above all, pay proper due to the gods with burnt-offerings, libations, and incense. With Hesiod morality has replaced the cult of honour and become a guiding principle in behaviour. This is combined with an unquestioning respect for the gods, who are the only hope for the oppressed and must on no account be offended. That is why even the most obscure taboos must be observed, such as those which insist that some days in the month are good and others bad. In such a world men must take no risks, and the most whimsical wishes of the gods must be obeyed.

Hesiod, whose life may have been close to Homer's, is in almost every significant respect his antithesis. Even when he tells of the portentous doings of the gods, such as the rout of the Titans by Zeus or the tale of Prometheus, he goes his own way. The rout of the Titans, who are cast down by thunderbolts and imprisoned in Tartarus, is conceived on a grander and more terrifying scale than anything in Homer, and shows a far more awe-stricken conception of divine power, while Prometheus' deception of Zeus by giving him bones wrapped in fat as his share of a sacrifice is in no sense comic but the cause of much trouble and evil in the world. Even in his manner, which owes much to epic tradition and was shaped for oral performance, Hesiod lacks the Homeric ease and flow and balance. Yet he has his own qualities. Much more than Homer, he delights in concise sayings, old saws, and scraps of proverbial wisdom, which may concern the weather or the jealousy of craftsmen or the duties of friends, and he expresses himself on such occasions with an engaging terseness. Just because he is not writing about the heroic doings of men, he may seem to use rather too high-flown a style for the difficulties of a farmer's life, but it is in spite of everything a good medium for what he has to say. It conveys his sense of urgency, of moral passion, of the need to pay attention to the smallest details of every day, of struggle and frustration and hope of reward. Above all, in his attempt to understand the place of man in the universe, he worked out his notion of what the gods ought to be, and found in them a consolation for the injured and the oppressed, a symbol and a guarantee of the ultimate triumph of order over disorder, of the radiant revelations, which, as he himself knew, sometimes come to men, and give them strength and insight. By speaking of the actual world which he knew Hesiod set an example, which was through the centuries not indeed to discredit the heroic past, but at least to provide an alternative to it by supplying a new source of material upon which poets could draw in their attempts to explain the ways of the gods with men.

Hesiod left behind him a school of poets who worked in his manner and dealt with mythological subjects. They need not have been very distinguished, but the wide scope of their themes did much to keep old tales alive and proved of much value when new forms of poetry looked to myth as a source for lyric or dramatic poetry. From this anonymous mass of poetry one complete poem survives, the *Shield of Heracles*. It dates from somewhere about 600 BC, and in 480 lines it tells of an episode in the career of Heracles, who was known to Homer but plays hardly any part in his poems. The poem is interesting as the only surviving specimen of a type, which must once have been common – the short heroic lay. Homer's own art shows many signs of it in the background, but this poem is an authentic example. Its nominal theme is the fight between Heracles and the monstrous Cycnus, son of Ares, whom after a splendid encounter Heracles kills. But the actual fight is preceded by preparations on a large scale, which call for attention in their own right. 178 lines are devoted to the description of Heracles' shield, and the whole description owes much to the shield of Achilles in the *Iliad*. It too is made by Hephaestus, but the Hesiodic poet is determined to outdo Homer. This shield is made of gypsum, ivory, electrum, gold, and enamel, and on it are emblazoned, not only a host of monsters and mythological figures, but scenes from common life closely drawn from Homer. Though the fight when it comes is lively enough, the shield dominates the poem and shows how at this date the old interest in heroic achievements has given place to an interest in imaginary works of art. The *Shield* is a highly derivative poem and shows what happened to the epic in its decline. It reverted to the old kind of composition on a small scale, and at the same time its art was more elaborate, more heavily loaded, and much less lively. What Homer knew of Mycenaean metal-work through his own tradition, the Hesiodic poet knows from Homer or someone working in the same manner. The heroic past has receded into a dim distance, and the poet is not very interested in it.

Hesiod's own performance shows that the emergence of the self in poetry was by no means confined to a few privileged nobles, and, though the poetry which comes after him was to forsake his traditional technique and fashion new kinds of verse, it still owed much to his precedent, not merely in its frankness and its concern with the present, but in its enquiring spirit and its attempts to define the end of life. Once personal poetry had begun to displace the epic, it was free to move in many unfamiliar directions and to look on one side to Hesiod and on the other to Homer in its interpretation of the forceful, adventurous spirit of the seventh and sixth centuries. One of its leading pioneers was Archilochus of Paros, who lived in the first half of the seventh century. At first sight he seems to be almost a reincarnation of a Homeric warrior, who lives for war and at the same time, like Achilles, is not ashamed to sing songs. He says of himself:

> I am the servant of him, the Master, the Lord of the War-cry,
> And the greatly belov'd gifts of the Muses I know.[11]

Yet the more closely we look at him, the clearer it becomes that Archilochus has transformed the heroic ideal to suit his own peculiar circumstances and made something entirely new of it. Unlike Hesiod, who stayed at home, Archilochus was a soldier of fortune, the only Greek poet known to us who took part in the colonizing enterprises of his time. From his home in Paros he joined a party which colonized the island of Thasos and spent much time and energy in fighting the barbarous Thracians there and on the mainland opposite. He was driven to this because, unlike Hesiod, he had no settled place in his own society. As the son of a free man and a slave-woman, he had to fend for himself and shape his own career, and he did so in a ruthlessly realistic spirit. He found no pleasure in leaving Paros 'with its figs and its life on the sea',[12] and he knew that his companions in adventure were the miserable dregs of Greece. He was equally hostile to enemies, 'the Thracian dogs'[13] and to his own commander, who enriched himself at the expense of his companions. He lacks the Homeric sense of comradeship, and, though when he first took to soldiering he must have hoped to make a fortune, he soon saw that he would not, but continued to fight because it had become his profession and there was little else that he could usefully do. He wrote directly from his own experience, neither exaggerating nor concealing anything, and, though we have almost no complete poem by him, his personality is in its main lines as forceful as that of any Greek poet. If this is partly because he wrote with an alarming candour, it is also because he had a remarkable gift for turning his moods into crisp, vigorous words. Sometimes, notably in his elegiacs, he uses the epic vocabulary, but in other forms of verse, which are closer to actual speech in their trochaic and iambic rhythms, he uses his own vernacular, and this gives an immediacy and intimacy to what he says.

Archilochus, who knows the demands of heroic honour, tests them by the brutality of facts and makes no attempt to live up to them. In later generations he was renowned for his savage tongue, and Pindar says of him:

> For in the past I see
> Archilochus the scold in poverty,
> Fattening his leanness with hate and heavy words.[14]

One of the chief objects of his hatred was Lycambes, the father of the girl, Neobule, whom Archilochus wished to marry, but was prevented from doing so, no doubt because of his equivocal social position. He conducted a feud with Lycambes in which he spared neither his opponent nor himself. If Achilles is ready to injure his friends in order to humiliate Agamemnon, at least he keeps his dignity in it, but Archilochus makes no such pretence and compares himself with the shifty fox in his desire to get his own back. He proudly asserts that he knows one great thing, which is to requite with fearful evils anyone who maltreats him, and in pursuing the subject he composes fables, which smack of popular lore and range from coarse abuse to exalted passion. Thus he tells of the eagle and the fox, and the eagle is Lycambes, and the fox himself. They begin by being friends, but become enemies; the eagle devours the fox's young, but in due course the eagle's young fall out of their nest, to be devoured by the fox. The savagery and the candour of the story are characteristic of Archilochus. The art of the Homeric simile has lost its detachment and its dignity. The result is sharp and bitter, and Archilochus twists his weapon in the wound. He feels far too strongly about his injuries and is far too conscious of being despised to allow any mercy for Lycambes.

If Archilochus unleashed his passions on Lycambes and others who derided him, he took the hazards and horrors of war in a much more equable spirit. He is a hard-bitten veteran, who has no illusions about the real nature of fighting, and if he dislikes his own higher command as much as the enemy, that is after all familiar enough in all ages. What is striking about him is that he sees no glory in war. When he loses his shield in battle, which was a perfectly sensible thing to do since it would only be an encumbrance in retreat, he is quite happy about it and says that he will soon get another just as good. His interest in war is realistic and professional. He sees it coming in Euboea and forecasts that the chief weapons will not be bows and arrows but swords; he foretells it elsewhere, possibly in Thrace, in the knowledgeable language of a weather-prophet, who knows that a cloud on a mountain on the island of Tenos portends storm. So, far from exulting in victory, he admits with shame that the slaughter of seven men by a large gang is nothing but murder. From campaigning he extracts occasional solaces in merriment, and tells of the delight of drinking aboard ship and the comfort which he derives, when at his station under arms, from a kneaded loaf, which is common but honest fare, and Ismarian wine, which is so good that he lies down, and drinks it as if he were at a feast. His most impressive quality is his ability to take disasters and defeats without complaining and to suggest, as he does after a shipwreck, that even for incurable woes the gods have given endurance as a medicine, or to point out in a time of trouble, when he is deeply disturbed, that just as it is wrong to exult too much in victory, it is equally wrong to lament in defeat; the right rule is to rejoice at things which call for rejoicing and not to be too distressed by evil fortune, for such is the rhythm in the ups and downs of life. This is not at all the heroic spirit with its exultation in success and its humiliation in defeat. Archilochus has worked out his own philosophy of action and lives according to its precepts. Though he is in every sense a professional soldier, he remains incorrigibly and splendidly himself. Most Greek poets, from Homer onwards, had divided minds about war, finding it both glorious and lamentable, but Archilochus avoids both extremes and presents his experiences with truth and balance and common sense.

Archilochus' hard-won knowledge of life in no way shook his trust in the gods. He was the servant alike of Ares and of Apollo, of war and of song, and these were the powers who ruled his being and claimed his devotion. To them he owed his talents, but he was not content with this and, like Hesiod, called for some divine governance of the world and especially for a justice that punished the wicked. In his quarrel with Lycambes he felt that he had been grossly maltreated, and in his fable of the fox and the eagle, he gives to the fox, in its moment of anguish at the slaughter of its young, words which ring far beyond the confines of fable and speak for the poet with complete sincerity:

> Zeus, father Zeus, the sky owns thy command:
> Thou watchest over what men do
> Both right and lawless, and for beasts also
> Pride and right doing feel thy power.[15]

Hesiod's trust in the righteousness of the gods is transferred from a social to a personal setting and the belief in individual honour is strengthened by attachment to a far-reaching belief in the gods. Archilochus is so unsocial that he looks at everything from his own point of view, and owes almost no allegiance to anything beyond it. The strength of his poetry lies in his gift for speaking of himself, not merely with all his pride and ambitions, but as he really is in his candour and his violence. In the reaction against the objective, impersonal art of the epic Archilochus takes a leading place. He knows that what he has to say is worth saying and that he alone can say it. Almost no other Greek poet has his arrogant individualism, and it is not surprising that later Greeks regarded him as a great innovator, comparable in his own sphere with Homer and Hesiod in theirs. For him song is an indispensable means of adjusting himself and making clear to other men how he stands in relation to his poetical calling, his profession of arms, his enemies, and his gods.

Archilochus does not accommodate his poetry to any ideal of what he ought to be, but puts the whole of himself into it, touching Homer on one side and Hesiod on another. The conflict in him may be seen in a wider context in much of the poetry of the same century. If it sometimes aimed at a lofty target, at other times it was content to be humble and domestic. The proverbial wisdom of Hesiod found successors in poets who looked round their situations, and made comments on them. Reft of the epic manner, these verses have little dignity or lyrical grace, but they succeed in being both ingenuous and ingenious. Just as Hesiod has some nasty things to say about women, so the theme was pursued at a lower level, and about 630 BC Semonides of Amorgos turned the Hesiodic maxim into neat, unpretentious satire, using not the stately hexameter but an iambic line close to the rhythm of common speech. The tone is unaffectedly lowly, and Semonides advances gaily to his theme as he compares different types of women in turn with sows, vixens, bitches, earth, the sea, and finally, in a cheering contrast, bees. There is plenty of malice and some observation in his lines, and his adroitness emerges when he compares a woman with the sea:

> One day she is all laughter and radiance:
> a stranger seeing her at home would praise her –
> 'There is no finer woman in existence
> anywhere in the earth, nor lovelier.'
> Another day she cannot be approached
> or looked upon – she is a maniac,
> berserk, like mother-dog above her whelps;
> implacable she is to all alike,
> a stumbling-block to enemies and friends.
> She is the sea; it lies in kindly calm,
> often in summer time, a boundless joy
> to sailors; yet it often turns to madness,
> sweeping along in thundershouting billows.[16]

This is not very exalted, but it is lively and genuine and makes its point with derision. The worldly wisdom which Hesiod imparted with some dignity has been elaborated and extended and lowered in tone. The high Homeric laughter has turned sour, and the poetry of contempt and denunciation, so manifest in Archilochus, has found a place in less unusual circles. Semonides had followers and influence. In the sixth century, Hipponax wrote in a similar spirit, and after them both came the wide, rich world of Attic comedy, which picked up its art where they left it and applied it in a dramatic form to mock the contemporary scene.

Semonides has rather a plebeian look, and can hardly have had any social pretensions. This is right enough in his succession to part of Hesiod's heritage, but in his time were other figures who owed more to Homer and spoke with standing and authority. Of very much the same date are Callinus of Ephesus and Tyrtaeus of Sparta, who were at work in the middle of the seventh century, to be followed a little later by Solon of Athens (c 624 to c 544 BC). All three of these were public figures, who used poetry as a means of political action and drew their strength less from their private idiosyncrasies than from a conviction that they spoke for their own people in a time of crisis. Of Callinus we know the least, but at least we know that in his time Asia Minor was devastated by an invasion of wild Cimmerians from the steppes, who overthrew the Lydian kingdom, and threatened the Greek cities of Ionia. Callinus speaks of them in a formidable line:

Now the Cimmerian host approaches us, workers of fury,[17]

and his only long fragment summons his countrymen to behave like men in the face of deadly danger. Tyrtaeus played a prominent part in Sparta, when she was threatened by the revolt of her Messenian subjects, and crushed them only after a long war. Solon was a pioneer of political reform at Athens, who succeeded in doing what he wished in restoring peace between rich and poor, but later saw much of his work undone by the growth of tyranny under Peisistratus. Different though their circumstances and their aims were, these three men had some important things in common. First, their words commanded attention, not because they themselves held political power, but because they spoke with such conviction and authority that men had to listen to them. At this date poetry did very much what oratory was to do later, and this gives it an unusual quality. These poets draw confidence from their mission and their conviction that the destiny of their people hangs on them. They speak with an exalted earnestness and sense of crisis, of public responsibility and a full persuasion that they are right. Callinus summons the Ephesians to rise from their feasting and fight and die for their country; Tyrtaeus addresses the Spartan army in the field and deals alike with immediate tactical problems and the wider issues, which they evoke; Solon is said to have delivered one of his first political poems from the market-place in Athens when he summoned his countrymen not to abandon the island of Salamis. The poet has ceased to be either an entertainer or the voice of his own troubles; he is a public figure who combines elements of the prophet, the preacher, and the public man in his manner and his message. In them there is something of the spirit of Homeric leaders, who rally their wavering comrades to fresh efforts, but it is now based on a considered theory of what a man owes to his country and to himself.

The elegiacs of these three poets owe much to the epic tradition, and this suggests that they are in their own day trying to revive a heroic outlook and to make it real in their present troubles. They call for great efforts, whether in war or in civil discord, but they have their own philosophies of worth and reward. When Callinus summons his countrymen to battle, he argues that since all men must die, it is better to die honoured in battle than dishonoured at home, and he sets out his ideal of what a man ought to be:

> All of the people mourn for a man high-hearted as he is,
> When he is dead; if he lives, breed of the gods he appears.
> Like a tower that rises before their eyes they behold him;
> For what is work to be done by many, he does alone.[18]

The reward of the man who dies in battle is that his people honour him, and this is not an idea to be found in Homer, who sets the reward in some wider and more lasting glory. Tyrtaeus says very much the same thing when he insists that it is better to die fighting than to run away:

> Noble is that man who falls and dies in the front press of battle,
> Proving his worth as a man should for his country in fight.
> But most wretched of all things known is to wander a beggar,
> Fleeing away from his own city and bountiful fields.[19]

While Callinus holds out glory as a reward, Tyrtaeus analyses an idea, that was to become dear to the Greeks, and gives his own views on it. He asks wherein lies the *areté* of man, the fulfilment of his nature, and he suggests various alternatives, as if this was a matter of common discussion. After considering in turn athletic prowess and strength and fleetness of foot, physical beauty, wealth, royal splendour, and eloquence of speech, he decides that *areté* is to be found in dying for one's country. In him the Spartan ideal of manhood, which was to play so large a part in Greek history, makes its first appearance, but the ideal was not confined to Sparta, and Tyrtaeus' conclusion lies behind many epitaphs on men who have fallen in battle for their cities. The ideal of personal prowess is attached to a city, and what Homer had foreshadowed in making Hector the antithesis of Achilles passes into a familiar pattern of thought. Though the seventh century saw the emergence of the individual in poetry, it related him to something larger than his own circle and his own honour and insisted that in the end he found himself in fulfilling his duties to his city.

This sense of civic responsibility is no less manifest in Solon, but is applied in a different field. His first concern is to give order to Athens, where the struggle between rich and poor is leading to anarchy. He was both a practical politician and a law-giver, indeed the only Greek law-giver whom we know from his own account of himself. His poems are poetical pamphlets attacking his enemies and defending his own policies, but they pass far beyond mere pamphleteering because they are based on a serious consideration of human values, and he sees more in man's duties than the call to die for his country. He works out a system which relates the doings of men to the gods and finds in this the inwardness of political events. On the one hand he sees men as their own worst enemies, who are seized by a blind infatuation and commit unjust actions in an arrogant spirit, with the result that in the end Zeus punishes not only them, but their children after them. He has built up a system of ethics, which is consistent and realistic, and gives first place to the gods' regard for men. On the other hand, he recognizes that they have their own admirable gifts and often put them to good use. In a long poem about himself he shows how men are able to surmount their natural blindness and ignorance, and, with the help of a god, to do something that is worth doing, in craftsmanship or poetry or prophecy or medicine. Though their success is limited by their ultimate ignorance and inability to foresee the future, and they are in the last resort at the mercy of fortune, yet there is a scale of enlightenment from the complete blindness of the proud through the more reputable ignorance of those who trust in chance to the partial knowledge of the learned professions. Solon's concern is with knowledge, and its special application is to the tasks that keep a city alive and flourishing.

In their different ways Callinus, Tyrtaeus, and Solon modify the Greek belief in the self by setting it at the service of the city. While Callinus and Tyrtaeus see the problem from the needs of war, and Solon from those of civic order, all three regard the man who shirks his public duty as contemptible or wicked. Yet this does not mean that they underrate the fullness of the individual life which was a central assumption and aim of all Greek thinking. Rather, they assume that this is impossible unless men are prepared to defend the system which allows and maintains it. In each case the perils were great. The Cimmerian invasion and the Messenian war were desperately dangerous, and the civil discord at Athens, where the nobles had lost their sense of responsibility, was hardly less menacing. In each case the poet was on the side that was ultimately victorious. The Cimmerians spent their force and vanished from history; the Messenians were crushed and reduced to bondage; Solon introduced reforms, which secured at least some years of quiet for his country. The poet has become a public man, and this is possible because he is not a professional but an amateur, eager, not to please patrons, but to impose his own ideas and his own will. He has the strength, which comes from knowing that others are with him and that his cause is just. This practical aim may mean that his poetry is not always at a high imaginative level. It is forced to say certain things plainly and forcibly, and this it does, but it cannot indulge in flights of fancy or delicate novelties. Tyrtaeus wrenches phrases from epic contexts and makes them serve new purposes in teaching Spartans how to fight; Solon's main doctrines are clear enough, but his details are not always shaped with precision. What counts in these poets is their sincerity and passion, their conviction that the situation is indeed urgent and must be faced in its reality. This essential seriousness, different alike from the heroic splendours of Homer and the dignified patience of Hesiod, has established itself in Greek poetry and come to stay.

Though the surviving pieces of Tyrtaeus suggest an almost exclusive concern with war and a belief in it as the only sphere in which a man truly fulfils himself, there is no need to assume that he was interested in nothing else. His poems are composed with a special purpose in an imperious national need, and for this he developed his theories and set them out with care. With Solon, of whom we know more, it is clear that in the intervals of politics he liked and shared the old aristocratic pleasures of the class in which he was born. He states his predilections with a natural simplicity, and they reflect his upbringing and his social circle:

> Happy is he who has sons that he loves, and clattering horses,
> Hounds who are keen on the scent, friends who live over the sea.[20]

Nor are all his pleasures so simple as these. He appreciates the claims of other, more absorbing delights:

> Dear to me are the works of the Cyprian and Dionysus,
> And of the Muses. These bring to me gladness and joy.[21]

If Tyrtaeus builds his theories round a core of patriotic sacrifice, Solon builds his on a respect for the natural man, whom he interprets by his own brand of political science. His aim is that every man should make the best of his gifts, and, though he recognizes that his accomplishments will change with the years, he sees no decline as full manhood is followed by ripe wisdom. Unlike most Greeks, he does not resent the coming of old age and hopes that he may live to be eighty, and even claims that as he grows old he is still learning something. Solon is a truly balanced man, carried away neither by heroic frenzy nor by excessive love of pleasure, and he speaks for the old aristocratic world at its best. In retrospect it soon became easy to condemn it as Solon condemned his own irresponsible contemporaries, but, after all, enough of them were in agreement with him to support his reforms, and he was by no means crying in a wilderness, but a successful statesman who based his ideas on a considered scheme of life and turned them into a grave, thoughtful poetry.

If public occasions might sometimes call for an impressive seriousness, the Greeks of this age were fully capable of other moods, and in their convivial relaxations they sang songs, which showed other sides of their nature. Mimnermus of Colophon (fl. 630 BC) came from a city not very far from the Ephesus of Callinus and gives from within a brilliant impression of Ionian civilization at its most congenial time. He too has a philosophy and asks what is the best thing for man, but he finds it not in duty and sacrifice nor even in a changing scale of activities with the years but in youth, its powers and its delights. At a first glance he seems to be an ir-repressible hedonist, as he asks his leading question:

> Ah, what life, what delight comes without Aphrodite the golden?
> May death be mine when no longer I care for such things,
> Love that is secret and hidden, and gifts like honey, and slumber.[22]

In the offing he sees old age and finds nothing good in it. He knows that the lives of men are as brief as the leaves of a tree and that the Dooms of age and death stand in waiting. When age comes, it is best to die; for it is full of sorrows and there is no man to whom Zeus does not give many evils. Mimnermus makes his variations on a theme of Homer:

> Like unto that of the leaves, so also are men's generations.[23]

This can be a text for a bleak pessimism, but Homer surmounts it by insisting that, since this is so, man must fill his time with prowess. Mimnermus offers a different solution, but his ideal of pleasure is neither so substantial nor so noble. Yet he was not entirely consistent in it. His poems on it may have been written when he was young and sung in convivial circles, where such opinions were in place because they caught the relaxed mood of the moment. So far as they went, they were apt enough, but they are not an embracing philosophy, and at times Mimnermus turned his mind to other matters and especially to the past glories of his country, both in the first years of its foundation by Greeks from the mainland and more recently when his countrymen fought the Lydians and defeated them. To both these struggles he gives an admiring praise and the qualities which he finds in his ancestors, remote or near, show his respect for powerful achievements, and notably for the pressure of high temper and brute force in them. Despite his professed cult of youth and pleasure, Mimnermus has a wide concept of human worth. It is the balance between action and relaxation, between effort and pleasure, which is central to his outlook, and this is why he is truly representative of the Ionian Greeks, who had dangerous enemies on their frontiers but, when they had inflicted some defeat on them and secured their own independence, sought to exploit the graces and the gaieties of an aristocratic existence. In the end his world is not very unlike Solon's and reflects a like balance, even if it is differently tilted. If the Greeks sought order, it was largely that they might enjoy their leisure with some assurance that it would last.

The meditative, purposeful, often didactic poetry of this age springs from the self-confidence of an aristocratic society before it began to fear that its security might be threatened from outside. In the sixth century the ancient hunger for land in a region where there is never enough led to prolonged civil struggles in which the old aristocrats were threatened and sometimes displaced by others, who coveted their possessions. In this struggle the voice of the defending side is amply heard in a collection of poems ascribed to Theognis of Megara. He was certainly a real figure in the latter part of the sixth century, an aristocrat and public official of Megara, who suffered from the intestine quarrels of his city, lost his lands, and went into exile. Under his name are preserved not mere fragments but a whole body of some 1400 elegiac verses, and we might hope that in these we could study in detail the work of a poet who worked in the middle years of the sixth century. Unfortunately, the authorship of these poems is fraught with problems. Pieces that can be dated seem to come from times so far apart that they cannot be the work of one man; some lines in the collection are known to be the work of earlier poets such as Solon and Mimnermus; the collection itself looks as if it had been put together in Athens. Yet this need not discourage us, and we can find some satisfaction in two conclusions. First, the collection is certainly built round a core of Theognis' own work and, though we cannot always say that this or that piece comes from him, there is much that we can identify as his and much more that we may suspect to be. Secondly, the collection displays through- out a remarkable unity of temper and outlook, and reflects an aristocratic society when it was on the defensive against the incursions of reformers and revolutionaries, and sharpened its convictions in self-justification against them. Theognis and his kind belong to a world more split than Solon's and inflamed with controversy and denunciation against those who attacked it. Theognis is a poet of the class-war and passionately committed to the challenged side. As the struggle continued and raged in other parts of Greece, his poems were much admired and widely known, and the collection ascribed to him is almost a *vade mecum* for the champions of the old ways.

The collection reveals a remarkable view of human relations. On the one side are the good, the just, the noble, on the other side the base, the unjust, and the ignoble. Yet the poet or poets are aware that politics engenders contradictions. Though they assume that men should be bred from good stocks like rams, asses and horses, and that these breeds should not be crossed with inferior ones, they admit that wealth, which ought to be a sign of nobility, is no longer one, and that nobles may be reduced to poverty and broken by it, since it is worse than old age or fever. Yet, though the old order is thus threatened and humiliated, it keeps all the more faithfully to its aristocratic creed and makes no concessions to new claimants for power. Its fundamental tenet is loyalty between members of a circle or class to one another, and this is peculiarly manifest in Theognis himself, who spends his affection and his counsel on a young man called Cyrnus. Their relation is not, like that of Achilles and Patroclus, between men of the same age, but between an older and a younger man. Theognis claims that by setting the name of Cyrnus on his poems he ensures that nobody will steal them or claim them as his own, and he is no less confident that they will give Cyrnus an immortality on the lips of men. Yet his poems are hardly concerned with love or even with affection, and are for the most part ethical or worldly-wise. Theognis preaches the doctrine of absolute candour and loyalty in friendship, and in the circles where such songs were sung this certainly had pride of place. A friend must hide nothing from a friend and must never distort or cloak his thoughts and feelings from him. The heroic standard of courtesy to enemies has been transformed by civic rancour into this black and white view of human beings. If friendship allows no concealment, hatred must allow no abatement:

> May in that hour the huge, brass sky from above crash upon me,
>   And strike terror in all men who are born of the earth,
> If ever I should fail to succour those men who love me
>   Or if I am not a great trouble and grief to my foes.[24]

This spirit has come to stay and remains a commonplace of Greek behaviour, not merely in politics, but in the whole range of personal relations. It was to be extended from private feuds to class struggles and beyond them to conflicts between one city and another, or between Greeks and barbarians. It has its roots in the aristocratic age and becomes a central point in applied ethics.

In their struggle for survival Theognis and his fellows are well aware that in their hard world goodness is not enough and insist that a man must temper his high ideals of nobility by taking the world as it is and turn its own weapons against the enemy's cause. Theognis himself tells Cyrnus that he must model himself on the cuttle-fish, the ancient counterpart of the chamaeleon, and take his colour from his company. In a like spirit he stresses the inescapable need of money, of flattering enemies to their faces, of speaking soft words. In all this we can see signs of decay in a society, which is losing its integrity through adverse circumstances and no longer believes in the practicability of what was once demanded by honour. Yet this school of poets has its other side in which much of the old grace of life survives unimpaired. Wine is drunk under the shadow of Taygetus to the music of pipe and flute, and even the wanderings of the exile bring consolations in the beauty of the places which he visits. But more striking is a certain austerity enforced by proper pride. Theognis himself lived in troubled times, when revolution at home and invasion from without were never far from his mind, and the events of every day are sufficiently dramatic to arouse excitement, as when he hears a 'voiceless herald' announcing war or laments that all has fallen to the crows and destruction, or pathos when abroad he hears the crane telling that it is time to plough and this sets his heart beating in black wrath because other men have seized his acres. In his misfortunes he keeps a certain dignity and regards himself as a follower of the Middle Way, because he thinks it equally right to kill a tyrant and to hold the populace in utter contempt. His poetry and that of others like him comes directly from personal experience, and its didactic messages are lessons which they have learned from their own sufferings. This direct approach to events is well mirrored in a language, which still derives words from the epic and gains a dignity from them, but has also its own vivid imagery, as when a brave man is compared with a citadel or a tower, or a girl with a ridden horse, or serfs in the fields with pasturing deer, or a faithless friend is said to nurse a cold snake in his bosom. Such poetry is eminently quotable, and was often quoted, because it embodied in short memorable lines sentiments, which were true enough to have many applications. It is not exactly a form of 'wisdom literature', but it combines matters of fierce contemporary interest with attempts to explain them by general rules and to deduce profitable lessons from them. But this practical purpose is always maintained at a genuinely poetical level. Many emotions are engaged and give a more than rhetorical or controversial interest to what is said.

This school of poets has its own ideas about the government of the world. At times Theognis blames everything on the gods, at other times he says that men are responsible for their own fortunes. The contradiction is natural enough in his outlook, and no doubt he found no more difficulty than other men in holding both views concurrently. But though he has theories about human events, he finds little comfort. The Theognidean poems are almost entirely lacking in hope for either this world or the next. At the best they assume that if life has occasional ups, it has plentiful downs; at the worst they deplore the whole business of living and set out a thesis, which was later to be taken up in a tragic spirit and made the basis of a whole, dark vision:

> Not to be born is the best of fates for earth's generations,
>> Never to turn their eyes up to the sun's cutting rays.
> But, if born, then quickly to pass through the gateway of Hades,
>> There to lie in the grave under a deep mass of earth.[25]

It is easy to explain such sentiments by claiming that the writers belonged to a defeated and declining class and lamented the loss of the felicities which had belonged to their fathers. Yet this black background was always more or less present in the Greek view of life, and these poets differ only in finding little or nothing to counter or alleviate their melancholy. Having rejected the heroic sense of grandeur and committed themselves to a system which set everything on wealth and position, they felt that, when they lost this, they were indeed lost themselves. Yet even this gloom would be impossible for men with zest and appetites less keen than those of Theognis. His fundamentally robust temperament, with its desire for affection and loyalty and the good life, takes its defeats much more to heart than would a man with thinner blood. The spirit of these poems is characteristically Greek, and their special emphasis rises from the Greek conviction that men must not expect too much and that, just because most delightful things are rare and short-lived, they are all the more worthy of pursuit.

4

LYRIC SONG

IN modern Europe the English word 'lyric' and its equivalents in other languages suggest little more than that a poem is short and melodious and probably personal, but for the Greeks, from whose word *lurikos* our own word is derived, the meaning was precise. It indicated simply that a song was accompanied by the lyre. Of course some songs might have no accompaniment, and others might be accompanied by the flute, but the lyre was commonly used, and 'lyric' song is poetry which is actually composed for singing. Its origins may lie in a remote past, for the lyre existed in the Mycenaean age, and it is hard to imagine any time when the Greeks, however primaeval, did not sing, but there is little reason to think that such songs were conscious or careful works of art. They are more likely to have been folk-songs of little complexity or improvised verses built round a refrain, such as we find in the early literature of many peoples. Homer knows of hymns to gods, laments for the dead, and songs at weddings, which are performed by a company but in which the main part belongs to a leader, who does most of the work while the rest support him at intervals. The earliest fragment of lyric song known to us is indeed the merest fragment, composed by Eumelus of Corinth *c* 730 BC for a choir of Messenians who sang it to Apollo at Delos. It comes from a dark time when the Messenians were offering a long and desperate resistance to the Spartans, and it must have been an appeal to the god for help, but, since it consists of only two lines, it tells almost nothing about early song. The transformation of song into a serious and impressive art seems to have been assisted by a musical revolution in the seventh century. When Terpander of Lesbos (fl. 676 BC) established a regular scale for the seven-stringed lyre, he made proper musical composition possible by giving it rules by which to work, and the seventh century took immediate advantage of his invention and inaugurated a bold and rapid growth of music and with it of lyric song. Of Terpander's own work almost nothing survives but he is primarily responsible for the way in which lyric song came to be a leading art in Greece and to take the place left empty by the decline of the epic. Of this great art far too much is lost, but what remains reveals its remarkable originality, vitality, and accomplishment. Though we inevitably compare it with the lyric poetry of Europe since the Middle Ages, the parallel is by no means close, and Greek song has characteristics to which it is hard to find parallels elsewhere.

Of the music which accompanied these songs not a note survives, and when we read the words, we must remember that they are only a part of a more complex art, which included also music and dancing or some kind of rhythmical action. In its intimate connection with music Greek lyric resembles that of the thirteenth and the sixteenth centuries, and when we consider how much poorer this would be without its tunes, we have a faint inkling of what we have lost in Greece. It is perhaps some consolation to think that, if we had the music, it would not sound in our ears as it did to the Greeks, since the seven-note scale is alien to us and the inequality of its tones and semitones might bewilder us. What remain, however scantily, are the words, and they have their own unusual appeal independently of their lost musical accompaniment. Even more than Elizabethan songs they live in their own right and are entirely satisfying as they are. Yet much of their appeal comes from their close association with music. They have their own verbal tune, their irresistible movement, which is that of a true song. The quantitative system of metric is turned to new purposes and inspires new patterns of sound, each of which has its own individual melody. No poetry which relies upon accent can begin to approximate to these effects, and, though not all Greek metres are easy to analyse or to catch in their full rhythm at a first reading, once we attune ourselves to them, they add a new dimension to the words and make them dance in our ears. Modern poetry, which once owed something of a like kind to music, may still keep some of the spirit of authentic song, but it lacks the endless variety and sprightliness which the Greeks gave to their songs.

Greek songs could be sung either by a choir or by an individual, and the distinction accounts for certain variations in them. Each kind developed in its own way and, though they influenced one another, they have different characteristics. The main difference is that while in monody, or solo-song, the poet sang about himself and his feelings, in choral song he was always to some degree the interpreter of a company or a society or a class and assumed duties which lay outside purely personal utterance. Both kinds must have gained much from the musical reforms of Terpander, but choral song is the first to catch our attention and to reveal its marked characteristics. Since choral song was accompanied by a dance, its character was deeply affected by it. Such dances were regular and formal, and the same movements were repeated to the same tune; therefore, the words must have a like formality, and this is true of Greek lyric until it begins to disintegrate towards 400 BC. It is composed in strophes, or stanzas, and in a single song each strophe is metrically identical with every other strophe. This may often be the case in modern lyrical poetry, but there is no absolute reason why it should be and, not only are exceptions common, but even so influential a form as the Italian *canzone* allows a considerable variation between the separate stanzas. When the Greeks felt that the repetition of strophes needed some adjustment, they solved the problem by making the unit, not the single strophe, but the triad of strophe, antistrophe, and epode, and each triad corresponded exactly with every other triad. Yet, though each poem is composed on a rigorous pattern, there is a great variety between one poem and another. Of the extant examples of choral song not one is composed on precisely the same plan as another. We can indeed divide them into classes according to the main principles of their metrical construction, but in effect each poem has its own scheme. Between Alcman in the seventh century and Pindar in the fifth there is a marked development in the variety and complexity of metrical schemes, but the formality remains and is indispensable to an art which includes music and dancing as well as words.

This external formality does not make Greek songs stiff or slow in their movement. On the contrary they take full advantage of their rich metrical resources to vary speed from one poem to another or indeed from one part of a single poem to another part, and this they are enabled to do by different balances in the relation of short and long syllables, but the lines never limp or halt, and indeed, compared with most English metres, Greek metres move at an unusual speed. We feel ourselves swept along to the movement, not of a march, but of a dance, in which every step is calculated and for this reason makes the whole progress light and easy and various. Nor does the complexity of metres interfere with the arrangement of words in a coherent and intelligible order. Greek song is not always easy to understand, but its difficulties do not come from forcing words into an unfamiliar order. In this of course the inflected nature of the Greek language is an enormous help, since it allows words to be placed in many more different orders than is possible in English or French, in which inflections are almost lacking. The form of Greek songs is essential to them. It keeps them shapely and orderly, but at the same time it allows within a given frame an extraordinary variety of movement and an ability to change their tone by a skilful exploitation of rhythm.

Greek choral song need not be short and often is not. Already in the seventh century Alcman composed songs of over a hundred lines, and the choirs can have had no difficulty in performing them. Late in the same century the scale was greatly extended by Stesichorus (*c* 630–*c* 553 BC), whose *Oresteia* must have contained several hundred lines, and was in antiquity edited as two books. The longest extant example of such a poem is Pindar's *Pythian* 4, which was composed in 462 BC for Arcesilas, king of Cyrene, and falls just short of four hundred lines. This was written for a special occasion and seems to be exceptional in Pindar's works. Construction on such a scale is partly an inheritance from the epic, and Stesichorus is known to have told with expansive energy of such heroic themes as the Sack of Troy, the quest of Cerberus by Heracles, the seizure by Heracles of the cattle of Geryon, the Calydonian Boar-hunt, the murder of Agamemnon and the vengeance of Orestes, while in *Pythian 4* Pindar tells, through selected scenes, of the Argonauts' quest for the Golden Fleece. Yet after Stesichorus the scope of choral song seems on the whole to have been restricted to not much more than a hundred lines. Even this implies a scale of composition considerably larger than that of most modern lyric poetry, and we may attribute this to the performance of such songs at grand occasions, such as feasts of men and festivals of the gods, when length was a token of respect and welcomed as such.

The character of choral songs was largely determined by the occasions at which they were sung. A poet did not compose one just because he felt like doing so; he waited until he was asked to celebrate some special event, and then he had to fit his manner to the need. The later Greeks divided choral songs into formal categories and, though these throw some light on the occasions of performance, they are a little too technical for our purpose, and there must have been much overlap between one kind and another. Choral songs must have begun as hymns to the gods, and such many of them remained. If gods had to be entreated or placated or praised, a choral hymn was a normal way to do it. But hymns to the gods may also concern men, and the fortunes and needs and doings of men almost inevitably have a part in them. Some indeed had a special character, notably Maiden-songs, which were sung by girls and reflected their interests and personalities, or Dance-songs, which were accompanied by a vigorous, mimetic action, or Laments, which naturally dwelt on grief and the shortness of human life. But in all songs divine influence impinged upon human affairs, and the singing of them brought men closer to the gods. Greek choral songs nearly always turn to the gods at some point, even when we do not expect it, and in this they resemble the epic on one side and tragedy on the other. The Greeks never forgot the gods for long and liked to set human achievements and ambitions in perspective against the divine powers which watched them and made them possible.

The earliest choral song of which we have any substantial remains was composed at Sparta in the seventh century by Alcman to be sung by maidens at the festival of some goddess. It is not complete, and the meaning of almost every phrase has been disputed, but its main characteristics are clear enough, and from them we can see how certain features of Greek choral song were already present in this early example. First, the song is part of a rite, which is conducted just before sunrise, and in it the maidens offer a plough to their goddess, who is not named but is connected with the dawn. The occasion is of some solemnity, and the maidens are conscious that they must do their best in an important task. Secondly, Alcman told in this poem a myth from the heroic past, how Heracles took a fierce vengeance from the sons of Hippocoön, who had killed a friend of his. After being forced by them to retreat, he returned and killed them. The story was appropriate, because the event was said to have taken place in Sparta, and illuminating, because it told how pride finds its own fall. Thirdly, Alcman introduces certain maxims to emphasize the point of his myth, and does this in an imaginative and striking way:

> Let no man ascend in flight on wings to heaven,
> Nor attempt to win in wedlock Aphrodite![1]

This sums up his doctrine of the Mean and finishes the myth and its consequences. Such maxims are an ancient feature in all Greek poetry, but Alcman gives them a new strength by clothing them in an appropriately lyrical dress. Fourthly, after the myth he turns to the present occasion, and his girls speak about each other and their leaders in words of charming and graceful badinage. We cannot hope to pick up all the clues, but it is clear that Alcman enters into their admirations and sees them as they see each other, notably when he praises through their mouths their leader, Hagesichora, who is like the sun rising, or a racing horse 'of the breed of winged dreams', and whose hair is like undefiled gold. The girls deprecate, not too seriously, their lack of fine ornaments and feel that other girls are more beautiful than they are, but they sing like the swan on the river Xanthus and trust in their leaders to win the contest. Fifthly, though Alcman speaks through the girls and probably takes no part himself in the actual song, he shapes their feelings into his own thoughts and directs them where he wishes. He is at once with them and outside them, the interpreter of their thoughts and the representative of Spartan society. It is he who makes the inner significance of the festival clear to everyone and who, at the same time, makes the girls speak frankly and gaily about themselves. Through them he finds an extension of his own personality, and through him they are able to reveal what lies in their hearts and stirs their hopes and affections. Alcman expresses the common consciousness of the choir, not by imagining what it ought ideally to feel, but by interpreting what it does.

These five elements are usually to be found in choral song, but their relative proportions vary, and sometimes one element is stressed at the expense of the rest. What we know of Stesichorus (*c* 630–*c* 553 BC) suggests that he paid great attention to the myths and told them on a generous scale with something of the epic amplitude of manner, not confining himself merely to high points, but spending time even on machining actions, as we can see from a recently discovered fragment in which Helen interprets an omen to Telemachus. Moreover, Stesichorus, who was a native of Sicily and worked in a tradition different from Alcman's, thought nothing of altering old stories with ingenious innovations. These do not interfere with the main lines of a story, but they show how the epic material could be kept alive by remodelling. For instance, he was the first to make Heracles wear a lion-skin and a club instead of armour and a bow and arrow, to say that Athene sprang fully armed from the head of Zeus, to give the monster Geryon wings as well as three heads and three bodies, to claim that, not Helen, but a phantom of her went to Troy. This last invention was a second thought, for legend told that he was stricken blind for his impiety in blaming Helen for the Trojan War and not healed until he recanted in a *Palinode*, in which he said:

> There is no truth in this story;
> You did not go on well-benched ships
> Nor come to Troy's citadel.[2]

For this he could put the blame on Homer, but he had also to recant for accusing Helen of having lovers, and for this he put the blame on Hesiod. Stesichorus' pictorial sense was much appreciated by painters and sculptors who saw the advantages of his innovations, but in poetry he was less influential. The choral ode became instead, more allusive, more concentrated, more elaborate. Stesichorus still sang in a Homeric strain, but other poets did not follow his example, and moved further away from the epic as they spoke more confidently and more intimately for new social conditions and changed ways of thought.

Soon after the choral ode had found itself with Alcman and in the actual lifetime of Stesichorus, lyrical monody also flowered with a striking brilliance in Terpander's island of Lesbos. About 600 BC Alcaeus and Sappho were already at work. They practised the art of song at an extraordinary level of accomplishment and belonged to very much the same social world as the composers of choral songs. Yet their art displays its own specialities because they sang, not for public occasions, but for themselves and their friends. They were not restricted by the needs of special occasions, and their main impulses came from their inner necessities. This means that their technique differs in several ways from that of the choral poets. First, they composed, not in a grand international language which could be understood in almost any Greek city, but in their own Lesbian vernacular. Their poetry is close to the speech of every day and their language is a selective and heightened version of it. This gives it a more immediate impact, a more instant effect, in which the emotions which inspire it are less disciplined by majestic words. Indeed, one of their most impressive characteristics is that, though they are adepts in melodious metres, they make their words fall into them in the easiest and most natural order, as if they were speaking without effort or premeditation. They have their small loans from the epic, their occasional adjectives from tradition, but even these look at home in the vernacular and strengthen the impression that this poetry is essentially personal and intimate, with no claims to pass beyond the immediate moment. Secondly, since the songs were sung by single individuals, probably by the poets themselves, there was no need to make adjustments for a choir, and they are considerably less elaborate in their structure. Their metres, which are more likely to have come from folk-song than from a dance, are simpler and more obviously musical, though they may lack some of the more impressive effects of choral song. The unit is still the strophe, but it seldom has more than four lines and often not more than two. In appearance these songs look much more like what we are accustomed to expect in lyric poetry. Thirdly, since they are personal utterances and reflect the mood of an individual at a certain moment, they lack the scale and scope of choral songs. They are not necessarily very short, but they handle their themes more economically and are sometimes content with half a dozen strophes. Nor in them does the poet feel that he must identify himself with the feelings of his choir on a public occasion. He speaks primarily for himself and expects his audience to listen to him. This art is rather different from that of choral song, and in reading it we feel that it comes from a more private but not less enthralling world.

Though we have only fragments of the work of Sappho and Alcaeus preserved in ancient quotations or recovered from broken pieces of papyrus in Egypt, we know their personalities from the inside. They complement one another, and each is a striking example of a way of life held with unshaken conviction and consistency. Alcaeus, the man, speaks for the life of action in its vigorous and often violent forms; Sappho, the woman, speaks for the life of the affections as she cultivated it in her own chosen circle. The two poets were born in Lesbos at about the same time and both belonged to the land-owning aristocracy. Both suffered from the political vicissitudes of a troubled age, when the aristocrats, who had displaced the monarchy and divided its powers among themselves, were challenged by other claimants to power, including their own discontented misfits, and threatened by an insurgent populace, which demanded a larger share of wealth and control. Alcaeus went into exile in Egypt, Sappho in Sicily, but both returned home, and round their own island and its activities, public and private, their poetry turns.

Alcaeus' poetry is the immediate, candid reflection of his tumultuous career. In the civil strife of Lesbos he was on the side of the conservatives, who wished to regain their former power but were frustrated by Pittacus, once their ally, who was voted into power by the people and in his ten years of office restored law and order. Though Alcaeus' opposition failed and, though his motives were not too reputable, his record of his feelings is entirely honest and shows what kind of man he was. He lacks any kind of moderation and exults in extremes. In his political controversies he has nothing too bad to say of Pittacus, whom he derides for his splay feet, his big belly, his low origin, his intemperate habits, his treachery to his old companions. On the other hand, he displays an unfaltering loyalty to his own comrades in arms, shares their sorrows with comfort and confidence, and pays them delicate and delightful tributes. Like Theognis, he prides himself on being as strong in his hates as in his loves, and this adds contrast and excitement to what he writes. Whatever he did, he did it with all his might, and his songs are the immediate reflection of his actions. They have the air of being composed on the spot for present calls, and their special skill is that, however ephemeral their theme, they have always a human interest and pass beyond their immediate stimulus to a more comprehensive vision.

In the very strength of his active interests Alcaeus lacks subtlety, and we must not look to him for illuminating flashes of insight. In him everything runs true to type in a straightforward, vigorous way, and his strength lies in the uninhibited immediacy of his responses to events and in his skill in transforming these into verse. However strong his passions may be, he does not allow them to run away with his words, but keeps an economical control of them, shaping them into lively and dramatic poems. Thus, when Pittacus was given dictatorial powers, it was a bitter blow to Alcaeus, but his account of it is admirably disciplined:

> him, who was lowly born,
> Pittacus, did they praise, each one and all, and they appointed him
> Lord and master of this city which lacks gall in its heavy doom.[3]

He rings many changes on the ups and downs of his fortunes, and makes each sufficiently individual to be interesting. His sense of style, not merely in words, but in action gives him a special distinction. When he looks at a hall packed with weapons, he notes with an affectionate, professional eye the plumed helmets, the bronze greaves, the linen jerkins, the Chalcidian swords, as each contributes to the glitter of the scene. He often writes about drinking wine and finds an excuse for it alike in the heat of summer and the chilling storms of winter, the exultation of success and the depression of defeat, and on each occasion he is ready with instructions for its proper ceremonial. More than once he compares the fortunes of his cause with those of a ship, and always knows exactly what point to make, whether the rough waves drive him into harbour, or the conflicting winds leave him perplexed as he struggles with great rents in the sail and water in the bilge. He has too his lighter moods as when he welcomes his brother, Antimenidas, home from fighting in the Babylonian army, and congratulates him on killing an adversary who was eight feet four inches high, or, when in exile away from his friends, he watches a beauty-competition for girls and marks their long robes and the loud cries of the women in the audience. His emotions may not have had a wide range, but they were enough to engage him in many matters and, when he was so engaged, he gave his full attention to a theme and presented it with a firm grasp of what it meant to him.

The same is true of his senses. Often enough his eye marked something and registered it firmly. Nature may have been no more to him than a background for action, but much of his life was passed out of doors, and more than once he is touched or delighted by what he sees. So he addresses a Macedonian river:

> Hebrus, most beautiful are you of rivers,
> Rolling by Aenus to the dark-blue waters
> Of the sea, surging through the Thracian country. . . .[4]

A flock of widgeon in flight makes him think that they have come from the end of the earth by the Ocean, but he does not fail to note their dappled necks and long wings. In his adventures at sea he marked the natural electric lights, thought to be Castor and Polydeuces, which shine on the rigging and foretell the end of a storm:

> Leaping on the peaks of the well-benched vessels,
> Brightly shine far off, running up the forestays,[5]

and equally in fine weather he speaks of the 'stormless breaths of gentle winds'.[6] Such things are hardly mentioned for their own sake, and their function is usually to set the scene of some action, as the flowering of the gillyflower and the noise of the cicada in high summer are a sign that it is time to drink but, even in this subordinate role, Alcaeus' touches from nature are part of his gift for seeing everything of a piece, for taking the world as he finds it and not asking too many questions about it.

From his varied experience Alcaeus drew lessons not indeed very exciting or profound, but true to his character and instinct with his usual candour. As a young man he played on the theme of enjoying youth while we can, and illustrated the point that a man has only one life by a lesson from Sisyphus, who did indeed escape once from the underworld, but, though he was the wisest of men, did not escape a second time. Like Theognis, Alcaeus knows that poverty breaks a man's spirit by robbing him of respect. He draws a contrast between the radiant Helen, who brought disaster and death to the Trojans, and Thetis, who was married to Peleus and gave birth to Achilles. He regards drink as the best medicine for human ills and equally as the best means to find out a man's true character. He states maxims and makes pronouncements and, though they are of a traditional kind, they are none the less true and worthy of his art. His language has a muscular strength and is capable of dealing admirably with his choice of themes. It is never elaborate, never pretentious. At times it may, as the ancient critics thought, come too near to political rhetoric, but that is more a fault of its matter than his manner. If Alcaeus has a generous share of Homeric echoes, that was not only fully permissible, but part of his straightforward approach to experience, dictated and justified by his attachment to old-fashioned ideals of manhood and his dependence on heroic precedents. At times he breaks into lines of unusual strength, as if his vision had been so held by something that he can think of nothing else and sees only what is central and most significant. The movement of his verse responds to the movement of his temperament and is in all its skilful variations always virile and lively. Few men who have given their lives to action have written so well as he did, and few have caught so faithfully the essential spirit of a life of action in words, which arise so directly and so naturally from it or reflect so spontaneously its thrills and disappointments, its determination to succeed and its relief when action is for the moment completed.

If Alcaeus draws the stuff of his poetry from his vigorous adventures, Sappho draws hers from the privacy of her emotions and the small circle which shared them. Though the political changes of her time touched her harshly, she hardly mentions them, and her whole being centres on her personal feelings. She lived on terms of passionate affection with young girls, and with them she shared the pastimes of her sex and her class, in song, in ceremonies, in happy relaxations, in a heightened intensity of consciousness which belonged to Aphrodite, the Muses, and the Graces. She was well aware that her tastes were different from those of men, and she might almost have Alcaeus in mind when she begins a poem with a statement of her creed, which is indeed the antithesis of his:

> On the black earth, say some, the thing most lovely
> Is a host of horsemen, or some, foot-soldiers,
> Others say of ships, but I – whatsoever
> Anyone loveth.[7]

The fount of her inspiration was love, and she treated it in the grateful and unquestioning conviction that it came from Aphrodite. In her longest extant poem she addresses a poem to the goddess and reveals on what intimate terms she is with her. She recalls how in the past Aphrodite has driven her chariot from heaven and appeared to her, asking about her troubles and assuring her that all will be well, and now Sappho makes this past occasion justify a new appeal for help in a new crisis. Though the goddess spoke to her in a mood of playful, teasing gentleness, there was a firm assurance in her promise:

> Though she now flies thee, yet she shall pursue thee:
> Though she takes no gifts, yet she soon shall give them;
> Though she yet love thee not, yet she shall love thee,
> Even unwilling.[8]

Aphrodite was the inspiring force of her life, and Sappho sees her as the author of all that is sweetest and most magical in it. When she summons her to take part in a ceremony among apple-trees by running water, she is confident that she will come. It was this belief that cast a celestial radiance on Sappho's passions. In following them, and making the most of them, she felt that she was obeying a divine will, and her service to it was the secret of her inspiration.

Passion took many forms for Sappho, and she watched it with an undeceived insight. In one place she tells how she sees a girl sitting next to a man and speaking and laughing with him. This fills her with an overmastering emotion, which shows itself in physical symptoms. She cannot speak; a flame runs underneath her skin; her ears are buzzing; she is paler than grass and feels herself on the edge of death. This shows how little premeditation there was in her love, and how absolutely she was the victim of her temperament. When she was in love, she wished to share all her pleasures with her beloved and her friends, but in such a system there must have been many dark hours of regret and parting. In song Sappho found relief, and more than once she speaks of girls who have left her perhaps to be married, and of the emptiness which she then feels in herself. We must take her at her word when she says that in all truth she wishes to die, but she recovers as little by little she recalls the happy hours of the past and finds comfort in them. Her love for her girls spread to their love for one another, and when one of them goes across the sea to Lydia, Sappho speaks of her to her friend, and compares her with the moon, which surpasses the stars in brightness, and as it sheds its light over land and sea, revives the flowers with dew. Even when her girls got married, she would write wedding-songs for them, and she compares one girl, who is wedded a little later than usual, with the sweet apple high on the tree which the gatherers have not reached till now, or another with the hyacinth, which shepherds tread on the mountains, and the purple blossom falls to the ground. She would even compose songs of a much simpler and more traditional kind in which the Bride and someone who takes the part of her Maidenhood sing in a duet:

Bride: Maidenhood, o maidenhood, where are you gone away from me?
Maidenhood: Never again shall I come back, never again back to you.[9]

There is nothing ultimately possessive in her love, and she knows that marriage is the right and inevitable end for those to whom she gives her devotion.

In her absorption in love Sappho sharpened her vision of the physical world as the scene in which she and her companions passed their days. Unlike Alcaeus, who treats nature almost accidentally, Sappho is keenly aware of it as the setting of her love and observes it with a tender affection. She likes to enumerate flowers; she compares a young bridegroom with a lithe sapling; she watches the stars hiding their faces when the moon rises;

she calls the nightingale 'the love-voiced herald of the spring'. [10] Yet what matters for her is less the visible scene than the invisible powers at work in it, who are present to the eye of her imagination and whom she believed that she actually saw. When she summons the Graces and the Muses to come to her, she means what she says; for these are the divine sources of her inspiration. It is this sense of present divinities which gives so radiant a quality to Sappho's words and transforms her every love into something at once passionately human and celestially exalted. She is indeed a poet of love in many moods, but for her all love was an expansion of the self in the being of another, the intensification of her faculties, of life throbbing through her. When she loses it, she is empty and almost dead. The Greeks regarded love as something irresistible, even merciless and savage, and attributed few tender qualities to it, but Sappho, who knows that it is 'a bitter-sweet, inescapable creature'[11] and falls upon her as a wind falls on oaks on a mountain, knows also its incalculable rewards, the soft and loving times that it brings. There is in her poetry a softness, which is hardly to be found elsewhere in Greek, and is all the sweeter because it is not self-indulgent or cloying. To live for the affections was the only life for her, and she knew that she was right.

Like Alcaeus, Sappho reacted to every impulse of her passionate and sensitive nature and made no attempt to conceal her feelings. If love for her girls was her chief theme, she had other, equally human affections. When her brother, Charaxus, wasted his money in Egypt on a notorious courtesan, she is said to have rated him for it, but she certainly forgave him, since in one poem she begs Aphrodite and the Nereids to see that he comes home safely and is reconciled to his sister. She had a daughter, Cleïs, 'like golden flowers',[12] whom she will not exchange for the wide realm of Lydia, and to whom she explains that she cannot afford to give a rich headband for a ceremonial occasion but that something simple is really better. In her cult of girls she had rivals, whose faults she was not averse from exposing. Yet, this other side of her character is somehow peripheral, even though it is quite consistent with what we know of her. She has even a kind of boisterous humour, which she used sometimes in wedding-songs, where it was traditional and expected, and encouraged her to make fun of the man who watches over the bridal-chamber for the size of his feet or even of the bridegroom for his clumsiness. Such jokes have long lost their savour, but they show that after all Sappho was a real woman in a real world and that the company of the gods had not spoiled her humbler characteristics.

The special claim of Sappho's poetry is the perfection with which powerful emotions are shaped into a highly disciplined art without losing any of their force. Even more than with Alcaeus, her melodious words, moving to sprightly and varied metres, seem to be absolutely natural, the speech of every day raised to an almost unprecedented purity and power. She seldom uses metaphor and relies for her most impressive effects on simple statements like: 'I loved you, Atthis, a time ago', or of Aphrodite: 'smiling with her undying lips', or 'from the quivering leaves sleep comes down' or 'to see her lovely gait and the bright sparkle of her face'.[13] This is an art, which hardly needs images to enrich it, because it has passed beyond them and moves in a world where everything is seen and felt so clearly that it needs no ornament or explanation, and is all the stronger for being purified and able to live in its own right. Other Greek poets often do something of the same kind, but Sappho does it often, even habitually, as if the divine forces at work in her compelled her to move at this exalted level of speech. We feel no gap and no conflict between her matter and its presentation, and it is hard to imagine how she composed poems, which at once look effortlessly simple and yet make every word do its task with uncommon strength and flawless truth.

The paradox of Sappho's art is that, though she was certainly moved deeply by physical passions, their physical aspect vanished in her treatment of them, and we feel that, though they may have a physical side, it is of no importance. What counts is their pure flame, their immediate intensity, which enhances the consciousness by making her see things, both visible and invisible, with a peculiar clairvoyance and mark what happens in herself with an unfaltering candour. Living, as she believed, in a world where divine presences were always near and at work, she has the exalted excitement which they evoke, and it was this that kept her poetry of love at so radiant a level. What the gods inspired in this way could not be wrong, and Sappho never even hints that it could be thought so. She has her moments of grief and regret, but these too are part of her calling and come from the gods. She knows that in the end she will have her reward. In addressing some woman whom she despises for her ignorance, she asserts that in the afterworld such a person, who has never shared in the roses of Pieria, will wander unremembered and unregretted among the unsubstantial dead. She implies that with herself it will be different, that somehow she will survive through her songs, which come from the gods and confer their own kind of immortality. There is no evidence that she held an official post as priestess of Aphrodite, but it is impossible to see her rightly unless we recognize that she was in her own way deeply religious, conscious of divine support and of the obligations which this laid upon her to make the utmost of her gifts, knowing that she was not as other women were. Nor did she lack recognition in her own world. Alcaeus, who differed from her in almost every way, addressed her as:

Violet-haired, holy, sweetly-smiling Sappho,[14]

and we may give to the word 'holy' as much meaning as we like. In it Alcaeus compares her with divine beings and, if she appeared such to him, it is not surprising that later generations regarded her as unique among women and indeed among poets. The coarse taste of a later age might fail to understand her motives or her outlook, but even when she had become a target for the gibes of comedy, there was still no doubt about the astonishing nature of her gifts. Even now, when so little of her work remains, we can see its unexampled worth and understand what Plato meant when he claimed that she was the Tenth Muse, as if she belonged to a company of celestial spirits who inspire the art of song. She did something which nobody was to do again, and though Greek song was to thrive and expand after her, it did not compete with her. It sought other avenues and other methods of speaking about the incalculable forces with which gods fill the hearts of men.

Though Alcaeus and Sappho lived in troubled times, they were quite sure of themselves and of the assumptions behind their pattern of life. They did not question the cult of certain virtues or the claims of song or the supremacy of the gods. Their rich personalities flourished in a society whose members knew each other so well that they accepted one another's idiosyncrasies and welcomed freedom of utterance between equals. This gives to their work an assurance and an equipoise which reflect a creative and energetic age, which had no misgivings about the traditional conception of the good life. Their conflicts were more with others than with themselves, and they were able to speak about their own feelings with unabashed knowledge and frankness and completeness. Though Alcaeus spits venom against Pittacus, and Sappho speaks sharply about ill-bred women who fall below her own standards, we do not feel in them the resentful uncertainty which is so marked in Theognis. In fighting for their hereditary privileges Alcaeus and his friends knew where they stood, and even the actual struggle brought recompenses and rewards to them. In Alcaeus and Sappho the world of the Greek aristocracies finds its fullest and purest expression, since its ways are taken for granted and provide an undivided outlook on experience.

This balance and this harmony could not last and began to be disturbed when the aristocracies yielded power to the single rulers called tyrants.

The name has a very wide range of connotation and in its first years was by no means associated with all the ugly ideas that gathered round it later. Tyrants were certainly dictators, but they might rule through the laws. Sometimes they represented the underprivileged, and sometimes they came from the aristocracy. Their main task was to keep some kind of civic order and, at a period when Greece was threatened by foreign enemies, to see that their cities were defended against them. Even if at times they got a bad name for their barbarities, they usually relied upon a large measure of popular support, and in order to make their doings known they were generous patrons of the arts and gave them protection and encouragement. But in so doing they affected the character of poetry. By imposing their own tastes on their guests, they helped to reduce the unfettered freedom which is apparent in Alcaeus and Sappho. What had been the candid art of a free society was touched by the atmosphere of the tyrant's court, and took a new direction. Of these patrons Polycrates of Samos, who held power from *c* 540 to *c* 522 BC, was an outstanding example. Famous alike as master of the Aegean Sea and the patron of architects, sculptors, engineers, and doctors, he did much for poets, and the effect on them is highly illuminating, as we can see from the fragments of two poets who worked for him.

The first, Ibycus, came from Rhegium in South Sicily, where he had practised poetry in the manner of Stesichorus and written choral odes which told stories of the heroic past in his master's tradition. About 530 BC he was summoned by Polycrates to Samos and adapted his manner to courtly needs. The remains of a longish poem show how he did it. It is addressed ultimately to the tyrant's young son, who has the same name, and it ends with a handsome compliment to his beauty. This was entirely consonant with Polycrates' own tastes and conformed to the special version of 'l'amour courtoise' as it was cultivated at Samos. But Ibycus leads up to his conclusion in an unexpected, even tortuous way. He touches lightly on many themes of heroic song, only to announce that this is what he is *not* going to sing:

> Them the Muses, who often have sung of them,
> Daughters of Helicon, could tell delightfully,
> But no mortal alive
> Can relate every tale among them.[15]

On the negative side Ibycus throws aside the old dependence on myths as if they were no longer of interest; on the positive, he accepts the claims of love as the best theme. In this poem the treatment of love is thin and almost formal, and we might well expect that in conforming to Samian conventions Ibycus was trying to force his genius into places where it was not naturally at home. But there were moments when he wrote very differently and, moved by undeniable passion, clothed it in a new style, which is indeed far from the direct approach of Sappho but has a peculiar power:

> In the spring the Cydonian
> Quinces, watered by river-streams
> Blossom, where the inviolate
> Maidens' garden is, and the shoots of vine
> Swell to ripeness and strength beneath
> Shady boughs of the vines, but my
> Love never slumbers at any season;
> But as the Thracian wind from the north,
> Flaming under the lightning stroke,
> It comes down with a rush from the Cyprian;
> Dark, and shameless, with shrivelling
> Madness it shakes all my soul in me
> Down to the roots.[16]

This is almost a metaphysical poem. Ibycus contrasts the ideal garden of the maidens, where love is a natural growth in the spring, with his own unseasonable, violent passion, which falls on him like the biting north wind. This is a new way to speak of love, and Ibycus means every word of it and achieves a striking effect. He has transformed the conception of love into something that moves almost outside ordinary human events and can be spoken of only in exalted language which stresses its strange strength. This is a tribute to its cult at the court of Polycrates, where, if it is to engage everyone's attention, it must be treated with more mystery than Sappho gives to it. Something of the old directness is lost, and its place is taken by a more conscious magnificence.

This cult of love left no large field for manoeuvre, but Polycrates' second distinguished poet, Anacreon of Teos (c 572–c 485 BC), applied a wonderful ease and dexterity in the choice of words and images to a poetry which caught a rather different aspect of courtly love. He too writes about very little else, and he too tries to accommodate his themes to the artificial and yet critical atmosphere of the court. Like Ibycus, he makes his themes more interesting by his use of myth and symbol which convey his complex states of mind. He personifies Love as a youth and presents him variously as sporting on the mountains with the Nymphs and Aphrodite, or as challenging him to love by throwing a golden ball

at him, or as striking him with an axe like a smith, or inciting him to a
boxing-match, or passing by him in the air on golden wings. Such symbols are more than metaphor and less than myth, and each of them conveys the inner character of a situation, giving to it just the degree of
excitement or anticipation or unwillingness which Anacreon feels. He
dramatizes his feelings by seeing himself in imaginary situations, which are
certainly fanciful and yet make use of old tales or common figures of
speech, as when he says that he throws himself from the Leucadian cliff,
whence unhappy lovers were said to throw themselves into the sea, or
implies that he swims in a sea of love after some desperate decision. When
he expresses his moderation in not wishing to be either very rich or very
old, he uses two lively figures, one drawn from myth, the other from
travellers' tales in his own time:

> I don't ask for Amalthea's
> Horn of plenty, or wish to live
> For a hundred and fifty years
> Like the king of Tartessus.[17]

If the situation is sufficiently absorbing, he develops his symbol and adds
something more to it, as when he likens a shy girl to a young sucking
fawn, which is frightened when its mother leaves it in a wood, or when he
tells of a boy who has escaped from his mother's protective care and finds
himself in a wonderful world of the imagination where Aphrodite has
tethered her horses in meadows of hyacinth. When he pursues a girl who
flies from him, he compares her with a filly, whom he will train and drive
around the course. Anacreon's symbols have the great advantage that they
catch the attention at once and make his purpose delightfully clear. Even a
single word will do the trick, as when after a plain statement to a boy that
he pursues him without avail, he tells him that he does not know that he is
the charioteer of Anacreon's soul. Such images and symbols are instruments for making the most of every situation, for extracting all that it has
to give and delving into it for unsuspected riches. If he had to conform to
the ways of the court, he made the most of the limitations which were
set on him, and remains both intimate and individual.

Beneath this brilliant exterior, which is always alluring and surprising,
Anacreon half-conceals feelings, which are not so uninhibited as those of
Alcaeus or so powerful as those of Sappho, but are undeniably authentic.
He might portray Love as a boy playing with dice, but he knew that the
dice were madness and turmoil. His loves might not have the purity of
pure flame, but they were genuine enough, and he often gives a hint

of tenderness for his beloved, praising him for his quiet ways or grace of behaviour. Circumstances decreed that he must write drinking-songs, and he was perfectly willing to do so, but, though he claims to throw away restraint and behave like a Bacchant, he soon recovers himself and says that men should not behave like Scythians, who in barbarous incontinence drink wine without water. His drinking lacks Alcaeus' hearty delight, and he was averse from the songs of war which were popular on convivial occasions, thinking it better to sing of the glorious gifts of the Muses and Aphrodite. Despite all its air of power and splendour the dominion of Polycrates was insecurely founded, for, over the narrow water from Samos, the Persian conquerors were in full control, and, while Anacreon was still with him, Polycrates was lured away by a Persian satrap and brutally crucified. Anacreon may have been conscious of this insecurity and for this very reason have concentrated on the passing hour and its satisfying delights. After the fall of Polycrates he went to Athens, where he became a notable and familiar figure, favoured by the great and liked by all parties. It was his task to sing to them in their hours of relaxation, and this was his special gift. It called for youth and strength, and he resented the coming of old age and the menace of death. When his hair had turned white and his teeth were old, he said:

> So I make my lamentation
> Often, because Hell affrights me;
> Ghastly is the pit of Hades
> And the path that goes down to it
> Is a hard one. It is certain,
> When you go, there's no returning.[18]

In his songs Anacreon carries to its limit the belief that pleasure is the chief end of man, and this is the main theme of his songs. No doubt, when he was not relaxing in this way, he had other convictions and other interests, but his special genius was fostered by this, and to it he gave his delightfully skilful art, with its reserve, its irony, its fancy, its underlying sincerity, its choice of telling words, and this exalts his work above most poems on such themes. His inspiring spirit is a kind of joy, worn indeed with a difference, but still joy, and though it has not the celestial exaltation of Sappho, it resembles in many ways the joy which the Greeks believed to belong to the gods at their feasts on Olympus. In a precarious world Anacreon was pleased to do what he could for this cause and to give to it an art which never overreaches itself and gains greatly from its conviction that the poet must indeed say what he feels but in a spirit that makes others feel it also.

When Anacreon came to Athens, power was still in the hands of the
sons of the tyrant Peisistratus, and with them Anacreon found conditions
not dissimilar to what he had known in Samos. Here too there was a local
art of convivial song, which men enjoyed among themselves. It consisted
of short catches. A man would sing one, and then another man would have
to cap him on a similar theme in a similar manner. A small song-book of
such pieces survives and shows what this limited and unpretentious art was.
Owing something to the example of Alcaeus, it spoke for a small aristocratic world, whose members, like Theognis, set a high value on friendship and loyalty and candour, and was not unaware of the dangers that
threatened it, but took them more calmly than he did. This art continued
to thrive after the murder of Peisistratus' son, Hipparchus, in 514 BC, and
the expulsion of his other son, Hippias, in 511 BC. Some of the most
stirring songs are written from the winning side, and their spirit is very
much the same as that of the losers. Composed for special occasions for
special points of view, they touch on contemporary matters and might
well have been short-lived if they had not a gift for seeing what is permanent in a passing theme. In substance and temper they are still the voice
of the aristocratic age, even though they welcome the coming of democracy with the murder of Hipparchus by Harmodius and Aristogriton.
They maintain the old view of the good life, as the seventh and sixth
centuries knew it, and sum it up neatly in a quatrain:

> For a man health is the first and best possession,
> Second best to be born with shapely beauty,
> And the third is wealth honestly won,
> Fourth are the days of youth spent in delight with friends.[19]

The Attic drinking-songs are a subsidiary art in a time when larger and
more splendid forms were being matured. Yet they are the true voice of a
passing age. They convey the refinement and the deeply personal attitudes
of an aristocratic society, which set a high value on human relations and
saw things from its own confident convictions. It could not last beyond
the society which nurtured it, and its place was taken in new conditions by
works of more ambitious scope and more extended range.

Meanwhile, much had happened to choral song, which pursued new
paths and elaborated its technique. Whereas most kinds of solo-song were
confined to local performances, choral song became a pan-Hellenic art.
It may already have been this with Stesichorus, but there is no doubt of it
with the three poets Simonides (556–467 BC), Pindar (512–c 448 BC), and
Bacchylides (c 505–c 450 BC). Simonides was the uncle of Bacchylides, who

must have learned much from him; they were both Ionians from the island of Ceos, and differed in origin and outlook from Pindar, who was a Boeotian aristocrat from Thebes. Yet, despite obvious differences, all three had much in common. Pindar learned his art in Athens, where Simonides spent many years and Bacchylides performed some of his songs; the richest patron of the age, the Sicilian tyrant, Hieron of Syracuse, invited all three to celebrate his great doings; their art, based on an ancient tradition, had strong common elements, and often enough they dealt with common themes. Though Pindar was a believer in aristocracy, he had, at least in his early years, friends in Athens, and he associated with the king of Cyrene and Thessalian princes; Simonides was almost the poet-laureate of Greece in the Persian Wars, but he too had royal and princely patrons, and saw himself as above the battle, speaking for eternal matters. All three poets were confident of themselves and their opinions and not afraid to speak out to their patrons, however powerful they might be. In the result their art stands for the transition from the old aristocratic age, many of whose virtues it embodies, into a new age of experiment and change. Yet despite its greater elaboration it kept the same main elements as we find in Alcman and enriched them with many lively innovations. The choral ode never ceased to develop in this period, and through it we can see what the imaginative thought of Greek poets was about the issues of the time.

Choral song is never far from the gods. In its simplest, perhaps oldest, form it is a direct hymn to them, which may beg something of them or tell of their power or bring them closer to men. But this spirit spread to almost every branch and its style is deeply engraven on all surviving pieces of choral song. At its simplest and most majestic it may be seen in some lines which take the form of a prayer and may have been written by Simonides, clearly for a city which is in trouble from war or civil strife, and summons the Fates, who are hardly Olympian deities but have a position and prestige almost equal to theirs:

> Listen, Fates, who sit nearest of gods to the throne of Zeus
> And weave with shuttles of adamant
> Inescapable devices for plans of every kind beyond counting,
> Aisa, Clotho, and Lachesis,
> Fine-armed daughters of Night,
> Hearken to our prayers, all-terrible goddesses
> Of sky and of earth;
> Send us rose-bosomed Lawfulness,
> And her sisters on glittering thrones,

Right and crowned Peace, and make this city
Forget the misfortunes which lie heavily on her heart.[20]

This is an authentic cry in a time of need, and in it the poet speaks for the city and pitches his words in the highest key. The Fates are summoned in all their power and glory because the city needs their aid, and the poet begs them to send the Graces, the guardians of civic order, whom he envisages in their sensuous beauty and splendour. The Hymn rises from the heart of Greek religion and, at the same time, abates nothing of its poetical richness; rather, the high demands of the occasion inspire a lofty temper and a no less lofty utterance. The poetry comes from the disturbed, tense mood of a poet who is at once deeply anxious for the city and conscious that only the most powerful gods can help.

If the hymn as such represents Greek lyric song at its grandest, its subjects spread over a large scale from other hymns down to purely human affairs. The Greeks made a main distinction between those songs which were addressed to gods and those which were addressed to men. This was sound enough and may be marked between the lines just quoted and the lines which Ibycus wrote for the young Polycrates. Yet, though there are obvious differences between two such extreme cases, lyric song has many abiding qualities, which appear in all its forms. In the sixth century it was no doubt extended to include praises for the tyrants and other great men of the time, but, even in such poems, it must have been difficult to say nothing of the gods, especially in songs which were sung at their festivals and at which they were themselves sometimes thought to be present. This is certainly the case with the Victory Songs which were composed to celebrate successes in the great Games and, by a strange whim of fortune, from the larger part of what is left of the poetry of both Bacchylides and Pindar. We might expect them to be unashamedly secular, but in fact the gods are never far from them. The Games were held in honour of the gods, notably Zeus, Apollo and Poseidon; the winners were regarded as enjoying a happiness almost divine in their success; the songs themselves were often sung in a temple or at a religious feast after the victor's return to his home. It was difficult to keep the gods out of them, and the poets, so far from attempting it, gave to these songs some qualities of a hymn. The religious spirit in choral song makes it different alike from the epic and from much lyric monody in being closer to the gods and more immediately concerned with them.

Simonides said that poetry is 'painting that speaks' and the words have both an immediate and a wider application. Even the scanty remains of his poetry show his skill in evoking a scene which appeals to the senses and combines the epic objectivity with an even finer perception. Thus, he makes Orpheus charm living creatures with his song:

> Innumerable birds
> Flew over his head, and caught by his beautiful song
> Fish leapt up straight out of the dark-blue sea.[21]

Even more effectively he catches the effect of sound as when a voice suddenly breaks into a deep calm:

> Then not even a breath of wind arose to stir the leaves,
> Which would by its quivering have stopped the honey-sweet voice
> From being fixed in the ears of men.[22]

This love of the senses means that Simonides looks on the visible world without seeing it as dependent on some unseen world greater than itself. Of course he accepts the gods as present in it, but his first concern is with what he sees and knows. Like all Greeks, he is fully aware of the uncertainty of the human condition, but his sense of this becomes more vivid by the precise image which he gives to it:

> Being a man, never say what to-morrow will be,
> Nor when you see a man happy, how long he will so remain;
> For not even the turn of the long-winged fly
> Is so swift a change as this.[23]

Simonides saw the events of human life in this concrete way and gave to each its own relevant poetry.

This pleasure in the senses extended to the human state, and in antiquity Simonides was renowned for his pathos. The depth of tenderness of which he is capable shows itself in some lines, from an unknown context, when Danaë has been locked in a chest with her small child, Perseus, and sent adrift on the sea in it:

> When on the carven chest
> The wind raved as it blew,
> And the troubled sea and fear cast her down,
> With cheeks not unwet
> She set round Perseus a loving hand
> And said: 'My child, what trouble is mine,
> But you sleep on,
> And in your baby heart
> Slumber in this joyless
> Bronze-bolted craft
> That shines in the dark,
> While you are stretched out in the blue twilight.

You heed not the deep salt-water
Of the waves that passes above your hair,
Nor the voice of the wind
As you lie in your purple garment,
Turning your beautiful face upward. If for you
Terror were indeed terrible,
You would turn your tiny ear to my words.
I bid you sleep, my child,
And sleep the sea, and sleep
Our immeasurable ill.
May some change of counsel come,
Father Zeus, from you.
Whatever word of prayer I utter
In boldness or without justice,
Forgive me.[24]

In the restrained pathos, which never attempts too much, in the skill with which Danaë's plight is caught at its darkest moment, in her love for her child, her modesty, and her courage in the visual impression of the half-light inside the chest, Simonides combines the essential qualities of dramatic narrative with the understanding and compassion which belong to tragedy. His art is more complex than that of the epic, and, since the myth is only part of the larger unity of the choral ode, Simonides gives it a full, independent worth and lets his imagination play in full strength on this strange theme.

The pathos of Simonides was also shown in rather a different art, epitaphs for the dead, especially for those who fell in the wars against Persia. In this he was such a master that many epitaphs, which he could not have written since they commemorate events after his death, were attributed to him, and he set a model, which later generations were proud to copy. He says in two or four lines all that he needs to say, and this is meant to show a man's worth and destiny in the eyes of eternity. He is less concerned with individual glory, as earlier epitaphs had been, than with some special splendour or distinction in the characters of those whom he celebrated such as the Spartan seer, Megistias, who at Thermopylae refused to leave his comrades in the battle and was killed with them, or of Archedice, daughter, wife and mother of princes, who did not lift up her heart to pride. The extreme simplicity of his form hides a powerful charge of emotion, and of all Greek poets he is the greatest master of under-statement. Thus, for the fallen at Thermopylae, he wrote no more than a couplet, which, translated literally, says: 'Tell, stranger, to the Lacedae-monians, that we lie here, in obedience to what they said,[25] Simonides is keenly aware of individual characteristics but he places them in a social setting and understands them in it. He marked the huge changes that took place in his time and was touched by the Ionian enlightenment, by the growth of science and philosophy in the sixth century and its gradual spread to religion and morality. Though he spent much of his time with royal and aristocratic patrons, he did not truckle to them but spoke out in a detached, courageous way. A remarkable case of this is a poem which he wrote for the Thessalian king Scopas. It concerns a maxim ascribed to Pittacus that 'it is hard to be good', and we may imagine that Scopas asked what this meant, hoping for the answer that it was indeed hard but that Scopas succeeded in it. Instead of this he gets rather a stiff lecture on the nature of the 'good man', about which the Greeks had been arguing since at least the time of Tyrtaeus. Simonides has put hard thought into the poem and shows limitations and contradictions inherent in the old meaning of 'good'. He argues that, since the old kinds of goodness, such as health, wealth, and the like do not last for ever, no man can be constantly 'good'. Against this he sets his own new ideal of the man who may properly be called 'good' because he acts for the city, knowing what he is doing. Simonides does not ask for too much, but what he asks for is sane and worthy of the age of city-states, when a man found his fulfilment in acting with his fellows for a common aim:

> He who is not base, nor too empty-witted,
> If he has in his heart the justice
> Which helps the city, is a sound man;
> Nor shall I blame him, for the generation
> Of fools is endless.
> All things are fair
> That are not mingled with baseness.[26]

This was hardly what Scopas would have expected, but it was a lesson which Simonides thought important and was not afraid to deliver.

Simonides also applied his speculations to certain received notions of his time and found them wanting. In thinking about the gods he found them even more powerful than most men believed and saw how helpless and futile men were in their hands. Men might seek to defy time by making monuments to themselves and so acquire some sort of equivalent to immortality, but what were these against the powers of nature and the gods at work in them?

> What that trusts in his wits would praise
> Cleobulus, who dwelt in Lindos,
> When against the everlasting rivers and the flowers of the spring,

The flame of the sun and of the golden moon,
And the eddies of the sea,
He set the might of a grave-stone?
For all things are less than the gods,
But a stone even mortal hands can smash.
The man who thought this was a fool.[27]

Yet, though Simonides derided the false pretences of men and knew their vast inferiority to the gods, this made him respect all the more their real glories, and recognize how they could best fulfil their natures in service and sacrifice. If on the one side he looks back to the aristocratic age with its high sense of style and its love of the good life, on the other he looks forward to the fifth century when probing questions into the nature of man, so far from discrediting him, made him an even more serious subject for study and added depth and range to speculations about him.

The sands of Egypt have given us substantial remains of the poetry of Simonides' nephew, Bacchylides, who clearly learned much from his uncle and has the same Ionian limpidity and grace. Pindar thought poorly of him and is said to have compared him variously with an ape and a jackdaw, and the later Greek critics thought him lacking in sublimity. He displays little of that deep interest in ultimate matters which we find in Simonides, and his maxims are a poor equivalent to Pindar's distilled wisdom. But as an exponent of the Ionian art of giving a refined pleasure, he has his place. His special gift is for narrative, and his myths may perhaps convey an idea of what those of Simonides were like. Bacchylides knows how to tell a story, to choose the right high-lights, and to make the details vivid and revealing. For Hieron of Syracuse, who was a generous patron of Apollo's shrine at Delphi, he tells the story of Croesus, who was an even more generous patron, but what interests Bacchylides is the thrilling tale of Croesus' last adventure. Hopelessly defeated by Cyrus, he builds a pyre and sets himself on it, and then comes the unexpected escape:

But when the shining strength
Of ruthless fire darted through it,
Zeus brought up a black rain-cloud
And quenched the yellow flame.[28]

In another poem, when Minos carries off Athenian youths and maidens to sacrifice them in Crete, the young Theseus is among them, and, being challenged by Minos, goes to recapture a ring thrown into the sea. He dives after it and is guided by dolphins to the palace of Poseidon, where he sees the sea-nymphs dancing and Amphitrite seated on her throne. They give him gifts and he returns safely to the ship, much to the amazement and the displeasure of Minos. Bacchylides likes excitement and danger, and knows how to thrill us. But he has other qualities of a finer worth. He makes Heracles visit the underworld to fetch the monstrous three-headed dog Cerberus, but of this he says little, and he gives all his powers to telling how Heracles meets the ghost of Meleager, who tells how he died when his mother, in vengeance for the death of her brothers, burns the torch which is doomed to be coincident with his life. Here indeed there is more than a touch of Simonidean pathos, especially when Meleager speaks of his last moments:

> My sweet life sank,
> And I knew my strength was short,
> Alas, and in my misery I wept and breathed my last,
> Leaving the brightness of my young manhood.[29]

Bacchylides is at his best when he is not trying to assume the grand manner or to establish eternal truths. He can advance from the single moment and see it in a wider context, as when, anticipating the tragic story of Deianira in the *Women of Trachis* by Sophocles, he tells how she prepares for Heracles the shirt which she thinks will bring him back to her but will in fact kill him in hideous agony:

> Ah, ill fated, ah unhappy one, what did she plan?
> Powerful jealousy ruined her,
> And a dark veil over things to come.[30]

Bacchylides works well enough within his limitations, and was perhaps unfortunate that he was a younger contemporary of Pindar, whose background and art were of a very different kind.

Pindar was an aristocrat who moved as an equal with the Sicilian tyrants and the king of Cyrene, but was most at home in Aegina, where noble families cultivated the games, and when they won in them asked Pindar to celebrate their victories. Just as in them he saw the blood of divine ancestors at work, so he claimed for himself a special calling to poetry. He assumed, without question, that poetry was given to him by the gods. He speaks often enough of his creative processes to show that he believed in divine inspiration and needed something of the kind both to start him at work and to keep him going, but in a typically Greek way he thought that this was futile unless he exerted to the utmost his own talents in making full use of what the Muse gave him. This was not so much the actual words, but the mood and the vision and the release of power which made it possible to summon themes from the depth of his being. He calls himself the Prophet of the Muses, because the Muses send him something which he has to put in order, rather as the prophetess of Apollo at Delphi has to put in order what the god gives to her. His conception of song, set out in a variety of images, is clear and convincing. On the one hand it must have a solid, shapely form, and of this he speaks when he compares it with the glittering porch of a temple, a treasure-house in a sheltered fold of a mountain, a piece of jewellery made of coral and gold and ivory, a woven garment, a garland of flowers. On the other hand song also lives and moves, and Pindar compares it with chariots and ships, with an eagle in flight, with bees gathering honey, with arrows and javelins that strike the target, with fire and light, with a river in spate. He understands the paradox that poetry must remain still and yet never cease to move, that it must have a monumental solidity and yet be lively and sprightly. Not all his ideas of it are likely to be his own, but no Greek poet speaks so often or so precisely about his art as Pindar, and none could have taken so much care to see that his patrons understood what he was giving them. His art is much richer than that of Bacchylides and, though we know too little of Simonides to compare Pindar with him, it is clear that the older poet wrote in an easier and more flowing style and aimed at simpler results.

Pindar has a clear notion of the purpose of poetry. Its first duty is to preserve the memory of great doings for later generations, and in this he restates Homer's belief in the power of song. Pindar claims that without song even the greatest doings are lost in darkness and that the noblest memories of the past exist only because song has immortalized them. Conversely, song gives to men something which they cannot get from elsewhere, and Pindar's favourite image for this is light. The radiance which his song casts on its themes is like that of the sun which illumines the world and makes it visible to all men. This light is itself divine, the child of holy Theia, who is the mother of the sun and the source of all light both physical and supernatural. Again and again Pindar makes variations on the theme of light, and, though its first purpose is to show that through song certain men are encompassed by a radiance like that of the gods, it has other associations. In a sense it gives life to the dead, not indeed full and active, but such life as is denied to ordinary men who have died and been forgotten. Pindar regards fame as a reality of which he does not analyse the nature, but which by some mysterious power, prolongs a man's existence in the minds of men. It may even penetrate to the shades of the dead, when their kinsmen win it, and Pindar more than once suggests that songs are heard by them as they listen in their tombs, or are brought to them by Echo. If song can do this, those who win it must deserve it, and Pindar is emphatic that he sings of great achievements, notably in action, by which a man proves his manhood to the full and wins the applause of his fellows. His concern is with the great ones of the earth, who have proved their inborn worth, and this worth is due either to their descent from gods or to being specially favoured by them. Pindar has his own metaphysic of aristocracy and is a confirmed believer in it at a time when it is being gravely questioned and challenged. He wrote his songs for aristocrats when they had done something which justified their exist-ence. He was a Panhellenic poet in the sense that he was at home anywhere in Greece with aristocratic hosts. For him ordinary people, if he thought of them at all, were 'the violent crowd', but on the whole he dismissed them from his mind. As the Greek aristocratic system fell into decay be-fore the rising power of Athens, Pindar put up a splendid rearguard defence for it, encouraging its members in their high sense of their own origins and of their ability to live up to them. Though he learned part of his art at Athens in boyhood and paid handsome tributes to her for her part in the Persian Wars, he could no longer like or admire her when she conquered both his own Boeotia and his beloved Aegina. Then he saw her as the arrogant Bellerophon, whose pride led him to a hideous fall, or as the Giants who defied the gods and were utterly crushed by them.

Pindar's art is highly complex and at a first reading his poetry seems, apart from its external formality, to be almost haphazard in its structure. Nor is it always easy to see what his main plan is or to disentangle the various themes which he brings into a poem. This is largely because he writes about a complex situation in which he has to celebrate, not only an athletic victor, his family, and his country, but also to explain his own views, illustrate them with a myth, and sometimes refer, however obliquely, to an existing political situation. At times he engages in con-troversy because he has said something that his patrons dislike or because he has at all costs to make his own views clear. He handles this mixed material with a good deal of concealed art. At the start of a poem he will set the tone of what is coming and even give a hint of it, but he varies this with contrasts and comments, and even when he tells a myth, he does not tell it with the simplicity of Bacchylides but makes full use of its in-structional possibilities and stresses certain points in it. In one or two of his poems his own violent feelings and controversial attitude run counter to his main theme, and we are left with a feeling that he has not resolved his discords. So, in *Pythian* 2, written for Hieron in 468 BC, he tries to praise him but fails because he has a nagging sense of injured dignity. But in the main he succeeds in creating a balanced result, in which the varia-

tion of mood as he proceeds adds to the imaginative experience and enriches it, approaching a complex subject from several sides and making his
points all the finer through his unexpected juxtapositions and sudden
changes of theme. The complexity of his art was imposed on him by circumstances but it was also part of an ancient tradition and can be seen in
Alcman. Pindar makes no attempt to simplify but prefers to touch on many
aspects of a rich subject and to bring the different threads together in a
resounding finale.

For this he fashioned a style which is very much his own. Though at
moments he is capable of a magnificent simplicity, he prefers to put as
much richness as possible into his words and to make each phrase and clause
carry a full burden of imaginative meaning. He draws his phraseology
from many sources and, though the epic is one of them, he uses it with
creative discretion and turns its stock epithets to new uses, as when he
speaks of a 'brazen-cheeked javelin' or 'the golden-crowned games' or
'loud-thundering lions' or 'a chariot that shook the earth'. His own
epithets are hardly ever otiose, and, though sometimes he accumulates
them for a special purpose, they are not even then overwhelming. Inside
a sentence he balances his words with great skill, giving special emphasis in
rarity or sound or length to what is most important and subordinating the
rest to it or, starting from a modest start, to lead up to some splendid close.
He has many small devices to mark emphasis or cause surprise or vary the
texture of his work. Some of these are certainly ancient, notably when he
uses a series of parallels to give the character of a varied occasion. So he
opens *Olympian* 1 with a row of paratactic sentences which lead to the
supreme glory of a victory in the Olympian Games:

> Water is the best thing of all, and gold
> Shines like flaming fire at night,
> More than all a great's man's wealth,
> But if, my heart, you would speak of athletic games,
> Seek no more in the empty sky for any star
> More warming than the sun.[31]

Pindar means that a victory of this kind is like water in its lasting nature,
like gold in its brightness, like the sun in its overwhelming glory. At times
he makes puns as if to draw attention to some inner connection between
things not commonly thought to be related; at other times he repeats the
same word at the beginning of two or three clauses with an almost oratorical insistence to drive a point home. He has behind him more than two
centuries of lyric song, and the many devices which poets evolved in this
time are at his full disposal. Yet, though Pindar's language and style are

extraordinarily rich and even elaborate, they are not overloaded. They keep their freshness even when he has to deal with themes so dull as lists of athletic victories, before which a less inventive poet might well shrink. His strength lies in his choice of words, his placing of them, and the unfailing, varied melody which he gives to their rhythm.

By a whim of chance the most fully preserved poems of Pindar are written in honour of victorious athletes, and we might think that so special a subject could not evoke all his powers. Yet these Epinicians reveal two important facets of his genius. First, he seems not to have been very interested in the actual Games, their skills and thrills. On such matters he seldom dwells, and his interest in the Games was his belief in them as tests of human ability and character. Secondly, into these poems Pindar put the whole range of his gifts. He makes a song cover a large range of mood and speculation and imaginative effect. He was able to do this because what he found in success was the fulfilment of human gifts, the positive proof that men could exert themselves as far as possible and in so doing reveal, not only their physical gifts, but self-control, courage, and a capacity for hard toil. In this they resemble the heroes of old, and Pindar does not shrink from equating victories in the Games with other ancient victories won on battlefields or against brutes and monsters. His supreme hero is Heracles, who, after a life of self-denial and prodigious labours, became a god and dwelt on Olympus. Pindar does not expect his athletes to become gods and expressly tells them that they must not aspire to, but he believes that in their moments of success and glory they enjoy a special felicity which is otherwise known only to the gods. In this they were aided by him, and his songs are indispensable to their full recognition and happiness. For him success is proof of a man's worth, and this is his version of older ideas of *aretê*. What other poets had found in fields such as war Pindar found in success in the Games, because it called even more qualities into action and was a fairer test of them. Even when he deals with actual war he sees in its champions the qualities needed for the Games, and is no less happy to celebrate them. His vision of mankind was not troubled by considerations of practical worth; what counted was the realization of a full human being to his utmost limits.

Pindar is keenly aware of the visible world, but he sees it illumined from time to time with a divine light, and his art aims at catching these special moments which belong to an intermediate sphere between men and gods. For him plain statement is seldom enough, and he uses image and metaphor and simile to convey what he sees, drawing his imagery from every kind of source for a number of different purposes. It helps to add something new to the visible scene, as when he says that Mount Etna 'suckles the biting frosts', but its chief use is to define more clearly the nature of his feelings, and in this he is a master. He varies his tone from saying that he is as untouched by evil speech as a cork is that rides on the surge, or that if a victor had stayed at home he would have been like a barn-yard cock, to comparing death with a wave that falls unforeseen even on him that foresees it, or saying that a ruined city is 'falling into a deep pit of doom' or bidding Hieron to 'forge an iron tongue on an anvil of truth'.[32] Pindar's unceasing use of imagery fills our minds with a series of vivid pictures, each of which conveys some subtle or delicate meaning beyond the reach of plain statement. At times it becomes almost a kind of mythology, as he develops his point through personification and works out the consequences. So, stirred to indignation by the slanders which led to the suicide of Ajax, he says:

> Of old too was hateful trickery,
> Walking with wheedling words, plotting deceit,
> Abuse working evil;
> She does violence to glory,
> And sets up a rotten renown for the unknown.[33]

Through imagery Pindar exalts his thoughts above any ordinary level and throws a magic light on them, making them so unusual that they are well fitted for the special realm between gods and men where he is most happily at work.

In a poem Pindar normally tells a myth. This was traditional and at least as old as Alcman, but Pindar practises it very much in his own way. His myths relate present events to past and so throw a special illumination on them. Not all his myths display their relevance at a first reading, but, in fact, he fits them skilfully into his dominating plan. Even when he tells the long story of the Argonauts in *Pythian* 4, it is because his patron, King Arcesilas IV of Cyrene, is descended from one of them and may be expected to show a heroic quality. More often the myth catches the tone of something central to the poem. In Pindar's earliest poem, *Pythian* 10, written in 498 BC for a young Thessalian, his myth of the care-free Hyperboreans at the end of the world is a counterpart to the happiness of the present occasion; when in *Pythian* 11, written in 454 BC, he tells with a tragic tension of Orestes' vengeance on Clytaemestra, he has in mind that Athens, which is at the moment oppressing Thebes, will be similarly punished; when in *Olympian* 1 he tells of the wicked Tantalus and his good son, Pelops, he hints to Hieron that he has it in his power to resemble one or the other, and the conclusion is left unsaid; when in *Isthmian* 8, written immediately after the Persian Wars in 478 BC, he tells of the danger which might have arisen in Olympus if Zeus or Poseidon had married Thetis and begotten a son greater than himself, he sets on a much vaster scene the dangers from which Greece has just escaped. Pindar's myths place his themes in a larger perspective and relate them to issues far beyond their actual occasions.

The myths themselves reveal a special side of Pindar's art. He seldom tells a story in the straightforward way of Bacchylides, but tends to choose a few salient points and to make the most of them, and what we remember are precisely these dazzling insights into a familiar story. The child Iamus is born in the open country and found in the bush and the brake:

> His delicate body soaked
> With gillyflowers' rays of yellow and deep purple.[34]

When Jason arrives, unknown, in the market-place of Iolcus, he makes an immediate and overwhelming impression:

> His bright locks of hair, not cut and cast away,
> Waved all down his back.
> And at once when he came,
> He stood, testing his never-flinching heart,
> When the people thronged in the main square.[35]

When in their last fight the Dioscuri fight the sons of Aphareus by the tomb of their father:

> From it they ripped death's ornament,
> A polished stone,
> And flung it on Polydeuces' breast,
> But they did not break him or drive him back.
> With his quick spear he jumped upon them
> And drove the bronze into Lynceus' lungs;
> And on Idas Zeus flung a fiery smoking thunderbolt.[36]

Pindar enjoys all kinds of action and presents even the strangest with a brilliant sense of their reality. He does not shrink from either the harshest or the most exalted themes. He rises, without apparent effort, to their various challenges and finds in each something that captures his imagination and sets it to work with unfaltering confidence. This is a very different art from the epic, but it is in its much smaller confines no less dramatic and exciting.

If men come near to the gods in certain hours of success, the song which celebrates them has also its celestial side. Pindar speaks with longing admiration for those wonderful occasions in the past when the gods attended the weddings of Peleus and Thetis or of Cadmus and Harmonia and sang at them, while Apollo led with his lyre. But even in his own performances the gods are not far away. Sometimes he believes that they are actually present at a feast in their honour, and other Greeks would have no difficulty in agreeing with him. But Pindar goes further than this. Through song he feels that he brings men closer to the gods and makes them conscious of their kinship with them, and it is this which gives so unusual a brilliance to much of his poetry. His fullest account of this may be seen in the opening of *Pythian* 1, which he wrote in 470 BC for Hieron of Syracuse. He addresses the lyre, which is the symbol of his art, and finds in the present celebration an occasion of celestial joy in which music and song unite heaven and earth in a single, flawless mood:

> O lyre of gold, Apollo's
> Treasure, shared with the violet-wreathed Muses,
> The light foot hears you, and the brightness begins:
> Your notes compel the singer
> When to lead out the dance
> The prelude is sounded on your trembling strings.
> You quench the warrior Thunderbolt's everlasting flame:
> On the sceptre of Zeus the eagle sleeps,
> Drooping his swift wings on either side,
>
> The King of Birds.
> You have poured a cloud on his beak and head,
> And darkened his face:
> His eyelids are shut with a sweet seal.
> He sleeps, his lithe back heaves:
> Your quivering song has conquered him.
> Even Ares the violent,
> Leaving aside his harsh and pointed spears,
> Comforts his heart in drowsiness.
> Your shafts enchant the souls even of the gods
> Through the wisdom of Lato's son
> And the deep-bosomed Muses.[37]

By such means Pindar transfigures the delight of the present occasion into a cosmic festival of which gods and men alike partake. This is the background of his poetry, and when he composes a choral song, he aims at bringing men and gods together.

In his songs Pindar insists that what he tells is the truth. Nothing else should perhaps be expected from the prophet of the Muses, but Pindar, almost unconsciously, agrees with grave spirits of his time who denounced Hesiod and Homer for the evil things which they said about the gods. For Pindar anything evil said of the gods cannot be true, and the man who speaks it is almost a lunatic. He implicitly denies Hesiod's belief that the Muses sometimes speak falsehoods and, though he admits that the Graces, who give much of its beauty to song, may lead men astray, he thinks it his first duty to resist this temptation, if only because it means impiety. That is why he rejects the old story that Tantalus served up his son, Pelops, as a dish to the gods and that Demeter ate his shoulder, and equally why he thinks it madness to say that Heracles, his ideal hero, fought in battle against Apollo, Poseidon, and Ares. In many small ways he tempers an old story to make the god's part in it more honourable or more powerful. His own position is quite clear:

> I cannot say, not I,
> That any Blessed God has a gluttonous belly –
> I stand aside.
> Those who speak evil have troubles thick upon them.[38]

What is a duty to the gods, gives greater strength to songs about men. Time tests the true from the false and in the end the true song survives even the most engaging of false inventions. Pindar's ideal of celestial joy includes truth as an essential element. It is, therefore, understandable that he makes Truth a daughter of Zeus, as if he had a divine obligation towards her.

If exalted joy is Pindar's driving force and conscious aim, he is fully capable of handling other emotions and using them as contrasts for his main purpose. He is well aware that joy is secured only by triumphing over dark and deleterious forces. Just as he sees music as uniting gods and men in a celestial harmony, so he also sees the monstrous, hundred-headed Typhos, the enemy of the gods, listening to it as he lies under Etna, a reminder of what obstacles have to be overcome before any triumph is complete. So too, just as his aim is to preserve the memory of great deeds in song, so he recognizes that there are other men, devoured by envy, who wish to keep them obscure and forgotten. His keen sense of this struggle for light and fame makes him all too aware of the obstacles which inevitably stand in the way. In his own lifetime he felt the appalling danger of the Persian invasion as a stone of Tantalus above his head, and later, when his own Boeotia and his beloved Aegina were conquered by Athens he saw her as a presumptuous giant whom the gods would inevitably humble. In private affairs, notably in his relations with Hieron of Syracuse, he found that the ideal state of joy was too easily frustrated by the intrigues and slanders of men, and he lashed out against them. The varieties of human conflict were matched by the matter of his myths, and in them he tells, with a brilliant selectiveness, what prowess needs for success and what hampers or halts it. At one end are the scenes of divine power and beauty, as when Apollo falls in love with a nymph while she wrestles with a lion or snatches an unborn child from his dead mother on her funeral-pyre, or Zeus brings back to life the dead Castor because of the entreaties of Polydeuces; at the other end are those who have been given great chances and make a monstrous use of them, as Ixion assaults Hera and sleeps instead with a cloud, from whom a hideous issue is born, or Tantalus is made to sit for ever with a stone above his head in sight of an Olympian feast which he can never touch, or Coronis, whom Apollo loves, betrays him for a mortal lover and is doomed to death. Pindar sees human life as oscillating between extremes of success and disaster, of joy and grief, and, though he thinks that there is more sorrow than joy, it is joy that concerns him more than anything else and is his to give. Through its very rarity it is indeed worth winning.

Pindar has no illusions about the security of the human condition or its chances of lasting happiness. At times indeed his imagination was caught by beliefs in some marvellous afterworld in which men of heroic stature would live beyond the western sea:

> Where the Airs, daughters of Ocean,
> Blow round the Island of the Blest,
> And the flowers are of gold,
> Some on land flaming from bright trees,
> Others the water feeds;
> They bind their hands with them and make crowns.[39]

But more often Pindar seems to accept the ancient view that man can expect little after death and that for this very reason he must make the most of his life on earth, not only by exerting himself to the utmost and thereby winning glory, but also by the familiar consolations of the human state. Pindar's concept of the good life included most forms of delight no less than loyalty and affection and noble toil. At the centre of his system was his belief that everything that matters for men comes from the gods, and that it is this which men must seek. They will never really resemble or rival the gods, but at unaccountable moments they will know, if only for a short time, what happiness the gods enjoy, and this gives solidity and sense to human life. In his old age he wrote some words which carry his chief message:

Man's life is a day. What is he?
What is he not? A shadow in a dream
Is man, but when Zeus sends a brightness
Shining light is on earth
And life is sweet as honey.[40]

He felt that when men were left to themselves, they were indeed unsubstantial, but when the light of the gods shone upon them, they found their full range and enjoyed a divine happiness. This was on the whole to be found in action and its results. It was in the full exercise of human faculties that Pindar found the stuff of his poetry, and that is why he achieves something which almost no other poet in the world does. Just because he saw human beings as in some small respects resembling the gods and had through his own religious experience a vivid sense of what this meant, he brings together gods and men as members of a single race, both being children of Earth, and shows how, despite all their differences and conflicts, they are able to come together, and this is the true fulfilment of life.

THE TRAGIC VISION

THE Greek word *tragôidia*, from which our own word 'tragedy' is derived, means nothing more than 'goat-song'. The Greeks disputed whether this was because a goat was the prize for the best song or because a goat was sacrificed when songs were sung, and modern speculations have added an alternative theory that the goat embodied Dionysus and the song was sung at his annual, ritual death. From a mass of obscure facts and ingenious theories a few solid facts emerge. All drama has its beginnings in mimetic dances in which the dancers identify themselves with certain characters and dress or daub or mask themselves to sustain the illusion. Their aim is religious or magical, a wish to enter into a closer relation with supernatural beings and usually to get them to do something. Such dances were common in Greece, and vases from the sixth century onwards have many pictures of men dancing in disguise. In Athens some dances were connected with Dionysus, the god, not only of wine, but of fertility and ecstatic excitement. To him songs were sung, accompanied by dances, and the whole complex, known as the Dithyramb, was at an early date standardized as an art-form, which told a story and no doubt illustrated it with action. The public performance of Dithyrambs was prominent in the second part of the sixth century and in the first half of the fifth Simonides, Bacchylides, and Pindar composed them. Though they were performed at the spring festival of Dionysus, their contents did not necessarily have much connection with him. On the one hand this kind of song became a special kind of choral lyric, but before it had reached its final form as such, it engendered a new and different form, which turned into tragedy. Soon after the middle of the sixth century a choir-leader called Thespis inserted into the performance pieces of spoken verse in which he assumed the part of one of the characters told of in the song. In 534 BC this art had developed sufficiently to be recognized officially at Athens and to have annual performances in the spring. At the start tragedy contained a large element of song and dance and a small element of acting done by a single actor, and no doubt closely related to the main theme of the song.

Of Thespis' work not a word has survived, and we know nothing at all about it. Even of his immediate successors we are equally ignorant, but it is clear that in the next fifty years the form of tragedy, helped by official approval from Peisistratus, was rapidly developed and more or less established. The number of actors was increased from one to two and eventually to three and four, but never to more, while the chorus was fixed at fifteen. The performance was held on a circular space, an orchestra or dancing-place, probably once a threshing-floor, from which at one end a thin slice was cut off and included in a tangential area to provide the equivalent of a stage, though it is not certain that an actual stage was regularly used. Behind this was a simple, conventional scene of a palace-front, with a large central door and entrances or exits at the sides. The performance was held under the open sky in a theatre, carved like a horse-shoe from the side of a hill, and the acoustics were excellent. Some of the acting, as well as the songs and dances, took place in the orchestra and to this extent the performance was 'in the round'. The use of masks and elaborate clothing need not have hampered the actors in a free play of gesture, and there is no reason to think that Greek acting was stiff or formalized. In the fifth century the guaranteed life of a play was a single performance in a series which lasted from dawn to dusk. Each dramatist produced four plays, of which the first three were tragedies, and the fourth was a satyric drama, that is, a less serious piece in which the chorus was played by Satyrs, the traditional companions of Dionysus. The dramatist whose play was adjudged best was awarded a prize. In these conditions tragedy kept its first features unimpaired. Though the speaking portions were continuously increased as the actors became more important, the chorus never ceased to have a central importance and almost to hold the play together. Just because originally events were narrated and not acted, much of importance takes place off stage and is reported by a messenger. A play often begins with a monologue by a god or goddess or chief character who sets out the situation, and almost equally often it ends with the epiphany of a divine being who tidies up the action and passes some judgment on it. Though Greek tragedy does not always obey the unities of time, place, and action as they were formulated by Boileau after Aristotle, it preserves a simplicity of structure which is quite unlike the generous and varied scope of Elizabethan drama. All the parts were taken by men or boys, and a single actor might often have to take two or three quite different parts in the same play.

It is hard to see how so serious a form as tragedy could have been born from the Dithyramb. It is true that, unlike modern tragedy, Greek need not have an unhappy ending, but that does not prevent it from dealing in a most searching spirit with problems that concern the relations of men with the gods. Most of the early dances, as we see them depicted on vases, are either boisterous or phallic or comic, and from them we can easily imagine how the antithetical art of comedy came into existence. Nor has extant tragedy much to do with Dionysus, except in the remarkable case of Euripides' *Bacchants*, in which Dionysus is the chief character and the chorus consists of his votaries. Euripides, who was something of an antiquarian, may possibly have gone back to the beginnings of his art in this last burst of his remarkable genius, but if he did, it is hard to see where he got his knowledge, and still harder to explain why in all other Attic tragedies Dionysus has almost no part at all. The answer is probably to be found in the special character which the Dithyramb had taken at Athens. From being a rowdy, improvised song it had developed a special dignity and told stories of high events from the heroic past. Almost by accident the cult of Dionysus was deeply infused with an epic tone, and this in its turn was applied to contemporary problems in a lofty spirit. Myths and legends were used to present in concrete form large issues which troubled the Athenian mind and called for a clear presentation in this dramatic way. Greek tragedy deals with conflict and confusion, but this may be resolved either by annihilation or by the restoration of order, and both solutions were common. What matters is the universal importance of the issues raised. With the single exception of Aeschylus' *Persians* the plots of extant Greek tragedies are taken from myth, but each myth is told, not simply for its own sake, in the epic way but for its implicit questions and lessons. It presents its problem from more than one angle and is fully aware of their dramatic character and the thrill of their episodes, but these take a deeper significance because they are made to illustrate vexed issues in the human state.

Greek tragedy belongs to Athens, and to Athens alone. If it was sometimes performed elsewhere, we know very little of it, but at Athens it incarnates the spirit of the fifth century from the defeat of the Persian invaders in 490 BC and 480–479 BC till the surrender to Sparta in 404 BC. This art is characteristic of Athens in that it keeps the fine sense of style and the lively curiosity of the aristocratic age and at the same time derives an adventurous strength from the new democracy, not least from its concern with ambition and power, and the belief that Athens had a civilizing mission to all Hellas. The abounding vitality of these years finds in tragedy an outlet, which is at once a fulfilment and a criticism of the Athenian outlook and provides a searching commentary on what Athenians thought about fundamental matters in their exuberant heyday and in the approaching shadows of their decline. Of its first fifty or so years we know next to nothing, and for us Greek tragedy is embodied in the surviving plays of the three dramatists whose work weathered the centuries successfully enough for a small proportion of it to be studied in the schools of Constantinople. Aeschylus (526–456 BC) grew up before Athens expelled its tyrants, and at the age of thirty-five fought against the Persians at Marathon, a fact recorded on his tomb to the exclusion of any mention of his poetry. He lived through the most glorious days of Athens after the democracy had reached its logical limit by making all free citizens take part in the government. His earliest surviving play, the *Persians*, was produced in 472 BC and his latest, the three plays of the *Oresteia*, in 458 BC, and this means that of his early work we know almost nothing. Yet, we can hardly doubt that he, more than anyone, laid the true foundations of tragedy and established the forms and the spirit which marked it out from other kinds of poetry. What survives from his work belongs to the years in which Athens established herself as a sea-power with an empire, reformed her constitution, and secured her system of liberty guaranteed by law. Sophocles (495–406 BC) was fortunate in that his life almost coincided with the great days of Athens. As a boy of fifteen he took part in a choir, which celebrated the victory of Salamis, and he died before the capitulation of his country to Sparta. Of the more than a hundred plays which he wrote seven survive and, though his first prize was won in 468 BC, when he defeated Aeschylus with his *Triptolemus*, his earliest surviving play, the *Ajax*, probably comes from the forties, and the other plays come at intervals up to the *Philoctetes* in 409 BC and the *Oedipus at Colonus*, which he finished just before his death. Thus what we have of his work comes from his mature years, and even when he wrote the *Ajax*, he may have been older than Shakespeare when he retired to silence and death at Stratford. Euripides (480–406 BC) wrote ninety-two plays, of which nineteen survive, ranging from the *Alcestis* in 438 BC to the *Iphigeneia in Aulis*, which he left unfinished to be completed by another hand. Each poet speaks for a different generation. Aeschylus, despite his concern with grave and enigmatic issues, is the veteran of Marathon, who believes that in the end most questions can be answered and that the darkest catastrophes have the promise of some comforting light. Sophocles, the friend of Pericles, reflects his seriousness and his interest in primary principles. He is more detached than Aeschylus from the contemporary scene and examines it with a more searching insight. Euripides speaks for more troubling forces, for the questions and doubts and uncertainties which were in the air before the Peloponnesian War and much aggravated by it. While Aeschylus and Sophocles are at home in their generations, Euripides sometimes seems to be a misfit or an oddity, but, despite this, he was in later times more widely read and quoted than they, and, even in his own time, he enjoyed an enormous, if critical, popularity. Enough has survived from these three poets to reveal typical qualities of their art, even if we cannot but lament the vast amount that has been lost and may have contained much of which we have no inkling. We must make the best of what we have, and this leaves no doubt about the extraordinary level of achievement of which these three men, with their quite different gifts, were capable, and the astonishing judgment of the Athenian people, who both expected such works to be written and understood them when they were.

Though the three tragedians differ greatly from one another in outlook and manner and technique, they are all controlled by the conditions of dramatic performance and have to conform to certain rules. These settled the length of a play, which may vary from about 1,100 to 1,700 lines, and is usually nearer the first than the second, and no play would take more than two hours to perform. This means that the dramatist must exercise economy and discrimination in deciding what he may put in and what he must leave out, and this is all the more insistent since a certain part of the play must be taken up with choral songs, which in their very nature are different from speeches and dialogue and limit even further the space allowed to these. The result is that any Greek tragedy not only operates with a small number of characters, but confines its action almost to a single crisis, which has indeed its preliminaries and its aftermath but is in itself complete and unelaborate. It cannot allow anything comparable to the wide sweep of persons and actions with which Shakespeare, for instance, builds up the first two acts of *Antony and Cleopatra*. Moreover, even economy of characters and action is not enough. To cram the full force of his drama into so short a space the Greek tragedian has to concentrate as much as possible into his words. There is no room for diversions, no matter how splendid, and the words spoken by the characters are directed immediately to the development of the action. This is assisted by a device, which may come from the beginnings of Greek tragedy. When characters converse on the stage, they often speak to one another by interchanging single complete lines. Less than a single line is very rare, and a normal method for conversation is this stately, formal intercourse. It looks archaic and may well be, but for the dramatist it has the advantage that he is almost forced to distil his words into a very short space. Each line caps or completes or contradicts the line before it, and, despite the obvious formality, this means a quick, rapidly changing, highly dramatic process by which the action develops through the shifts of thought and feeling in the actors. Even when the poet goes to the other extreme and makes a messenger tell a full and varied story, he must still see that every word is on the point. In its very nature Greek tragedy practises selection and exclusion, and this calls for a high degree of attention in watching it. If the spectator allows his mind to wander, he will miss something indispensable to the whole development of the action.

Secondly, tradition laid down that every tragedy must have in it a Chorus, whose task was to sing about the action, to play some part in it, and in general to provide some kind of continuity since it is always present from soon after the beginning to the end, when it usually has the last word. The Chorus represents some suitable general role, such as old men or captive women or in special cases Oceanids or Bacchants. As tragedy developed through the fifth century, there was a tendency, not only to reduce the time given to choral songs, but to relate the Chorus more closely to the action, but throughout, it has a central part, and its importance may be gauged from the fact that four plays of Aeschylus, one of Sophocles, and five of Euripides are named after it. It is not an entirely impersonal body, but it is not very fully individualized and it can vary from expressing the poet's own ideas to saying what ordinary people might feel in an extraordinary situation, or even, as in Aeschylus' *Eumenides* or Euripides' *Bacchants*, to presenting an unusual point of view. What happens to the other characters must be judged against the background of the Chorus, which provides a setting for it, passes comments and judgments, and often sets an emotional tone, which affects our response to the actual events. Sometimes it is the central actor in a play, as in Aeschylus' *Suppliant Women*, and this may be an inheritance from the first days of tragedy. The mere existence of the Chorus means that the dramatic action is set in a certain perspective and hardly ever moves in a self-sufficient world of its own as it does in Shakespeare and Racine. However strongly we respond to the actual events of a play, we must take them in conjunction with what the Chorus says about them. It gives to them a greater depth and a richer significance by relating them to other issues, even if these issues are no more than the usual thoughts of men on such subjects, and the Chorus is certainly not meant to give final answers on any matter. The degree of this relation may vary from play to play even in the works of a single dramatist, but it is always there and must be reckoned with in any attempt to understand Greek tragedy. The Chorus is not an appendage to the other actors but, like them, part of a single design. We are right to see it as belonging to the whole imaginary world in which the dramatic action takes place, and just because it is so little individualized it suggests all the more forcibly what reactions are possible to the striking and disturbing episodes of tragic action.

Thirdly, we must not expect to find in Greek drama characters so fully personal as those of Shakespeare. This is impossible, partly because of the much smaller scale on which the Greek poets work, but also because they were primarily concerned with depicting human destinies as what might happen to anyone through his human nature and his place in the world. Tragedy speaks, as Aristotle saw, of universal matters, and to these a high degree of personality and minor idiosyncrasies are alien. This general character was enhanced by the use of masks. Even if a character changed his mask during a play, as Oedipus may have done after blinding himself, the mere wearing of it imposes a permanence on a character and makes us look at him from a single angle and not expect anything discordant with it in what he says or does. In the Greek theatre the mask is almost the man, but not quite. After all, he speaks, and his words, though not inconsistent with such a part as a mask suggests, certainly amplify and enrich it. Yet, when we compare the characters of Greek tragedy with those of modern drama, still more with those of novelists who work on a large scale like Tolstoy or Proust, we feel that what concerns us is not so much their personalities, as their destinies, not what they are, but what they do and have done to them. The top moments of Greek tragedy come when through the force of circumstances men and women represent in their single selves a whole human destiny and, even if they have brought it on themselves, their motives are like those of other human beings and remarkable more for their strength than for their subtlety. They are presented as examples of behaviour seen from without rather than from within and, though this sooner or later invites us to discern special characteristics, we may doubt whether their creators were much concerned with them. So, far from acting on the principle of Heraclitus that 'character is destiny',[1] the Greek tragedians almost insist that destiny is character.

This does not mean that the persons of tragedy are mere abstractions, but it does mean that they are highly simplified and that their special kind of vitality comes from the omission of much that we take for granted in human beings. This simplification strengthens their impact on us and concentrates our attention on those few qualities which are indispensable to their fate. They are far from being types of the kind favoured by the comedy of manners; for a type is created by a different kind of simplification, in which everything is dominated and determined by a single quality, visible in a character's every action and infused through his whole being. In Greek tragic characters something is needed to explain why they are in their actual situations and why they act or suffer as they do. They have qualities, which we know in ourselves and others, and these keep them alive before us, but we do not have to look for cryptic or complex motives or take notice of irrelevant, if engaging, superfluities. The tragedian's task is to show men and women in their universal characteristics as crisis tests and reveals them. When we see a Greek play acted, we interpret the actions of the characters by the familiar rules of human nature, and we are right to do so, but we need not look for anything paradoxical or unfamiliar. The tragedian's task is to illuminate the familiar, recurrent, recognizable situation, not to seek out unexplored recesses in the soul. In the end this is a great strength. Because tragedy eschews the odd and the unusual and gives its full powers to matters with which we are all acquainted, it makes special exertions to keep to the truth and to make it more impressive even to those who think that they are well acquainted with it.

Aeschylus differs from Sophocles and Euripides in making his unit of composition, not the single play, but the trilogy, or three plays in succession on a comprehensive subject. This gives him a remarkable breadth and scope in his main design and enables him to show unseen powers at work in more than one generation. Though he seems to have composed almost entirely in trilogies, only one complete example survives, the *Oresteia*, which consists of the *Agamemnon*, *Libation-bearers*, and *Eumenides*. From this it is clear that a trilogy is not a long, three-act play but three separate plays, united by a single dominating theme. Each play is a well-conceived unit, which can be acted quite satisfactorily by itself, but between them they tell a single story at three stages, the murder of Agamemnon by his wife, Clytaemestra, the vengeance which their son, Orestes, takes by killing her, his final acquittal from the crime of murder in the eyes of gods and men. From this single example we must surmise as best we can how his other surviving plays were fitted into similarly grandiose schemes. The *Suppliant Women*, which survives, was the first play of a trilogy and tells how Danaüs and his fifty daughters have escaped from Egypt to Argos, and are in peril from their suitors coming in pursuit. They are finally welcomed in Argos, and the play catches the excitement, uncertainty, and fear of their reception there. The second play, the *Egyptians*, told of the arrival of the Egyptian suitors, their battle with the Argives, whose king was killed, and their taking to marriage the daughters of Danaüs. The daughters, then, at their father's command kill their husbands, with the exception of Hypermestra who accepts the marriage. In the third play, the *Daughters of Danaüs*, Hypermestra, who has disobeyed her father, and invited trouble by her disobedience, seems to have been tried and acquitted through the intervention of Aphrodite. On the other hand the *Seven against Thebes* is the last play of a trilogy, which turns on the doom of the house of Laius. In the first play, the *Laius*, Laius hearing that he will be killed by his son, has him exposed, but the child none the less survives. He is Oedipus, who in the play called after him has grown up and accidentally kills Laius, not knowing who he is. The hideous truth comes out, and at the end of the play Oedipus curses his children for their harsh treatment of him. In the *Seven against Thebes* the curse is at work. One son, Polynices, has attacked Thebes, which is ruled by his brother, Eteocles. They meet in battle, and both are killed, and the play ends with prognostications of evil for the other members of the house of Laius.

The *Prometheus Bound* presents more complex problems. It deals with the punishment of Prometheus, himself a divine being, by Zeus for having stolen fire from Olympus and given it to men. It was followed by the lost *Prometheus Delivered*, in which Prometheus was freed by Zeus because he knew a secret, that, if Zeus married Thetis, they would have a son who would overthrow him. But the rest is almost hopelessly obscure. It is possible that there was a third play, *Prometheus the Fire-bearer*, which may have brought the action to earth and told of the establishment of fire-festivals, but almost all that we know of it is that in it Aeschylus said that Prometheus had been chained for thirty thousand years. It is even possible that the third play was never completed, and that this accounts for our ignorance of it. What we do know is that the two plays, of which we have the first and some information on the second, told of the punishment of Prometheus and then of his deliverance, and were certainly parts of a single plan. On the other hand the *Persians* was written as a single play and, though it was produced with two others, the *Phineus* and the *Glaucus Potnieus*, its connection with both cannot have been related to its subject, since this was contemporary and theirs was mythical. They may of course have touched on some superficial connections, but it is hard to say how they can have, and not necessary to think that they did.

From the little that we can construct from these imperfect trilogies and from the extant *Oresteia* certain points emerge. Since a trilogy can extend beyond a single generation and can make each play deal with a self-contained topic, it is free to develop a theme on a large scale, and in this it differs from a single play. The individual plays were independent and complete wholes in themselves, comparable with the single plays of the other two dramatists, but the trilogy held them together by some large, uniting concept. In the *Oresteia* the question is of vengeance for murder in a family. Clytaemestra kills Agamemnon for sacrificing their daughter, Iphigeneia; Orestes kills Clytaemestra; what then should happen to Orestes? By the old rules, embodied in the Furies, blood calls for blood, and Orestes should be killed. But Aeschylus in the *Eumenides* has Orestes acquitted of murder and a new rule of order established under law. The Laius trilogy dramatized a curse which visits the sins of the fathers upon the children to the third generation. The idea was at least as old as Solon, and Aeschylus shows how it worked in practice. In the three plays on the daughters of Danaüs the central theme seems to be built on the relations between the sexes and to claim that a woman has a right to marry the man she loves. No doubt there was much more than this, including a conflict between filial obedience and personal passion, but that is about all that we can say. The central theme of the Prometheus plays was certainly the conflict between Prometheus and Zeus, which began in the punishment of Prometheus by Zeus but seems to have ended in some sort of reconciliation, though how this came we can only guess. It is at least not impossible that Zeus was displayed as growing milder as he grew older. The scale of structure in the trilogy corresponds with the sweep of Aeschylus' dramatic vision. He sees events in a large outline and detects divine laws at work in them, and for this, the trilogy is a more capacious field than the single play.

Though Aeschylus builds his trilogies on a single dominating theme, this is only part of their structure, and he must not be treated as a philosopher or a theologian. His ideas are transformed into drama and poetry and make their effect through the individual, concrete shapes which they take. What engages us is not the mere idea but its significance in special situations, which have their own fascinating appeal. Thus, though the theme of vengeance runs through the three plays of the *Oresteia*, what is really significant is the actual sequence of events, the murder of Agamemnon, the madness of Orestes, the uncertainty whether he will in the end be acquitted. In the *Persians*, where the punishment of pride is amply displayed, we see what it means not merely to Xerxes himself in his humiliation but to his aged mother and to the Ghost of his father, who stand for wiser policies and convey almost historical lessons as they deplore the excesses of their son. In the *Prometheus Bound* what first concerns us is the fate of Prometheus, which is presented almost entirely from his point of view, so that we cannot but sympathize with him and admire him. In the *Seven against Thebes* Eteocles may indeed be doomed to die, but before his death he is magnificently in control of his people and, when he goes out to battle, it is with a truly heroic ardour and desperation. Whatever Aeschylus' own processes of composition may have been the effect which he makes on us is to feel the impact of his dramatic events first and then to ask what interpretation, if any, he offers of them. And indeed the same may have been true of his own processes. When he chose a myth for a drama, he seems first to have felt its claims on the emotions and then to have shaped these into some guiding but never very interfering plan. He certainly does not use his dramatic persons to embody abstract situations or to illustrate lessons. They have their own extraordinary life and appeal to us by their own natures, which may well run counter to the designs of the gods and the laws of men but are none the less human and enthralling in their own right. Even Clytaemestra, who lives with a paramour and has long plotted her husband's murder before she commits it on his return from Troy, has an overwhelming splendour in the force of her hatred and the brazen effrontery of her speech. Zeus may have his own reasons for having Prometheus nailed to a rock in the Caucasus, but the scene of the nailing, with which the play begins, spares nothing of its cruelty or of the silent fortitude with which Prometheus endures it. The first appeal is to our human feelings, and through these we are eventually led to think about the vast issues involved in the action.

Aeschylus reinforces this method by using the Chorus to raise questions which are relevant to his drama. We must not assume that his Chorus always speaks for himself. It certainly does not in the *Suppliant Women*, where the Chorus are important actors in the drama, and the comments made by the Oceanids to Prometheus throw a new light on Prometheus' fate but are not necessarily final. But in the *Agamemnon* the long choral songs, which deal with large abstract conceptions, have been thought to be the poet's own comment on the events. So, to a considerable extent, they are, but these comments are not the exegesis of an abstract thinker but the imaginative musings of a poet at full stretch. The dark forces of doom and heredity, of pride and humiliation, which he sees at work fill him with awe and wonder, and he is less concerned to make them clear than to convey their mysterious power. They belong to an order halfway between gods and men, and they are relevant to both. Aeschylus presents their strange movements and gives to them a mythological reality, but his first interest is to catch their nature from more than one angle and to convey their character through a rich array of symbols and metaphors. They add to the drama by enhancing its less intelligible sides and make us look at the events in the knowledge that far more is at work than meets the immediate eye. They are indeed highly intellectual poetry in the sense that much hard thought has gone into them, but this thought is not explanatory but pictorial, not analytical but impressionist, not factual but imaginative. Though there are moments when Aeschylus by his sheer visual power reminds us of Dante, he differs from him in making us form our own conclusions from the many hints which he throws out and does not throughout assume a single, consistent system in which everything is clear.

Aeschylus' notion of dramatic action is not the same as our own. In some plays he might even seem, by modern standards, to be unduly undramatic. In the *Prometheus Bound*, the actual drama is confined to the beginning, when Prometheus is nailed to the rock, and the end, when he is engulfed by an earthquake. But the rest of the play consists of conversations between him and first Oceanus, then Io, and finally Hermes, and of these only the last has any dramatic results, since Prometheus' refusal to tell Hermes his terrific secret leads to his being swallowed under the earth. In the *Seven Against Thebes* the larger part of the play consists of speeches in which Eteocles hears in turn of his main opponents and learns about their appearance and their characters. It is only after this that he moves into action and displays his full being. Much of the *Suppliant Women* consists of songs and debates, and it is not till the end that a real crisis emerges. Yet, despite the lack of action on the stage and even of descriptions of it off, these long passages are certainly not dull nor, strictly speaking, static. What they do is to present with much force and imagination states of consciousness, both mental and emotional, and present issues which cannot fail to catch our attention. Their dramatic quality lies in the play and counterplay of vivid prospects and retrospects, of fears and hopes equally uncertain and unfulfilled, of large controversies reduced to individual discussions and yet alike far-ranging and inexorably present. The fascination of these long discussions lies in their rich and loaded poetry which transforms everything that it touches and raises it to an exalted, visionary level, in which every theme is at once clairvoyantly vivid and yet rich in vast associations beyond itself. Aeschylus does not need to fill his plays with obviously dramatic moments; there is drama enough in his shifts of mood and his brilliant presentation of them to engage all our attention.

At the same time Aeschylus can, when he chooses, present scenes of an unusually dramatic power, firmly conceived and economically worked out. His bold, confident imagination finds no difficulty in giving verisimilitude to the strange creations of myth but thrives on making them at once striking and plausible, or perhaps so striking that they become plausible in their own world. When, in the *Persians*, the ghost of Darius is summoned at his tomb, there is no attempt to enforce the unearthly character of his appearance. He speaks as the great conqueror, the king of kings, who recalls with pride his own achievements and condemns the reckless effrontery of Xerxes. When Hephaestus helps to nail Prometheus to his rock, he does so unwillingly, but there is a relentless determination in his performance of his duty. When at the beginning of the *Eumenides* the Furies wait outside Apollo's temple to snatch Orestes as their victim, they are indeed true children of Hell and bestially convincing as the agents of the old rule that blood calls for blood. But it is not only the supernatural which sets Aeschylus' finest powers to work. In dealing with a purely human situation he displays powers no less formidable and exalts his scenes to a superhuman simplicity and power. In the *Agamemnon*, which abounds in dramatic episodes, one of the most striking is that in which Clytaemestra compels her husband to walk on a purple carpet and thus to show an arrogance which he would gladly avoid. She does it by pure power of will and shows that he is even at this moment her victim. A little later Cassandra, whom Agamemnon has brought from Troy to be his concubine and who has hitherto kept a complete silence, bursts into words and tells of the butcheries which haunt the house of Atreus, until Clytaemestra summons her into the palace. Then to our surprise she refuses to go, and Clytaemestra leaves her outside. But Cassandra knows that she is doomed, and soon goes of her own accord, a predestined victim, to her death. Aeschylus is keenly aware of the advantages of surprise and knows how to exploit them. When, in the *Libation-bearers*, Orestes is about to kill his mother, he falters and asks whether he should have pity on her, but he is kept to his task by his friend Pylades, who says:

> Where then shall be Apollos's oracles,
> The solemn covenants giv'n at his shrine?
> Let all men hate you rather than the gods.[2]

These are the only words spoken by Pylades in the whole play, and for that reason all the more impressive and terrible. When, in the *Seven against*

Thebes, Eteocles has heard the long accounts of the warriors who await battle against him, he makes up his mind to fight them, but at this moment he is filled with a savage desperation and knows that the doom of the House of Laius is on him:

> Now that a god mightily drives things on,
> Let all of Laius' breed, that Phoebus hates,
> Drive with the wind into Cocytus' waves.[3]

There is a sudden change both in the action of the play and in the mood of Eteocles. The crisis has come with irresistible suddenness and the whole play reveals its essential shape. Yet here too what counts is the powerful, poetical impact, by which words, straining to their limit, convey the full meaning of this moment of decision. In Aeschylus the poetry holds everything together and blends the moments of high crisis with the mental conflicts and preparations of which they are the culmination.

In his concentration on this all-important point Aeschylus may seem to pay insufficient attention to the actual details of his plots. We might of course surmise that, since he was largely the creator of tragedy and was among the first to give it a plot, he had not divined how much is gained by making this clear and convincing. But this does not seem to be the case, for, when he chooses, as in the carpet-scene in the Agamemnon, he provides an entirely satisfying episode. It is more likely that in his concentration on the changing moods in his drama, he chose to sacrifice the secondary interest of dramatic intrigue. Thus, in the *Eumenides*, Orestes is tried for matricide, of which he is unquestionably guilty, and we might expect that he would be acquitted because he is the only man who can exact vengeance for his father's murder. But this is not what Aeschylus says. Orestes is acquitted by the single vote of Athene on the strength of Apollo's argument that a man's mother is not really his parent, and, therefore, it was not wrong to kill Clytaemestra. This is in itself unsatisfying and neglects much that has been said in this and the previous plays. But Aeschylus seems to do it because he wishes above all to show that the gods approve of Orestes' action and must protect him from the dark powers which pursue him. In a similar spirit Aeschylus deals unexpectedly with the recognition of one another by Orestes and his sister, Electra, in the *Libation-bearers*. The Greek tragedians excelled at such scenes, and Aristotle thought of them as one of the essential points in a tragedy. But Aeschylus treats this one in what seems almost too artless a way. Electra finds a lock of hair on her father's tomb and says that it is very like that of Orestes, whom in fact she has not seen for many years. Her suspicion is confirmed when she finds footprints, which are of the same shape and size as her own. On the strength of these two rather scanty pieces of evidence she concludes that Orestes is about, and before long she is united to him. As a recognition-scene this does not compare with some far more skilful scenes in Euripides, but Aeschylus has something else in mind than the mere excitement of a brother and sister recognizing each other. The hair and the footmarks are signs of the unbreakable ties which bind Orestes and Electra together and of the common task which awaits them. This calls for emphasis and he secures it by a rather artless device.

Aeschylus enforced his effects with a generous use of spectacle, on which he relies much more than Sophocles and Euripides. In the *Suppliant Women* the fifty daughters of Danaüs are pursued by an army of Egyptian slaves. The daughters flee, and the Egyptians are put to flight by an Argive army. This must have called for a large number on the scene at the same time, and the soldiers would presumably be equipped with glittering military accoutrements. In the *Prometheus Bound* the action takes place, not before the usual palace, but on a rocky crag. The daughters of Ocean, who form the Chorus, arrive on chariots at a higher level and descend from them to speak to Prometheus; Ocean himself arrives on a four-legged bird, and Io comes pursued by a monstrous gad-fly. All this called for inventive ingenuity in the stage-craftsmen and enhanced the effect of remoteness and strangeness. In the *Agamemnon* the victorious king comes home with a following worthy of his triumph. He himself rides in a chariot and is followed by his men-at-arms, who are presumably on foot, and by the prophetess Cassandra in a second chariot. The *Eumenides* opens at the temple of Apollo. By it are the Furies, black and ugly, who make weird unintelligible noises and display their lust for blood in their dripping eyes and drooling mouths. Soon afterwards the ghost of Clytaemestra appears and with a savagery worthy of her living self calls on the Furies to do their fell task, and they reply with suitable grunts. To be able to present such scenes Aeschylus must have had rich patrons, and they are notable evidence for the wealth of Athens after the Persian Wars. Though convention limited him to four actors with speaking parts, he employed a large number of mutes who at times must have filled the whole orchestra as well as the tangential area which served as the stage. The spectacle dazzled the eyes, while the words caught and held the ear, but the spectacle was essentially secondary to the words.

With Aeschylus it is the poetry that counts. Like Pindar, he writes in a rich metaphorical style, which makes no concessions to vulgar realism. It is this which sets the distance between his subjects and the common world and places them in their own majestic sphere of the imagination. Yet, though his language is always rich and elaborate, it has an extraordinary variety of temper and effect. Aeschylus proves what we might otherwise find hard to believe, that the consciously grand style can adapt itself to a whole range of different needs without losing any of its grandeur. Though he is magnificently eloquent, he is not rhetorical, and his words do not try to say more than they really mean. When later writers tried to imitate him, they fell into bombast, but he himself is in full control of his adventurous and amazing speech. Its range may be illustrated from three small cases in the *Agamemnon*. First, when the play opens, the Watchman on the roof of the palace is on duty waiting for the bonfire to tell that Troy has been captured. To his enormous surprise he suddenly sees it, and he expresses his delight in words which are homely and yet vastly expressive:

> And I will dance the overture myself.
> My master's dice have fallen well, and I
> For this night's work shall score a treble six.[4]

The images suit the Watchman's humble station, but they are not the less lively for that. Next, when Cassandra goes to her death, her last words are about her doom which she sees as an example of the whole human state:

> Ah, for the life of man! in happiness
> It may be like a shadow – in unhappiness
> A wet sponge drips and rubs the picture out.[5]

The image is again simple and even humble, but just for this reason it stresses the futility of life, which is no more important than a casual action of this kind. Thirdly, when Clytaemestra comes out of the palace, having killed her husband and glorying in it, she says:

> There he lay prostrate, gasping out his soul,
> And pouring forth a sudden spurt of blood
> Rained thick these drops of deathly dew upon me,
> While I rejoiced like cornfields at the flow
> Of heavenly moisture in birth-pangs of the bud.[6]

The murderess exults in what she has done and feels that life revives in her as it does in the earth in spring time.

Though imagery is central to Aeschylus' language and enables him to catch the precise tone and temper of almost any occasion, there are moments when he uses a much simpler statement and yet maintains his habitual majesty. When Clytaemestra brushes aside Agamemnon's doubts about walking on a purple carpet, she argues for it in a spirit of reckless extravagance on the grounds that there is plenty more purple dye where it came from:

> There is the sea, and who shall drain it dry?[7]

When Prometheus is left alone by his gaolers to whom he has said nothing, he bursts into speech and addresses the whole wide world around him:

> O holy sky, and breezes swift of wing,
> O river-springs, and multitudinous laughter
> Of ocean waves, and you, all-mother Earth,
> And on the Sun's all-seeing orb I call:
> See what, a god, I suffer from the gods.[8]

Imagery plays a part in this, but the whole effect is of a boundless simplicity and spaciousness, worthy of the vast solitude in which Prometheus is imprisoned. At the opposite end of the scale we may set words which Orestes' old nurse speaks when she has heard a false rumour of his death and recalls his childhood and what it meant to her:

> A child in swaddling clothes cannot declare
> His wants, that he would eat, or drink, or make
> Water, and childish bellies will not wait
> Upon attendance.[9]

This is innocent and touching and entirely true to life. So too in a fragment of *The Net-Haulers*, which is a satyric play and might be expected not to maintain the high Aeschylean manner, there is a charming scene in which Silenus, seeing Danaë and the infant Perseus thrown on land from the sea in their chest, tries to cheer the child:

> Don't be afraid. Why are you whimpering?
> Over here to my sons let us go,
> And you can come, my pretty one,
> To my protecting arms – I'll be kind to you,
> You'll delight in the martens and fawns,
> And the young of the porcupines.[10]

Though Aeschylus' language is remarkably his own, it is surprisingly adaptable and able to express a whole gamut of moods and effects. Once we have assimilated its commanding tone, we see of what variations it is capable. If we say that it has something archaic about it, this is true only in the sense that it is always experimenting and finding its way and that it takes risks which a more mature or more sophisticated art might avoid. In its own realm it is in complete command, and it has the great advantage that it is doing many things for the first time. Though Aeschylus has something in common with Pindar, he goes far beyond him in his use of words, for drama called for a more adventurous style than choral song and had to maintain it on a much larger scale.

Aeschylus was consciously proud of being an Athenian at a time when Athens had begun to dominate Greece. His patriotism is confidently to the fore in the *Persians*, when the queen Atossa asks the Chorus about whom Xerxes is attacking and hears only about Athens. Even when the Chorus sings of the many places which have been liberated from the Persians, they are precisely those which had at the time of the play's production joined the Delian League under Athens. But Aeschylus is also a Panhellenic poet, and the account of the Persian defeat at Plataea does ample honour to the other Greek states, who took part. Nor are contemporary references lacking in other plays, though we must be careful of reading too much into them. The most notable is the reference in the *Eumenides*, produced in 458 BC, to the court of the Areopagus at Athens, which had two years earlier been transformed from a last stronghold of the aristocracy into a high court of justice, and there is no doubt that Aeschylus' sympathies are with the reformers. Indeed the whole conclusion of the play is like an Athenian festival in which the gods, especially Athene, display their love for Athens, and the reformed Furies, now become guardians of law and order, sing as they march in a torchlit procession of the happy prospects which await the city:

> Joy to you, joy of your justly appointed riches,
> Joy to all the people blest
> With the Virgin's love, who sits
> Next beside her Father's throne.
> Wisdom ye have learned at last.
> Folded under Pallas' wing,
> Yours at last the grace of Zeus.[11]

Even here high politics are transformed and transcended in far more important issues, and this, outside the *Persians*, is as near as Aeschylus gets to speaking of contemporary events. It is conceivable that the *Suppliant Women*, in which the action takes place in Argos, comes from a time about 464 BC when Athens was encouraging Argos to abandon her neutrality and support Athens against Sparta, but there is no sign that the main issue of the trilogy is political. In the *Prometheus Bound* the conflict between Zeus and Prometheus may possibly have been suggested by the sudden growth of Athenian power after the Persian Wars and by the problems which it raised, but, if so, these are seen from an exalted, universal standpoint with no references to the present. Aeschylus may have found some of his starting-points in contemporary events but he looked far beyond them to the lasting principles which they illustrated and which could best be presented in a mythical form without any distracting local or ephemeral details. If Pindar illuminates the events of his own time by myths, Aeschylus goes further and makes myths illustrate matters which pass far beyond the present and are often everlasting principles behind the changing scene.

Aeschylus' conception of tragedy can to some extent be deduced from his practice of it. No more for him than for Sophocles and Euripides is it an art which necessarily ends in disaster and death. Rather it tries to grasp the main issues of life and death and to face the problems of human fortune with its contrasts of good and evil, of prosperity and disaster. Its main material is conflict, which is usually between human beings, but can be, as in the *Prometheus Bound*, between a greater and a lesser immortal, and in all such conflicts the gods are in some way at work. Aeschylus suggests explanations for his conflicts at two levels. The human actors behave in accordance with their human nature, and what they do is perfectly intelligible to anyone. But behind them are darker forces, which compel them to act as they do, through a hereditary curse as in the house of Laius or through the claims of blood for blood as in the house of Agamemnon. Aeschylus thus presents us with the familiar paradox that, though men think themselves to be acting by free choice, their actual decisions are determined by forces beyond their control and almost beyond their knowledge. Aeschylus was not worried any more than most Greeks by attempts to distinguish between free will and determinism, and assumes that, though men make their own decisions, they are largely forced to do so by divine powers. In this there is of course an ultimate inconsistency, but most of us are not troubled by it, and it need not trouble us in Aeschylus. What it does is to show human actions from two points of view, in their immediate character and in their remoter significance. In this way Aeschylus builds up his plots and makes them both individual and universal, though they always keep the particularity of presentation which is necessary to true art. Having built up his complex patterns of dramatic action he comes to a conclusion, and in the *Eumenides* it is not merely happy but radiantly positive and constructive. Out of much evil even greater good will come. We may suspect that if there was a third play in the trilogy of Prometheus the end was similarly satisfying, while in what we know of the *Daughters of Danaüs* doubts were dispelled and quarrels healed. Aeschylus seems to have welcomed the idea that tragic actions could end in some grand restoration of life and order. This enabled him to show the gods in a beneficent light and to favour the Hesiodic rather than the Homeric view of them. On our scanty evidence the only exception to this rule is the *Seven against Thebes*, which ends with the extinction of the House of Laius. Yet even this has its own kind of consolation. The curse started by Laius himself was deserved, and, even though it passed to his grandchildren, the Greeks would have accepted this as right enough. When at last it is worked out, we have a sense of relief because the gods' will is done and there is nothing more to fear. More than this, Eteocles dies heroically in battle, and no end is more honourable than that.

The second great tragedian of Athens, Sophocles, learned much from Aeschylus and in his first years, on his own statement, imitated his majesty.[12] But he moved away from this and formed not only his own style but his own kind of tragic drama. His unit was not the trilogy but the single play, and to this he applied his concentrated and subtle art. His seven surviving plays show that what he has lost in breadth he has gained in depth, that he is able not only to put more action into a play but to present it with a keener insight and a more intimate poetry. Despite their conventions his plays can still hold the stage and enthral us, even when most of their poetry has been lost in translation and the music of their words stirs hardly an echo. Sophocles, who said of Aeschylus: 'Even if he does the right thing, it is without knowing it',[13] was a much more conscious artist who sought to put much more into a play and to make it as shapely and rich as possible. But his idea of shapeliness was inventive and adventurous, and he took risks, fully justified in the result, to stress the formative idea in a tragic story. Thus, in his *Ajax*, the hero kills himself well before the end of the play, and the rest of it consists of a dispute whether he should be buried or not. This is not an anti-climax, nor is it otiose. It is essential to the whole drama, which turns on the worth of Ajax's heroic career and the judgment which men should pass on him, and the upshot is that, though in his last madness he has behaved as no hero should, it is not his fault and quite outweighted by his previous achievements and services. In the *Antigone* the heroine goes to her death well before the end, and the rest of the play is taken up with the humiliation and punishment of Creon who has sent her to it. This is needed to make amends for what has happened and to show Antigone's death in its right perspective. In the *Women of Trachis* the first part is occupied with

Deianira, who unwittingly devises the death of her husband in his absence, and the second part with his actual dying agonies after she has killed herself. The remarkable shape of the play emphasizes the nature of its subject, the unbridgeable gap between the all too womanly woman and the prodigious, more than human man. Sophocles shapes his main design to suit the nature of his theme and what he finds in it.

Both in these plays and in others which have a more straightforward plan Sophocles gets his dramatic tension by making each stage of the action rise directly from what has preceded it, but in moving from his start to his conclusion he uses a special kind of irony which shows how different the reality of things is from their appearance. This irony pierces very deep and accounts for much that is most perceptive and striking in Sophocles' conception of human life. In the *Ajax* the hero is humiliated by Athene, whom he has derided in battle, and made to slaughter cattle, believing them to be his fellow warriors, but in the end this terrible abasement is transformed after death into a recognition of his heroic worth. In the *Antigone* we start by thinking that Creon must be right in forbidding burial to the dead traitor Polynices and that Antigone must be wrong to disobey him, but inexorably we learn that it is Creon who is wrong and Antigone who is right. In the *Women of Trachis* Deianira, who thinks that she can win back the love of her husband Heracles by magic, ends by killing him, and he, who thinks that at last he can end his days in peace, finds this end in a hideous, torturing death. In *King Oedipus*, Oedipus, who seems to be the wise man in full command of his people and himself, is shown to be living in fatal ignorance of his real state as a creature abhorred by the gods and ends by blinding himself and leaving his city as an outcast. In the *Electra* the criminals, Aegisthus and Clytaemestra, who are afraid that Orestes will exact vengeance from them, are led to believe that he is dead, only to find that he is alive and among them, and it is they who are killed. In the *Philoctetes* Odysseus, who tries to get hold of the bow of Philoctetes, since without it Troy cannot be taken, is the experienced master of stratagem, but it is precisely through this that he fails, since the young Neoptolemus, who begins by entering gladly into his plan, turns against it when he sees its effect on Philoctetes, and all the assumptions on which the play begins are destroyed by the emergence of truth in words and feelings. In *Oedipus at Colonus* the old Oedipus seeks asylum at Colonus, but his troubles are by no means at an end. His doom seems to be that he must suffer to the last, and we fear that his end will be as hard as his beginning, but then we learn that all his final agonies are but preliminary to his transformation into a *daemon*, a tutelary spirit, who is to live under the earth and watch over Athens. His last ordeals reveal the daemonic character which is to be his and prepare the way for him, who has been hated by the gods and rejected by men, to pass invisibly to his supernatural status. Sophoclean irony is an instrument for bringing out the contrast between the illusions in which men, especially the powerful and the great, live and the inexorable reality which sooner or later destroys them. In this lies the tragic conflict, and this is the central point of Sophocles' tragic world.

Sophocles, like Aeschylus, does not always make his plays end unhappily, and indeed of the surviving seven only the *Antigone, Women of Trachis*, and *King Oedipus*, may be said to do so. But in all his plays the action leads to a crisis of discovery in which the leading person or persons find themselves forced to see things as they are. Sophocles prepares the way to this by showing them in their various states of ignorance, but in due course comes the appalling, enthralling moment when all is made clear, and the price has to be paid. He achieves this effect by many different ways. In the *Electra* the illumination comes with joy to Orestes and Electra, when they recognize one another after a long separation, and with horror to Clytaemestra and Aegisthus, whom they are going to kill. In *King Oedipus* almost the whole play is concerned with Oedipus' discovery of his own identity and of the hideous consequences which this means to him as the man who has killed his father and married his mother. The irony is given a new dimension because Oedipus sets out, as he thinks, to find out the truth about the death of Laius, but is prevented by his own blindness from seeing it even when Teiresias tells him what it is. In the end the facts are brought inexorably home to him, and he then knows who he is and that his whole life is as nothing. Against this background of ignorance Sophocles sets mankind in its relations with the gods, and to it his whole art is shaped.

Like Aeschylus, Sophocles reveals his dramatic personalities through their situations. They are what they should be if they are to fit the legends about them. They are presented in broad lines and, though we must not expect too many refinements or subtleties in their delineation, they act from recognizable motives and are always of a piece with themselves. Antigone is no more than a girl, who acts without hesitation on a point of final principle – that her brother must be buried because that is the law of the gods. She never questions her decision and despises her sister for not acting with her, but when at last she is led off to be buried alive in a cove, she breaks down, not indeed to excuse herself, but to lament what a doom is hers. Oedipus is a great king, a man of action who shows foresight and decision and is ready to do all that his people asks. He is the kind of man who would have answered the riddle of the Sphinx and been made king of Thebes for doing so, and it is his hideous fate that all this impedes his discovery of the truth and makes it even more terrible when it comes. Even his marriage to his mother is depicted with consummate tact and insight; for Jocasta is older than he and looks after him with the anxious care of a wife who is also a mother. When the young Neoptolemus is persuaded to trick Philoctetes, he agrees because he is avid for honour and not for nothing the son of Achilles, and for a time he plays the part as if it were a mere game, but Philoctetes' sufferings awake something deep and noble in him, and he throws the whole trick aside. Philoctetes himself is cast in a heroic mould, a man of deep affections and admirations, but capable of lasting hatred against those, especially Odysseus, who have wronged him and condemned him to solitary exile on a deserted island. When Oedipus gets to Colonus, he is an old man, who has suffered for many years, but he has also something truly heroic and daemonic about him, and that is why he turns with savage curses on the son who has dishonoured him and with deep affection to the daughters who have accompanied him in all his wanderings. The reality of Sophocles' characters is that they fit into their situations and their destinies. They are in their way highly simplified, but that does not detract from their reality in their own world. We can see why they act as they do, and form our own feelings and judgments on them.

Behind the way in which Sophocles shapes his characters to suit the action we can see certain tendencies of his age at work. Both his Ajax and his Heracles are figures of heroic legend, but he fashions each in an unexpected shape. Both are remote from other men, obsessed with the thought of their own honour, and both come to hideous ends. Ajax is driven mad by shame and must perish because he has incurred the enmity of Athene. He solves his problem by killing himself, but in his last hours he shows almost no human weakness or even tenderness. His concubine, Tecmessa, is deeply attached to him but he treats her with an inconsiderate brusqueness; his little son appeals to him only because he may restore his father's honour, and it is right that when Ajax falls on his sword, it should be in a solitary place and that his last words should be about his reputation. Ajax is a great hero, as Sophocles imagined that he ought to be, but in the *Women of Trachis* Heracles, who is even greater, is more remote and more inhuman. It is true that we see him only when he is dying in agony and his magnificent body is slowly being eaten by a devilish poison. He refuses to forgive his wife for causing his death,

139

although he knows that she has done it in ignorance hoping to win back his love; he sternly makes his son marry the woman he himself has intended to make his concubine. He is a hero in that he stands above and beyond human standards and embodies a terrific force which brings him close to the gods. He cannot show tenderness and does not wish to be liked or even loved, and to this degree he embodies the imperial spirit of Athens, which sought power and fame, even at the cost of hatred and envy. Sophocles understood what power is, whether in men or in cities, and set it on the scene as he saw it. If the Athenians of his time asked what kind of man was Heracles, this was his answer. So too in the *Electra*, when Orestes has, at the bidding of Apollo, to kill his mother, he does so without qualms or hesitations. He has, indeed, his tender and human side, which finds fulfilment in his newly discovered love for his sister Electra, but in taking vengeance on his mother he does what he has to do with a steely determination and allows no qualms to deter him.

Sophocles presents his characters with a detached fairness and cannot be said to divide them into good and bad. If his obvious villains have their redeeming qualities, his most attractive creations have touches of weakness or inhumanity. Antigone is harsh on her sister when she refuses to join in burying their brother; Deianira, who radiates gentleness and affection, should not try to win back her husband by magic; Neoptolemus enters too easily and too gaily into the plot to cheat Philoctetes. Sophocles' nearest approach to a moral judgment is the debate after the death of Ajax between Agamemnon and Menelaus on the one side and Odysseus on the other. Ajax has menaced his comrades-in-arms, and deserves, so the kings argue, to be punished after death, but against them Odysseus argues that his faults are outweighed by his merits, and in the end he triumphs. In general Sophocles leaves his audience to make their own judgments on his characters, and, if these judgments are mixed, that is all the better, for it reflects actual life. But this does not mean that Sophocles is not concerned with the doings of men in the eyes of the gods. Every surviving play gives some part to the gods, either explicitly or implicitly, and in each divine purposes are displayed at work. Ajax has to die because he has insulted Athene; Creon is broken because he has defied the laws of the gods about burial; Deianira may act in all innocence, but the death of Heracles comes from her action, and the whole ghastly end has been ordained by Zeus; in *King Oedipus* Oedipus has been doomed from the beginning to kill his father and marry his mother, and, since this makes him a defiled and hideous creature in the eyes of the gods, he assists their purpose by blinding himself and so cutting himself off from the light of day; Electra drives her brother to kill their mother because Apollo has commanded it; Philoctetes is fated to go to Troy, though Odysseus' stratagem to get him there breaks down; in *Oedipus at Colonus* the old Oedipus passes through many moods and situations before his end, because he is fated after life to become a demi-god, and he already shows what this means in his out-bursts of touching gratitude and savage condemnation.

Though the gods set the plan for the action, we do not have them in mind in our feelings for the human characters. To these our responses are immediate and at a purely human level. Their destinies would concern us just as much if the gods had not decided them. If we pass judgments on the characters and their actions, we have every right to do so, but we must not think that the gods view them in the same spirit as we do. In fact one of the chief characteristics of Sophoclean tragedy is that it emphasizes the gap between human and divine judgments, and from this draws much of its mystery and its strength. He writes throughout in the conviction that the laws of the gods are not the same as the laws of men, and what may seem right enough to men may be utterly wrong for the gods. In *King Oedipus* Sophocles presents Oedipus as an outstanding figure of remarkable gifts, but because he has killed his father and married his mother, he is a creature of horror to the gods and must be punished. It does not matter that legally and morally he is innocent; he remains hideously polluted and defiles the light of day. The gods hate him, but this does not mean that we must not symphathize with him in his appalling situation. In fact, we cannot help doing so, and as human beings we have every right to do so. It is precisely the vast gap between what the gods think and what men think that makes Oedipus so poignant and disturbing a figure. In the *Women of Trachis* Heracles ends a life of suffering and effort in hideous torment, for which there is no justification, and yet at the end his son, Hyllus, speaking of what has happened, concludes:

And nothing of these that is not Zeus.[14]

While we share the feelings of his characters, Sophocles indicates quietly but surely how the gods are at work and fulfil their designs. By this means he creates the conflicts of his tragic world. It is one in which men, acting by their human nature, are countered and corrected, for evil or for good, by powers outside themselves. They may fight against these or try to work with them, but in the end they are at their mercy. On the one hand this brings them to a terrible doom like Oedipus and Ajax and Heracles, on the other to unforeseen success like Orestes and Philoctetes. While we watch the action and respond to it with our human feelings, the gods are at work at a different level, and it is not till the end that their full designs are revealed.

In his famous analysis of Attic tragedy Aristotle lays emphasis on what he calls Discovery and defines as 'a change from ignorance to knowledge, and thus to either love or hate, in the personage marked for good or evil fortune'.[15] Sophocles indeed practises Discovery, but not in Aristotle's special sense. What matters with him is much less that one character discovers another, as Orestes and Electra discover one another, than that a character discovers himself. Oedipus discovers that he is the son of Laius and Jocasta, and that is why he blinds himself. Ajax finds that he has been the victim of insane delusions, Creon that he has acted with gross injustice, Heracles that the gods have kept him, not for peace, but for a hideous death, Philoctetes that he has been obstructing the divine will, the old Oedipus that he, a beggar and an outcast, will become after death a demigod. Moreover, in this moment of self-discovery lies the crisis of the drama and what follows from it is the solution of the action. It may mean that, like Creon, a man is so overwhelmed that he no longer wishes to live, but it may equally be a challenge, as it is to Oedipus, who assists the gods in their plans against him, or to Philoctetes who subdues his own feelings and, despite the way in which he has been treated, agrees to help the Greeks to take Troy. In Sophocles Discovery is intimately associated with Reversal, which Aristotle regards as equally important to tragedy and treats as the change from good to bad fortune or from bad to good. In Sophocles the moment of change is fused into the moment of self-discovery, and each promotes the other.

Though the gods are at work in Sophocles' plays, he makes little attempt to explain their reasons for doing what they do. Athene, indeed, is within her rights when she drives Ajax mad, and Apollo is determined that Clytaemestra shall be punished for killing her husband, but there is no explanation of the doom which harries Oedipus from before his birth or of the hideous end of Heracles. Sophocles accepts what the gods do, and expects us to do the same. It is not for men to criticize them, or even to hope to understand them. What is required is a mood of unquestioning awe and respect, and this provides the background of Sophoclean tragedy. Its unique strength is that though the gods are inscrutable and often treat men savagely, men keep their dignity and their own kind of grandeur. Yet, despite his refusal to provide any ultimate explanation of the gods, Sophocles has a clear notion of what tragedy is. For him the tragic issue comes from some breach in the divine order of the world. Whether a play ends unhappily or happily, the conflict which it presents arises because someone has gone too far and upset the balance of life. In the *Ajax* and *Antigone* Ajax and Creon transgress the rules of the gods, turn to violence, and bring destruction to others and to themselves. In the *Women of Trachis* Deianira's womanly but presumptuous decision to win back Heracles leads to her own doom and to his. In *King Oedipus* the actions of Oedipus before the play begins are such that the gods must punish him. They send a plague, and when he tries to stop it, he finds out who he is. In the *Electra* the murder of Agamemnon can be cured only by more bloodshed; the original injustice done to Philoctetes by leaving him alone on a deserted island is responsible for the first collapse of the attempt to bring him to Troy; the pollution of Oedipus and his expulsions from Thebes create a situation in the *Oedipus at Colonus* in which he curses his sons and shows a terrible ferocity. In Sophocles the tragic situation is a breach in the order of things, and promotes angry passions which cloud the judgment. It does not matter whether it is made deliberately or not. The evil caused by the innocent Oedipus is as great as that caused by Clytaemestra. What matters is that disorder is created:

> Not order but disorder, luckless one,
> It seems to be, and madness in your heart.[16]

Some act of man destroys an existing order and substitutes chaos and unreason for it. In different shapes this is the fundamental pattern of all Sophocles' surviving plays.

The solution to tragic conflicts which Sophocles finds in the restoration of an ultimate order creates indeed a calm of mind, and it is perhaps this which had led to some extraordinary misjudgments on him. He is too often treated as an exemplar of classic detachment, of sublime remoteness, and this has been thought to receive support from ancient accounts of him as a happy and contented man. But this picture of him, however true it may have been of his behaviour among his friends, tells nothing about his art and is indeed as irrelevant to it as the contemporary description of Shakespeare as 'a handsome well shaped man, very good company and of very ready and pleasant smooth wit' is to the author of *King Lear* and *Hamlet*. We know nothing of the inner forces which drove either poet to create what he did, but we know what they wrote, and this is the reflection of their truest selves. In his concern with the conflicts between divine order and human action Sophocles displays many savage elements in his choice of themes. Homer would surely have avoided them, but they were relevant to the hard struggles of the Periclean age and enabled Sophocles to make his contrasts sharper and his conclusions more complete. His refusal to shirk harsh elements, as legend presented them, is manifest in the suicide of Ajax and the burial of Antigone alive, in the dying agonies of Heracles, and the self-blinding of Oedipus, in the pitiful humiliation of Electra and the unforgiving hatred which it has bred in her for her mother, in the physical sufferings of Philoctetes, in the savage outbursts of the old Oedipus against his son and his treacherous kinsman, Creon. Sophocles has indeed his moments of pathos, but he plays for something harsher and less comforting. He wishes to show beyond doubt what suffering is and allows no easy consolations. The Sophoclean world is undeniably brutal in its events and in many of its moods. The Athenians lived close to violence and death, and one of the functions of tragedy was to make men look at these without flinching and see them for what they are. The more violent the tests to which a man is subjected, the greater is his opportunity to display himself in his true nature.

Though Sophocles does not indulge in the spectacular effects of Aeschylus, his sense of a dramatic situation is even stronger than his master's and achieved with an even keener eye for an overwhelming situation. When Antigone is brought in by a guard to Creon for defying his decree, she bursts into an unanswerable defence of her action:

> It was not Zeus, I think, made this decree,
> Nor Justice, dweller with the gods below,
> Who made appointment of such laws to men.[17]

Against this Creon's worthy platitudes sound hollow, and the true nature of the conflict is revealed. When Jocasta, hearing the story of Oedipus' exposure as a child, sees the truth about him long before he does, she first tries to stop him asking any more questions, and then leaves the stage to kill herself, saying as she goes:

> Alas, alas, accursèd one! That name alone
> I give you, and none other any more.[18]

The whole hideous character of Oedipus' predicament is contained in these words, and with them the fool's paradise in which Jocasta has lived is annihilated. When, to her incredulous surprise, Electra finds that Orestes is not dead but at her side, brother and sister are so moved that they have almost nothing to say, and yet what they say meets every need:

Electra: O happy light!
Orestes: A light of joy indeed!
Electra: Voice, you have come!
Orestes: My voice shall be your answer.
Electra: Here in my arms?
Orestes: Here, where I still would be.[19]

When the Messenger tells of the passing of the old Oedipus into his super-natural state, he strikes a deep note of mystery when he reports a voice calling from the sky:

> Oedipus, Oedipus, why dost delay
> To go? Too long hast thou been lingering,[20]

and yet the whole scene is absolutely firm and clear. Sophocles rises to his high occasions with a consummate ease and naturalness, with a matchless economy which knows exactly how far to go and what to emphasize and what to omit.

Sophocles' language, as we know it, has advanced very far from that of Aeschylus. If it lacks some of the Aeschylean majesty, it makes up for it in subtlety and compression and variety. It maintains a uniform level of high expressiveness, and at its most dramatic moments it succeeds by an overwhelming simplicity. When Oedipus at last sees that he himself may be the murderer of Laius, he cries out:

> O Zeus, what have you planned to do with me?[21]

and in this moment, without fully knowing it, he reveals his destiny. At such times Sophocles passes beyond the limits of characterization to a universal utterance, but much of his poetry is exquisitely adapted to the characters of those who speak it, and at the same time suggests unknown possibilities beyond the actual moment. When Deianira, having felt pity for the captive Iolë, sees why she has been sent by Heracles, she feels the first pangs of jealousy and says:

> I see her youth has not yet come to bloom,
> While mine is failing. Men's eyes love to pick
> The bud, but from the other turn away.[22]

It is this slight change of mood, so truly and so delicately stated, which leads to hideous consequences. When Neoptolemus watches Philoctetes raving in the delirium of his sickness, he says:

> Long have I felt your woes and pitied them,[23]

and it is this which causes his change of heart and ruins all the ingenious stratagem of Odysseus. The horror and hatred which Electra feels for Clytaemestra is fully present in her words to Orestes:

> Mother in name, in nothing like one she,[24]

and we know that she will work with her brother for vengeance. The poetry of the essential revealing statement is a central feature in Sophocles, but it is varied from person to person and from situation to situation. The Guard who arrests Antigone is a very simple soldier, and has the thoughts and feelings of his kind, while at the other end of the scale the old Oedipus or the dying Heracles speaks with almost a superhuman authority.

Nor does Sophocles confine his poetry to the actual dramatic action. There are times when his Messengers report what has taken place behind the scenes and for this he has his own special kind of narrative, which spares no horrors and yet is rich in compassion and understanding. In the *Electra* there is a full account of a chariot-race in which Orestes, quite falsely, is said to have been killed, and, though it is all a trick, it is extremely exciting and realistic. When Deianira leaves the scene to kill herself, knowing that she has destroyed her husband, she goes into her room and takes her farewell:

> O bed and bridal room of mine,
> Good-bye for always now; for never shall
> You welcome me to sleep in you again.[25]

But intimate though he can be and so transform his situations into high poetry, Sophocles is never unaware of the wider issues which lie beyond them. In *Oedipus at Colonus* the old Oedipus is welcomed by Theseus to Athens and offered a resting-place there. He is deeply touched and grateful, but his sense of reality prevents him from expecting too much, and he answers:

> Dear son of Aegeus, to the gods alone
> Belongs immunity from death and age:
> All else doth all-controlling time confound.
> Earth's strength decays, the body's strength decays,
> Faith dies and faithlessness bursts into flower,
> And never does the same wind blow for long
> Steadfast from friend to friend, from town to town.[26]

This is the true Sophoclean temper, which has no illusions about man's destiny but takes the passing moment for all that it is worth and finds in it a poetry which gives it a transforming and illuminating strength. He could write with equal understanding of innocent girlhood and impotent old age, of abounding vitality and shattered hopes, of headstrong youth and ripe wisdom. From each theme he drew what he found in it, and we can never be sure that he speaks merely for himself. His choral songs may lack the vast sweep of Aeschylus' winged meditations, and their first task is not to reveal his own feelings but to act as a background of common opinion against which the enigmatic actions of the tragedies may be set. When Antigone confounds everyone by disobeying Creon's edict and burying her brother, the Chorus, not yet awake to its real significance, still sees that it is an act of astonishing courage and discourses on the strange character of man; when the old men of Colonus watch the dangers and difficulties which beset Oedipus, they lament the misery of life and say, as the Greeks often did, that it is better not to be born, but even so they cannot but admire the spirit with which Oedipus endures one shock after another:

> So on him without respite
> Dread, like great billows breaking,
> Shocks fall upon him and shake him,
> Some from the side where the sun sinks,
> Some from its orient dawning,
> Some by the midday glow,
> Some from the Arctic night.[27]

Their first thoughts about him, though justifiable enough, are not to the point, and what matters is their respect for his unbroken resistance to the last.

Sophocles is regarded, not without justice, as the authentic poet of Periclean Athens. Yet he lived long after the death of Pericles and saw the long, wearying, in the end hopeless years after the renewal of war in 415 BC. Yet into this age of doubt and sophistry he brought his own outlook formed in an earlier generation and able to face with courage the woes of his old age. His belief in the gods never wavered, and in *Oedipus at Colonus* his theme is that of a much-suffering, much-tormented man who is rewarded at the last by becoming a tutelary deity of Athens. Sophocles' art is indeed a criticism of life, not from any personal or even national point of view, but from a grave consciousness that few things are as clear as they seem to be and that, even when the cosmic order is broken by the acts of men, there is still much to be said on both sides. His interest in human nature extends beyond its immediate manifestations with all their varied appeal to their place in the scheme of things, and the essence of his tragic vision is that, no matter how hideous the waste and the wickedness may have been, something emerges from them which exalts and redeems the human state.

Both Aeschylus and Sophocles accepted the traditional form of tragedy and turned it into a vehicle for vivid drama by tempering some of its more recalcitrant elements. Euripides, who was fifteen years younger than Sophocles and in many ways belongs to a later, less assured generation, might have been expected to make substantial alterations in the interests of modernity. Yet, though he used tragedy to express many modern ideas, he not only kept its traditional form but even emphasized some of its more archaic features. His questing, questioning spirit seems to have felt the need for this formality as a means to keep himself in control and to adapt his modern thoughts to an ancient art. By insisting on the primitive character of tragedy he could make his own effects more striking and yet contain them inside an accepted form. In particular he made use of the formal Prologue, in which a character gives in simple outline the situation with which the play is concerned and adds a few hints on what is going to happen. The Prologue must go back to Thespis and the time when a single actor stood out from the Chorus and told what the plot was going to be. It is a natural device for drama and can be found equally in some oriental plays and in miracle-plays of the Middle Ages. Its purpose is to give some notion of what the subject of the play is going to be and prepare the audience for it. Aeschylus makes a special use of it in the *Eumenides*, where the Priestess of Apollo tells of his shrine at Delphi and then of the monstrous Furies who gather round it. Sophocles does not use the device at all, but Euripides uses it in almost every surviving play. Sometimes it is highly dramatic and inventive; sometimes it may seem a little too formal for the violence which is to come after it. It has the great advantage for Euripides that it removes the action from the immediate present to a formalized past of art, and legend, and that is, no doubt, why he writes his Prologues with a studied simplicity suited to their archaic character. Since tragedy was almost the only available means for him to say to a large public much that was on his mind, he wrote it according to the recognized rules and so let his new effects stand out the more boldly by contrast.

If a Euripidean tragedy begins with a formal Prologue, it often ends with an almost equally formal epiphany of a god or goddess, the so-called 'deus ex machinâ'. Euripides uses this in ten plays, and it is likely to be as archaic as the formal Prologue. The first tragedies were closely connected with religious rites and the impersonation of a god or goddess at the end of them would set out their conclusions and any morals that should be drawn from the action. In the *Philoctetes* Sophocles make Heracles, who is now a god, appear and solve the hopeless tangle into which Neoptolemus and Philoctetes have got themselves. But this is not quite what Euripides does. Even in the *Hippolytus*, where, in a scene of great pathos and beauty, Artemis appears and tells Theseus that Hippolytus is not guilty of the crime for which Theseus has cursed him, her effect could have been secured by other means. In most other cases the epiphany adds nothing to

1 Lion-gateway of Mycenae, main seat of Achaean power from *c* 1500 to
c 1200 BC. See p. 3.

2 Ruins of Mycenaean palace near Pylos, destroyed by fire *c* 1200 BC and thought to be traditional seat of Homer's Nestor.

3 Ivory model of Mycenaean warrior's head, with helmet made of boars' teeth, as described by Homer when Odysseus goes out on night operations.

4 Attic jug, *c* 700 BC, of shipwreck, in which a figure rides on the keel as Homer's Odysseus does.

5 Attic jug, c 700 BC, showing fight for ships.
6 Large terra-cotta vase, c 620 BC, showing the Trojan Horse.

7 Rhodian plate, *c* 600 BC, showing Hector and Menelaus fighting over the
body of Euphorbus, a variant on an episode in the *Iliad*.

8 Argive mixing-bowl, *c* 650 BC, showing blinding of Polyphemus.

9 Reverse, showing contemporary sea-fight.

10 Argive bronze mirror handle, *c* 600 BC, showing Priam ransoming the body of Hector.

11 (*below*) Thetis visits Achilles, *c* 575–550 BC.

12a and b Geometric wine-jug from Athens, c 720 BC, with earliest known inscription in Greek alphabet.

13 Stone lions erected by Naxians on Delos, facing the sacred lake where Apollo was believed to have been born. See p. 56.

14 Man carrying calf, *c* 600 BC.

17 Temple of Apollo at Corinth, *c* 550–525 BC.

15 (*opposite*, *left*) Marble statue of young male figure, *c* 615–600 BC.

16 (*opposite*, *right*) Marble statue of woman from Crete *c* 620 BC.

18 Europa riding on bull, on metope from temple at Selinus, Sicily, middle of sixth century.

19 Perseus, aided by Athene, cuts off the head of Medusa, on metope from temple at Selinus, Sicily, middle of sixth century.

20 The Calydonian boar, on metope from Sicyonian Treasury at Delphi, 575–550 BC. See p. 83.

21 Painted limestone figure of three-bodied monster, from pediment of archaic temple at Athens, 560–550 BC.

22 Clytaemestra with Cassandra.
Bronze relief from Prosymna, *c* 650 BC.

23 Perseus cuts off head of Medusa,
ivory relief from Samos, early
sixth century.

24 Centaurs attacking Caineus,
bronze relief at Olympia, 650–625 BC.

25 Croesus on pyre, Attic amphora
by Myson, early fifth century. See p. 105.

26 The young Theseus, with Athene, visits the sea-goddess Amphitite, on Attic cup by Onesimos, early fifth century. See p. 105.

27 Chariot-race at the funeral-games of Pelias, on Corinthian mixing-bowl, 575–550 BC.

28 Youths wrestling, relief on marble statue-base at Athens, c 510 BC.

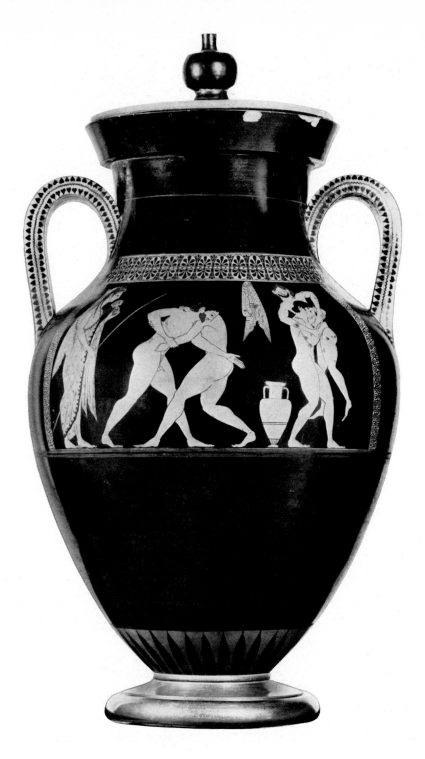

29 Wrestling practice, on Attic amphora, *c* 500 BC.

30 Jumper in mid air, on Attic cup.

31 Youth finishing a jump, Attic
bronze statuette, fifth century.

32 Grave-stone of athlete from Sunium, fifth century.

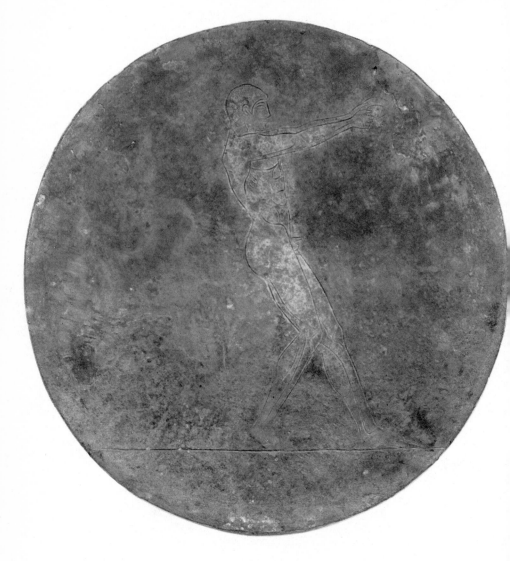

33 Bronze-discus, incised with picture of discus-thrower.

34 (*right, above*) Theatre at Epidaurus, able to hold some 15,000 spectators, fourth century. See p. 118.

35 (*right, below*) Theatre at Delphi, with temple of Apollo just below it.

36 Fat-man riding on phallus-pole in fertility rite, on Attic amphora of sixth century. See p. 191.

37 Chorus of men as mounted knights. Late sixth century. See p. 191.

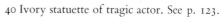
40 Ivory statuette of tragic actor. See p. 123.

38 Chorus of feathered men. See p. 191.

39 Bronze statuette of actor from Athens.

41 The Acropolis at Athens.

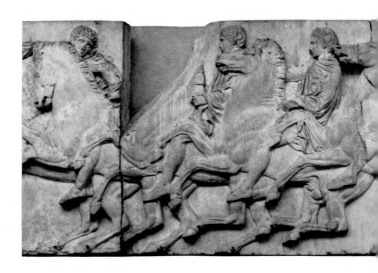

42 The Parthenon at Athens seen from the west.

43 Young horsemen on the Parthenon frieze.

44 Young men carrying jars on Parthenon frieze.

45 Darius, seated on throne, receives a guest through his vizier. Frieze of Persepolis.

46 Frieze of tribute-payers, soldiers and officials at Persepolis.

47 Pillared hall of Persepolis. The pillars supported a wooden roof.

49 Attic plate of young man in Persian clothing, inscribed 'Miltiades'.

48 (*left*) Relief of Xerxes at Persepolis with mythical animal.

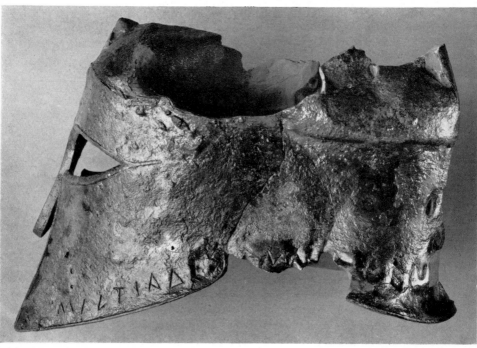

52 Alexander in battle on sarchophagus found at Sidon and now in Istanbul.

50 (*left, above*) Persian helmet dedicated at Olympia, presumably from spoils of Marathon or Plataea.

51 (*left, below*) Bronze helmet of Miltiades, inscribed with his name, dedicated at Olympia.

54 Head of Pericles.

53 (*left*) Marble statuette of Socrates.

55 Statue of Demosthenes in Copenhagen, probably copy of original by Polyeuctus.

the action, and its chief task is to be an epilogue which tells the future
fortunes of the various characters. But Euripides does this in his own way.
The myth which has provided the substance for a tragedy is often connected with some religious rite in Attica or elsewhere, and to this Euripides
refers. It is a kind of antiquarianism, an interest in local archaeology, but it
is justified because it brings the remote past of legend into contact with the
present by showing how memories of it survive in local belief. Moreover,
the appearance of a divinity on the scene brings the action back to the
traditional sphere of tragedy in which gods and men act together, and
since in his action Euripides sets the gods sometimes in unexpected lights
and sometimes in no light at all, he forestalls any charge of neglecting the
essential nature of tragedy. Like the formal Prologue, the epiphany keeps
the proprieties and lets the audience know in what sphere of existence the
dramatic events take place. Perhaps for this reason Euripides lets himself go
far more than in the Prologues and sometimes achieves in them his most
touching effects.

In handling a third traditional element, the Chorus, Euripides had before him the rich examples of Aeschylus and Sophocles, but he did not in
every respect follow them. He gives a large part to it, but he seldom allows
it to express grave meditations on what takes place in the dramatic action,
and avoids considerations of universal laws. If he uses it for general ideas,
it is for more mundane matters such as the position of women, the value of
noble birth, the uselessness of war, and the pains and troubles of marriage.
The Chorus underlines what happens and makes general remarks about it,
but the remarks do not reach very far. This did not content Euripides, and
his irresistible songfulness carried him often in other directions, until
the choral songs seem to be lyrical interludes, which take our attention
away from the action into realms of fancy and delight. In the *Medea* the
terrifying action is broken by a hymn in praise to Athens, which has for us
a special claim since it was written in 431 BC in the last months of peace
before the Peloponnesian War. In the *Phoenician Women* the tragic quarrel
of Eteocles and Polynices is followed by an account of their ancestor Cadmus who slaughtered a dragon. In the *Electra* the murder of Clytaemestra
is preceded by a resplendent account of the shield of Achilles. In the *Hippolytus*, after Phaedra has gone out to kill herself, the Chorus sing a mira-
culous song wishing that they were like birds and could fly to the end of
the earth. Euripides needed such songs to realize part of his creative genius,
but another part of it called for a different use. He tries at times to bring
the Chorus closer into the action and, if he had done so, it would have
been in full accord with tradition. Yet though his Chorus often converses

with the main actors, it takes little part in their doings. Indeed at times Euripides, who likes realistic effects, is remarkably unrealistic in his use of it. Though it is horrified by the atrocious designs of Medea to kill the girl whom her husband is taking as his second wife, it omits to say a single word which might have prevented her. In the *Hippolytus* the Chorus knows throughout that Hippolytus is innocent of the charge of seduction which Phaedra has levelled against him, but does nothing about it, and the truth is kept hidden until Artemis reveals it at the end of the play. In his later plays Euripides made various experiments with the Chorus and may well have wished it to provide more a musical than a dramatic interlude, but in his *Bacchants*, written at the end of his life, the Chorus, which gives its name to the play, is one of the chief characters, since its members are followers of the god Dionysus, of whose ecstatic religion they sing in words of fire and frenzy. In his use of the Chorus Euripides showed the experimental, at times uncertain spirit which is characteristic of him and differentiates him from his predecessors.

Euripides' realism is based on a strong sense of reality and provides him with a special strength. He had to find his subject in ancient legends which might contain elements of horror or absurdity, and in dealing with them he seems to have asked himself: 'How did it really happen?' He lacks Sophocles' gift of making even the most fantastic plots seem true, but he makes up for this by a ruthless examination of his material and a determination to relate it to life as he knows it. So, in his *Alcestis* (438 BC), he takes a legend which on the surface is charming and dramatic. Admetus, king of Thessaly, has been promised by Apollo that, if he is stricken by a mortal sickness, he has only to get someone to die for him and he will survive. His wife Alcestis agrees to do this, but fortunately is saved by the arrival of Heracles, who wrestles with Death and defeats him, and brings back Alcestis from the grave. Euripides thinks out what this would mean in practice, and his Alcestis is a devoted wife who gives her life for her husband, but what about Admetus? He sees nothing wrong in sacrificing his wife and, though he laments her with an abundance of self-pity, he never attempts to stop her, and when his old father refuses to take her place, Admetus blames him for selfishness and gets soundly rated in return. Admetus is in fact a selfish prig and, though he has excellent manners and a convincing style, the play shows him up, not indeed at all savagely but with an ironical humour. In his *Heracles* (c 423 BC) Euripides handles the grim and fearful story that Heracles went mad and slew his wife and children. Euripides sees the whole ghastliness of the story and shirks nothing in it. He makes Heracles return from his visit to Hades and find that his family are on the point of being killed by the usurper Lycus. He kills Lycus and frees his family, but at this point, when all seems to be well, he is driven mad by a supernatural frenzy and kills his wife and children. It is an action of unredeemed horror, agonizing and terrible, but Euripides makes it convincing because Heracles has spent so much of his life in acts of violence that it is but natural that in the end his way of life should turn against him and that he should in his excess of strength and fury not know what he is doing. But Euripides does not leave it at this. He asks how guilty Heracles really is, and, through the figure of Theseus, he convinces us that he is not guilty at all. In the *Electra* (*c* 413 BC) Euripides treats a theme already treated by Aeschylus and Sophocles, and follows tradition in making Orestes, abetted by his sister, kill their mother and her lover. But the climax is not, as with Sophocles, the actual murders, but the disillusion and unhappiness which follow them. Apollo may have commanded the murder, but if it was committed, this is the effect which it would have on the murderers. Euripides sees the dark story from the inside, and it is hard not to accept the essential truth of his presentation.

This urge to see things as they are took Euripides into dark places of the soul. Epic had told how Jason, in his quest of the Golden Fleece, had been helped by the Colchian princess Medea, who saved him by her magic and returned home with him as his wife. No doubt she was always an ambiguous figure, since her magic had already worked more than one death. Euripides asks what kind of woman she really was, and what was her life with Jason. His drama comes from the moment when their marriage has broken up and Jason is about to marry the young daughter of the king of Corinth. Medea's love for him turns to deadly hatred. With a poisoned crown and robe she kills the princess and her father with her, and then, that her own children may not live with Jason, kills them also. She is driven by murderous fury and nothing can hold her, but at the end she triumphs. She has secured a safe refuge in Athens and at the end of the play, from a chariot drawn by dragons, she exults over the broken Jason. The *Medea* (431 BC) made a bad impression when it was first produced, but we cannot deny its remarkable power. Euripides is intent on portraying a foreign woman who is also a sorceress, and to Medea he gives all the uncontrolled passion and savagery of a barbarian. He presents her with such understanding in her humiliation that we cannot but feel sympathy for her. At the same time he does not spare Jason, who is moved by low motives of ambition and quite unable to tell the truth to Medea or to make any proper case for himself. In the end vengeance and destruction prevail, and we do not merely accept them, we even feel that Medea is a better human being than Jason. We might argue that a marriage like theirs, which began with bloodshed, must end in it, and perhaps Euripides means us to feel this. But it does not abate the final impression of triumphant savagery and uncontrolled passion. This, Euripides seems to say, is how it must have happened, and we must take it at that.

The *Medea* is not so much an amoral play, as the presentation of a conflict between two kinds of evil, of which the stronger and more instinctive wins. But in the work of Euripides it stands alone, and perhaps he felt that he had gone too far for what was essentially a religious rite. But in other plays he turns the same intensity of passion to more sympathetic uses and thereby achieves some of his most truly tragic effects. In the *Hecuba* (*c* 425 BC) his chief character, whose fate provides the unity of the play, is the old queen of Troy, whose city has been sacked and whose husband and children slaughtered. In the play she begins by retaining some of her royal majesty, but first she hears that her lost son, whom she thought to be safe abroad, has been murdered, and later her daughter, Polyxena, is sacrificed on the funeral mound of Achilles. These appalling misfortunes distort her nature and leave her a bitter, savage old woman, who blinds her son's murderer and will, in the end, be transformed into a Hell-hound with fiery eyes to frighten sailors at night. Yet, though Hecuba has something in common with Medea and is no less formidable, her wrongs are such that they explain and excuse everything in her. Euripides' compassion in no way blinds him to the dark results of suffering. He knows what it is and what it costs.

In treating large themes of this kind Euripides inevitably came up against the question of the gods and the part which they play in human lives. In this he was certainly touched by the enquiring spirit of his time and often makes his characters question the goodness and the justice of the gods. But this does not prove that he was an atheist or an agnostic or a rationalist; for Sophocles sometimes does very much the same thing, and of his devout faith there is no doubt. But, just as Euripides sought to see how events really must have happened, so he sought to see what part the gods really took in the affairs of men. He had to deal with them, and he did not shirk the responsibility. He must of course avoid open impiety in his presentation of them, but there is no reason to think that he felt any strong leanings towards it. In asking what the gods were he formed a perfectly normal opinion that they were embodiments of immeasurable power, and that this was their essential quality. He saw this displayed in legends of them, and with it a vast difference from men. Like Sophocles, he evidently felt that their ways could be in some respects discerned but not really explained, and that they must be accepted as they were. He realized that by ordinary human judgments some of their actions might be thought reprehensible, but they were not men and not to be judged by the standards of men. So in the *Ion* (*c* 418 BC) he tells with much delicacy and insight the story of a woman who has a child, Ion, by Apollo, and thinks that the god has deserted both him and her. In this frame of mind she denounces the god, as she is fully entitled to do, but in the end the god puts everything right and Ion comes into his inheritance. There is no need to think that the happy ending to a skilful and dramatic play is a bit of hypocrisy put in to avoid imputations of impiety; it is much more satisfactory if we accept it as it is and see that in the end the gods do not desert their children and that even the Delphic Oracle is justified in its forecasts.

We cannot say what kind or degree of reality Euripides attributed to Apollo, but there is no doubt how deeply he believed in the reality of some other gods. His *Hippolytus* (428 BC) is the story of a virginal young man, who adores Artemis and despises Aphrodite. He insults Aphrodite by refusing her service, and she, in the traditional way of gods, decides that he must be destroyed. This is done by making his step-mother Phaedra fall in love with him and try, through magic, to win his love in return. He is appalled to the depths of his being, but swears to say nothing of it. Phaedra, out of shame, hangs herself, but before death denounces Hippolytus in a letter to her husband, Theseus. Theseus curses Hippolytus to Poseidon, who sends a monstrous bull out of the sea, which so terrifies his horses that he is thrown and dragged and hideously mutilated. He is brought back dying, and then Artemis speaks. She makes it clear that she can do nothing for him, and he pathetically chides her for her desertion of him:

Lightly you leave our long companionship.[28]

Here Euripides shows two goddesses at work in a real world. Aphrodite is the force of natural passion which turns to violence when it is opposed, Artemis the rarer instinct of purity, which ordinary Greeks would think inhuman and even wrong and certainly likely to foster, as it does in Hippolytus, an unbecoming pride. The tragedy of Hippolytus is that, though he is innocent of the charge for which he is killed, he has tried to resist a powerful goddess and failed. In his *Bacchants* Euripides faces an even fiercer issue and produces what is in many respects his masterpiece. The young god Dionysus, who is the god, not only of wine, but of ecstasy, has come to Thebes and won a large following. The young king Pentheus does not recognize him for what he is but treats him as a dangerous impostor who wants only women. Dionysus takes a hideous revenge on Pentheus, first hypnotizing him into putting on a woman's dress and going to visit the Bacchants at their revels, then inspiring the Bacchants to tear him to pieces. Now Pentheus is a poor creature, and we feel very little sympathy for him in his ignorance and his arrogance, and, at first, we respect Dionysus. But as Dionysus shows his power, we see how deadly he is. Like Aphrodite, he is unquestionably real and, though he inspires his followers to ecstatic delight, even this may turn to a bitter aftermath of disillusion and regret, and he is merciless to anyone who withstands him. Euripides shirks nothing in his presentation of him, from his first appearance of seeming innocence, through his brutal mockery of Pentheus, to his final appearance when he foretells the dark fates which await even some who have supported him. His Bacchants, who reflect at a human level his astonishing power, move from enthralled delight in his service on the mountains to outspoken, murderous hatred for those who do not share their beliefs and especially for the impious Pentheus. Here Euripides makes a god the chief character of a play and, though he is beyond good and evil, there is no doubt that he is a god and that those who resist him will come to a hideous end.

The view of the gods which emerges from Euripides' plays is consistent and even traditional, but it is certainly not comforting. He seems to have reduced a mass of religious beliefs to a basic minimum and to have founded his tragic outlook on this. There is no need to believe that he accepted all tales about the gods, for, after all, even the pious Pindar did not, and there was no obligation to do so. Euripides even follows Pindar when he makes his Iphigeneia say that legend must be wrong in saying that a god could delight in eating human flesh. He displays his own tentative enquiries through the lips of some characters. He may well agree with his Heracles, who on his return to sanity says:

> Say not there be adulterers in Heaven
> Nor prisoner gods and gaoler. Long ago
> My heart has known it false and will not alter.
> God, if he be God, lacketh naught. All these
> Are dead unhappy tales of minstrelsy.[29]

But this is not after all saying very much. The *Heracles* shows Hera as responsible for the hero's madness, and for this there is no ultimate explanation. Euripides knows that some men and women believe that the gods must be just, and he can see the force of their belief in the *Trojan Women* when he makes the hideously wronged Hecuba exclaim:

> Bearer of earth, who hast thy seat on earth,
> Whoe'er thou art, hard to discern or know,
> Zeus, whether nature's law or mind of men,
> To thee I pray, for on a soundless path
> Thou goest, guiding mortal things in right.[30]

Hecuba then calls upon Menelaus to kill Helen who is the source of all the evils of the Trojan War but, though he starts by intending to do so, he puts off his decision, and so Hecuba's prayer is shown to be useless. In the end perhaps their actions are by their own rules just, but it is not for men to lay down how they should act. In the *Suppliant Women* Theseus, who more than any other character of Euripides may be taken to speak for his creator, says:

> But wisdom seeks to be more powerful
> Than God. With empty vanity in our hearts
> We think that we are wiser than the gods.[31]

Euripides was certainly much interested in theological speculations, and often gives them to his characters, but in the end his tragic vision allowed few consolations. The gods are what they are, and men must act in this knowledge and beware of them.

Euripides was fully awake to the society in which he lived and makes many more direct or half-concealed references to current issues than does either Aeschylus or Sophocles. In particular he was much concerned with the Peloponnesian War between Athens and Sparta. In its beginning he wrote his *Heraclidae*, which, despite a lamentably defective text, tells a story from the legendary past of Athens. The play turns on the generous spirit in which the Athenians have treated the sons of Heracles and are rewarded by ingratitude, and this is Euripides' way of denouncing the present Spartans for their ingratitude to Athens. When Athens is attacked she is right to defend herself, and at this date Euripides has no qualms or misgivings about the war. In the *Suppliant Women*, which he wrote in 424 BC towards the end of the first part of the war, his attitude has somewhat changed. The play condemns war between one Greek and another, and this is indeed its main theme. But, much though peace may be desired, it is not yet possible, and meanwhile Athens is ready to uphold her ancient traditions even at the cost of war. Euripides has learned something about war and sees more deeply into its implications, but he is still a patriotic Athenian, eager that his country should be true to herself and resist those who wish for her destruction. He believed in the mission of Athens and was to this degree faithful to the memory of Pericles after his death. But when the war was renewed Euripides had clearly changed his view. His *Trojan Women* was produced in 415 BC in the spring after the winter in which the Athenians had slaughtered the male inhabitants of Melos and sold the women and children into slavery. It is impossible to doubt that Euripides has this in his mind. He says nothing about it, but the *Trojan Women* is a deeply tragic play about a conquered city, in which the men are dead and the women are allotted to the victors as slaves and concubines. The scales are weighted heavily on the side of the defeated Trojans, and especially on behalf of the old queen Hecuba, the prophetess Cassandra, and the widowed Andromache, whose little son is thrown to death over the city-walls. The compassion and the indignation which the play arouses amount to a denunciation of war or at least of the treatment of the vanquished by the victors. But Euripides goes further than this. Though the Trojans are indeed stricken, the Greeks also are doomed to future disasters, and at the start this is emphasized by the appearance of Athene, who has hitherto supported them but now turns against them for their impiety and successfully begs Poseidon to raise a storm which shall wreck their ships on their return to Greece. Euripides suggests that war of this kind ruins conquered and conquerors alike. We cannot say that at the time he had in mind the great expedition which was sailing to Sicily, but we may be sure that the renewal of war was almost abhorrent to him and that he had few illusions left about it.

The hideous disaster of the Syracusan expedition evoked no satisfaction in Euripides. Instead, in this dark period he turned his creative gifts in a new direction, as if the best comfort he could give to his countrymen was to write tragedies which were close to what we would call romantic comedies and move in a world of ingenious fancy. In his *Iphigeneia in Tauris* (c 413 BC) Euripides tells of an adventure on the edge of the known world. Orestes and his friend Pylades come to a temple where his long-lost sister Iphigeneia is priestess and the inhabitants sacrifice all strangers to their goddess. It is a gruesome situation, and Euripides does not play it down. The two men are in real danger, but the play does not merely extricate them from it by an ingenious trick played on the barbarian king, it gains a special depth through the remarkable scene, much admired by Aristotle, in which Orestes and Iphigeneia recognize each other. Euripides touches on real emotions and catches the ugly paradox of Iphigeneia as the priestess of a bloodthirsty cult. But his happy ending comes neatly and happily, and there is no sense of waste or loss. In the *Helen* (412 BC) Euripides carries this romantic art a stage further. His theme comes from Stesichorus – that Helen stayed in Egypt while a phantom of her went to Troy. In the play her husband, Menelaus, is washed up in Egypt, and Helen, despite all that has passed, welcomes him and saves his life from the Egyptians. The action is admirably exciting and various, but hardly any deep note is touched. The triumphant character is Helen, whose womanly wisdom and courage outweigh the blustering antics of the men around her. Euripides, who had treated her harshly in the *Trojan Women*, now presents a picture of her close to Homer's, charming, courageous, resourceful, and in the best sense feminine.

As the war drew slowly to its close, Euripides seems to have found life in Athens uncongenial and both the *Phoenician Women* (*c* 410 BC) and the *Orestes* (408 BC) show signs of uncertainty and weariness. In 408 BC, when he was seventy-two years old, he went to Macedon, and there found a new life in writing his *Bacchants*, which may draw on local rites which he witnessed, and beginning his *Iphigeneia in Aulis*, which was finished by his son after his death. Its theme is the proposed sacrifice of Iphigeneia by her father Agamemnon in order to get fair winds to take his fleet to Troy, and this gives it a fundamental seriousness outside the range of romance. But Euripides enriches the theme with his deft characterization of the feeble and dishonest Agamemnon, the outraged mother Clytaemestra, the young, honourable, and easily deceived Achilles, to whom Iphigeneia thinks that she is to be married, and Iphigeneia herself, brave and candid and devoted. The disaster of human sacrifice was probably averted by the appearance of a god, and the play is not truly tragic, but it shows that even at the end of his life Euripides was still attempting new effects and preparing the way for a more domestic, more intimate, and more psychological drama.

Compared with Aeschylus and Sophocles Euripides lacks confidence in himself both as a man and an artist. He does not share their single-minded outlooks on the world, but seeks eagerly for new points of view, only to abandon them for something else. This means that his poetry is very uneven. Even his choral songs, which often have an effortless spontaneous flight, can at times fall into empty periphrasis and ineffective moralizing. Though his language is much less simple than it appears to be and has many moments of concentrated power in which much is said in a very few words, it can also be unduly pompous, as if he felt that poetry ought to be more remote than he made it. But his most flagrant inequalities come from his interest in contemporary intellectual activities, which were not easily brought into poetry. He knew something of the new movements in philosophy, but at a low, popularized level, and he cannot refrain from introducing hints of these even when they are quite inappropriate. When in the *Suppliant Women* the refugee Adrastus makes a poignant appeal for help, Theseus answers with a discourse on the ingratitude of men, the constitution of states, and the blessings of the Middle Way in politics. When the body of the murdered Aegisthus is brought in, Electra vents her hatred in a speech, but instead of a passionate outburst we get a meditation on the folly of unequal marriages, the insecurity of wealth, and the vanity of bodily beauty. This taste for general ideas is matched by a taste for argument and debate of a kind much loved by the Athenians in the political assembly and the law-courts, but too abstract and too impersonal for tragedy. When Jason is denounced by Medea for his heartless treatment of her love, he answers that she loved him not of her own free-will but under the compulsion of passion and, though Jason is a poor creature, the words ring flat even from him. When, in the *Trojan Women*, Helen is confronted with the husband whom she has betrayed, Euripides does not turn to any account the emotional possibilities of the occasion, but presents a scene like a law-court in which Menelaus is the judge, Hecuba the counsel for the prosecution, and Helen the accused who conducts her own defence, with the result that Menelaus passes judgment against her but postpones its execution until she gets back to Greece. We cannot doubt that, if he had chosen, Euripides could have made a great dramatic success of this episode, but his actual treatment reflects a certain perversity of judgment, a wish to be up-to-date and contemporary in defiance of the established tone of tragedy. His contemporaries, such as Aristophanes, were as fully aware of these faults as we are, but they are clearly due to his uncertainty about how to treat tragedy. He wished to put into it much that it could not easily hold, and this makes him an uncertain artist, but it was from his experiments that later dramatists were to learn how to broaden the scope of drama.

The real strength of Euripides is his ability to see how legendary events must have happened. Sophocles also had this gift but, whereas he made his persons and episodes conform to a self-consistent heroic world, Euripides relied on his knowledge of the contemporary scene and his sharp moments of insight into it. He applied these to the legendary past with paradoxical but striking effect, and he underlined his lessons by making the gods even more inscrutable than Aeschylus or Sophocles had made them. When Aristotle calls him 'the most tragic of the poets',[32] he seems to mean no more than that Euripides had a preference for unhappy endings, but the words can carry more meaning than that. Euripides is a truly tragic poet because he offers no consolation for what happens. Sophocles suggests that a rift in the scheme of things has somehow been mended, but Euripides leaves us with a sense of inexplicable waste and disaster, of the hideous dooms to which men are brought by their circumstances and their characters. In their moments of catastrophe his persons are most themselves and display the richness of their natures. They are not heroes in the Homeric sense, but they attain a peculiar grandeur just because their sufferings are so appalling. Euripides plumbs the depths of human insecurity, and, because he allows no anodynes or consolations, he too is a true child of the fifth century, an Athenian, who has learned the hard lessons of his time and not been afraid of facing their consequences.

Sophocles and Euripides both died shortly before the fall of Athens in 404 BC, and with them Attic tragedy came to a close. In the fourth century economic difficulties meant that it could not be produced with the old splendour, but in any case poets ceased to write it, no doubt because in the disillusioned post-war years they lacked the spirit to face its fierce issues and the vitality to create on so generous a scale. Such tragedies as were written, were more literary exercises than positive criticisms of life. But while it throve, Attic tragedy not only produced a series of enduring masterpieces, but brought together in a peculiarly Athenian way different threads from past achievement and worked them into a single pattern. It gave a new life to heroic legends by giving them a new interpretation without debasing their high sense of human worth. It turned choral song into a dramatic medium admirable for its own sake and also able to pass new comments on many aspects of human behaviour and destiny; it picked up themes from philosophy and transformed them into poetry, thus bringing them into closer touch with ordinary men. It is also characteristically Athenian in its grand design, its scale and depth, its generous humanity and its searching seriousness. If it lacks the gracious, expansive ease of the epic, that is because it reflects a more troubled outlook and more anxious thought. In its gravity and its confidence it is the true reflection of the Athenian people in its magnificent heyday, and it reveals the self-questioning and the close examination of ultimate issues which tempered the quest for imperial power.

6

FROM MYTH TO SCIENCE

THE Greek genius for adapting traditional forms to new uses accounts for their success alike in epic, lyric, and dramatic poetry. In each an ancient form was developed and elaborated into a high art, and each throve because it met some social or individual need. But the rapid growth of Greek civilization in the seventh and sixth centuries created new needs which called for satisfaction in words but for which there was no obvious form already in existence. This was the case with the first beginnings of science and philosophy, which are already visible at the start of the sixth century. If science asked how things *become*, philosophy asked how things *are* and, though in their first years the two pursuits were almost indistinguishable, both needed appropriate means to express their problems. The father of Greek science, Thales, who foretold an eclipse on 28 May 585 BC, seems not to have put down his speculations in writing, and his teaching, such as that all things come ultimately from water, must have been delivered by word of mouth and remembered because of its remarkable character. But others were not content with this and had to find a suitable medium. Since he and his successors were Ionian Greeks, they had behind them a long tradition of poetry, and it is not surprising that some early thinkers wrote in verse. In this they continued in new conditions what Hesiod had done when he explained the world in mythical genealogies, or Alcman, when, with a curious anticipation of Thales, he said that Thetis, the sea-goddess, had in the beginning set things in order. Poetry was an established form, and it was natural to turn it to formulate matters of intellectual enquiry.

Xenophanes of Colophon (570–479 BC) used elegiacs to criticize social faults, such as the high rewards given to successful athletes or the need to sing serious songs at feasts, but when he was drawn to subjects of larger interest, he set them forth in hexameters, no doubt, because this was a recognized means for displaying cosmologies. He was particularly interested in the gods and had bold and original ideas about them. He dismissed all tales that they steal and fornicate and cheat. He argued that the anthropomorphic conception of them was quite wrong, and that, if horses and oxen had hands, they would make images of gods like them-selves. He believed in a single god, who seems to have been both physical and mental, the totality of things at all levels:

All of him sees, and all of him thinks, and all of him listens.[1]

His vigorous arguments and his well-chosen examples fall easily into his lucid and melodious lines, if only because he avoids highly abstract arguments and uses no technical terms. He was at once theologian, philosopher, and scientist, and combined all three roles without any trouble. But his methods could not be used by everyone. Parmenides of Elea (*c* 520–*c* 450 BC) attempted a much more difficult task when he set out in hexameters his remarkable view of reality as a single, unchanging unity and of appearance as a mass of contradictions, about which we can only make guesses. The importance which he attaches to his theme is clear from his opening lines in which he portrays himself as setting out on a chariot to the Gates of Night and Day, where a goddess welcomes him and makes a revelation to him. But, though he has a remarkable command of words, his taut, tough argument is more than hexameters can easily carry, and this, not merely the fragmentary state of his text, is one of the reasons why his message is so hard to unravel. Nor did any philosopher after him use verse again. For science and religion it had a longer lease. Empedocles of Acragas (494–434 BC) wrote two works in hexameters, *Purifications* and *On Nature*. The first deals with religious beliefs current in Sicily in his time and especially with the transmigration of souls, in which he ardently believed. Here the poetical form adds conviction and splendour to the doctrine and we need not be too surprised that he should begin by addressing his fellow-citizens with a remarkable claim:

Hail! to you I am a god undying, no longer a mortal.[2]

But *On Nature* deals with more technical matters and attempts to reduce reality to four elements of earth, water, air, and fire, a theory which remained unquestioned for many centuries. It has stiff passages of argu-ment and proof, but it maintains its poetical zest and makes use of a mythical machinery as it sees the world governed by Love and Strife, which bring the birth and the death of mortal things. The substantial remains of this work show that Empedocles was able to write well even on the most unpromising subjects; so adaptable was the Greek hexameter and so abundant the vocabulary at a poet's disposal.

Brilliant though these achievements were in extending the activities of words, they would surely, if they had been continued, have hampered the free growth of intellectual enquiry. Fortunately, the early thinkers did not all follow the same pattern. Some of them, notably Anaximander (610–c 540 BC) and his pupil Anaximenes (fl. 546 BC), both of Miletus, wrote in prose about the structure of the universe, and they must have derived their manner from common speech, with an eye for its vivid figures. Thus Anaximenes said: 'Just as our soul, being air, holds us together, so do breath and air encompass the whole world',[3] and uses a very simple image to make his meaning plain. To these first thinkers Greek prose owed its beginnings, and it is significant that their straightforward manner, which is the reflection of their sharp intelligences, was taken up in the next hundred years by other enquirers, such as Democritus (c 460–c 370 BC), the putative father of atomic physics. Even so not all philosophers wrote as they did. One at least felt that his special task called for a special style. Heraclitus of Ephesus (fl. 500 BC), who saw reality as a perpetual flux, wrote in an oracular manner in which he half conceals his meaning in imagery and paradox and thereby creates, as he no doubt intended, effects which are often imaginative and impressive, as when he says that 'The way up and the way down is one and the same'[4] or 'Time is a child playing draughts, the kingly power is a child's',[5] or 'Mortals are immortals and immortals are mortals, the one living the others' death and dying the others' life'.[6] From its first conscious beginnings Greek prose moved in more than one direction, and when it came to maturity, its practitioners had many possibilities open to them from which to choose what most suited their purpose and their gifts.

At this stage the Greeks hardly distinguished between scientists and philosophers and regarded all men who enquired into the nature of things as practising what they called *historiê*, which simply means 'enquiry'. This naturally included enquiry into the nature of man, his doings, his home on the earth, and it was this that led to the creation of what we know as history. At the start it had no such narrow bounds as we tend to give it. Its founder is Hecataeus of Miletus, who was active in anti-Persian politics from 500 to 494 BC and wrote two books, of which considerable remains survive. In his *Genealogies* he tried to make for men a counterpart to what Hesiod had done for the gods and worked out a number of pedigrees. In his *Tour of the Earth* he described the geography of parts of Europe, Asia, and Africa with some details on their inhabitants, touching Tartessus in Spain on one side and India on the other, but most of his material is Mediterranean. Yet he laid the foundations of history because he placed the present generation of men in relation to a long past and realized that peoples must be seen in their geographical setting. Though he was criticized by his successors for his bad judgment and his wholesale borrowing, his intentions were excellent; for, as he said at the beginning of his *Genealogies*: 'What I write here is the account which I considered to be true. For the stories of the Greeks are numerous and in my opinion ridiculous.'[7] This fine independence reveals his Ionian curiosity, and it was in such a spirit that his work was to be continued by others.

Herodotus of Halicarnassus (*c* 485–*c* 428 BC) was called by Cicero the 'father of history' and such in the record of western civilization he deservedly remains. He left his home early and travelled extensively, in the Black Sea to the Crimea and inland beyond it, in the western regions of Asia Minor, on the main caravan-route from Palestine to Egypt, in Egypt as far south as Assuan. He spent some years at Thurii in south-western Italy, but his spiritual home was Athens. For her he conceived an early, admiring love which he never lost. In writing his *History* he knew what he wanted to do and set out his aims in his opening paragraph:

This is the record of the enquiry (*historiē*) of Herodotus of Halicarnassus, that neither what men have done in the past may be obliterated nor great and wonderful actions, some of them performed by Greeks and some by barbarians, may lose their glory, and above all why they fought with one another.[8]

Herodotus' main theme is the relations between Greeks and foreign peoples, and the culmination of this is the Persian Wars of 490 and 480–479 BC. He sees that these can be placed in their proper context only if he relates previous contacts and conflicts and sets out the main movements which made the Greeks what they were at the time of the Persian invasions. He sets the foundations of his history on a generous scale, beginning with the first menace from Lydia in the seventh century and taking it down through the conquest of Lydia by Cyrus the Mede, through Cyrus' successors, Darius and Cambyses, until he reaches Xerxes. But in his deep interest in the Persians he gives full accounts, not merely of their political history, but of the huge realms, which they conquered in Babylonia and Egypt, and of their attempt to conquer Scythia. Then he turns to Africa, part of which was conquered by Cambyses, and gives an equally ample treatment to it. In the first part of his great work the Greeks are often introduced, and we hear about their history in the seventh and sixth centuries, but it is not till the Persians come into conflict with the Ionians of Asia Minor that Herodotus gives an equal part to each contending people and in his final books simplifies his manner as he tells in detail of the battles and political actions of the Persian Wars. The exuberant expansiveness of the first books is a calculated means to set the coming events in a correct perspective and to show on how wide a stage events were played. In it he has many diversions, partly because his conditions of publication precluded footnotes, which had to be included in the text, and maps, which had to be made not by diagrams but by words, but more because his material is so diverse that it cannot be fitted into a straightforward narrative. If he had treated his enormous subject in a more economical manner, we should have been immeasurably the poorer.

Herodotus' conception of history included a great deal more than the record of political and military events. He was convinced that men were largely the creatures of their environment, and that he must make clear what this is. He used what few maps were available, but they were schematic diagrams more than accurate maps. They gave him his notion of a world divided into three continents, Europe, Asia, and Africa, but he was not moved by *a priori* considerations into saying what shape they must have. He doubted the existence of the River of Ocean, which was supposed to flow round the earth, and he did not believe in the mythical Hyperboreans who were said to live beyond the north wind. He knew that Africa was surrounded by sea, because it had been circumnavigated by Phoenician sailors, but he was not convinced that the Cassiterides, or Tin Islands, which seem to have been Britain, were really islands or that the Eridanus, which has been variously identified with the Rhone, the Rhine, and the Po, flowed northwards. He was greatly interested in the Nile and especially in the silt which it brings down to form the Egyptian Delta. He reckoned that in time the Nile-mouths would be blocked and the river would create a second Egypt in the Red Sea. He showed his sense of time when he reckoned that this would take twenty-thousand years, and thought nothing odd in it. His information, collected from every kind of source, included the route across the Sahara to the Bahr-el Ghazal and its Pygmies, the vast extension of Asia eastward, the crocodiles in an Indian river, perhaps the Indus or even the Ganges, the amber-trade over land from the north-west, the changing landscape of modern Russia at least as far as the Urals. He has a keen eye for physical conditions, from the well-watered lands of Mesopotamia to the deserts of Africa, and he noted what wild animals flourished in various regions. He visited the battlefields of the Persian Wars and made his narrative fit the geographical setting. He saw men as the creation of their circumstances and had his own theories about the connection between the one and the other.

Herodotus knew from his own travels that there are many kinds of men, and his curiosity about them made him the father of anthropology. Some of the differences between one people and another he ascribed to physical causes, claiming that the sun blackens faces and hardens skulls. But he makes a bold and successful attempt to classify men by blood-kinship or physique, speech, cults and rituals, and mode of life. For each he gives good examples. First, he noticed that some Scythians at Ascalon were beardless and that the same phenomenon was to be seen in Scythia. Secondly, he often quotes foreign words and tells an interesting story how Pharaoh Psammetichus of Egypt tried to find out what was the oldest language by isolating two children from birth. Their first utterance was the word *bekos*, which was the Phrygian word for bread, and that settled the question. Thirdly, Herodotus notes many religious rites, describing them in detail for Persians and Egyptians and Scythians. Fourthly, he is much interested in diet, and notes that different peoples eat corn, or acorns, or fruit, or monkeys, or lice, as do the nomad Boudini of north Africa, or their elderly relatives, as do the Callatian Indians. In all these matters he is wonderfully tolerant and quite unshocked by what many Greeks would have regarded as disgusting barbarian practices. He quotes for his own purposes Pindar's words: 'Custom is king of everything' and, though Pindar used them to prove that the gods may do what men may not, Herodotus applies them in a much more generous spirit to prove that men must act according to their upbringing and traditions. His four tests for differentiating one people from another are by no means outmoded, and in each he made full use of his keen personal observations. He was well aware that even these tests were not final and that 'anything may happen in the length of years',[9] but, just because he was so well aware of human differences, he was able to contrast the vast multi-racial empires of Asia with the divided but none the less homogeneous Greeks. His anthropology, like his geography, was an invaluable background to the story of conflict which he had to tell.

A third branch of enquiry relating to man was what the Greeks called 'politics'. It was the study of methods and principles of government and was in due course to become a leading topic with philosophers. In Herodotus we can see it at work in an early stage. After the overthrow of the Magi, who had seized power in Persia, the leading conspirators discuss what kind of government should be instituted. In turn Otanes, Megabyzus, and Darius plead respectively for the virtues of democracy, oligarchy, and autocracy. The four others, who have not spoken, vote for the last, and it wins the day. Now it is most improbable that such speeches were made, or, that, if they were, Herodotus could have heard about them, but he insists that, 'though some of our countrymen refuse to believe that they were made, they were made nevertheless'.[10] He must have believed his authority for them, and that he did so is remarkable, but more relevant is that this short discussion, in which each speaker puts with some force the familiar arguments for his choice of government, is an attempt to settle their relative merits. Herodotus wishes the issue to be made clear and succeeds by this means. But he himself does not agree with its conclusion. Tolerant though he was of all manners of men and governments, his own admiration was given to the Athenian democracy as it emerged during the Persian Wars, and he believed that the emergence of democratic freedom was largely responsible for the defeat of Persia. In fact he seems more than once to have accepted a little too readily the Athenian version of recent events at the expense of Sparta or Corinth or Thebes. But, if his democratic convictions occasionally led him astray, he was able to see all kinds of men in their human worth and variety and was very far from thinking that tyrants and great kings were necessarily bad men. In his main plan his political interests give shape to the main issues between Greeks and barbarians and add yet another element to his rich and variegated pattern. Though he was never an Athenian citizen, and may not have spent very many years at Athens, he speaks from the Athenian point of view at the time of Athens' greatest splendour.

Herodotus saw much for himself, but he extended it enormously by hearsay and enquiry. He does not seem to have relied, as modern historians do, very much on written documents. He may have learned something from them in Egypt, but he did not know the language and was at the mercy of what the guides told him. He did not visit Persia, and his excellent information on Persian affairs must have been got from Persians whom he met elsewhere, and in that case documents would hardly be in question. He read his few predecessors, notably Hecataeus, but had no great opinion of him. His main source of supply was talk, and this he pursued with an extraordinary zest in all manner of quarters. On his own admission he spoke with men from more than forty Greek cities and regions, from Cyprus to Syracuse, and from more than thirty other countries, from Arabia and the Oasis of Ammon to the Caucasus and Scythia, and from Persia to Carthage. He was well aware that he could not accept everything that he heard and, though his methods may not have been what we should call scientific, he saw the need for tests and criteria, and formulated them in his own way. Perhaps his wisest decision was to record what he had heard, even if he doubted or disbelieved it. Thus, when the Phoenicians sailed round Africa, they reported that after a certain point the sun rose on their right. This was of course correct, but Herodotus, not knowing the spheroid shape of the earth, could not accept it. He was a friend of the great Alcmaeonid clan at Athens and could not believe that they had planned to collaborate with the Persians if they won at Marathon, but he reports as evidence for it the story that a shield was used to flash the news of the battle to them. He liked, when possible, to get more than one account of an event, and if these conflicted he would set out both sides fairly, as when he notes the Athenian story that the Corinthians ran away at Salamis, but adds: 'they themselves do not admit its truth . . . and the rest of Greece testifies in their favour'.[11] He did not regard his own conclusions as nearly so important as his reporting of what he heard. His first duty was to his evidence, and this he presented with admirable impartiality. Other historians, who are more sure of their own judgment, might well learn from him that a first duty is to set out the material on which judgments are made.

The material which Herodotus gathered by such means is magnificent and multifarious, but, having gathered it, he had to arrange it in an attractive form. His grand design provided a frame but inside it he had to decide how this or that kind of episode was to be treated. So far as the purely geographical information was concerned, the answer was easy. It could be arranged like a running commentary on a map, running from east to west with north Africa or from south to north with Scythia. But stories of action called for more special treatment and, in dealing with them, Herodotus made use of more than one literary type current in his time. It is likely that he himself recited his work in public, and if so, he had to bear in mind the needs of public recitation and the susceptibilities of an audience. The Greeks were trained to listening to more than one kind of recitation, and the humblest were simple stories, told perhaps by professional story-tellers, in open places to a mixed public. Such stories exist in most parts of the world, and Herodotus certainly picked up some of them. From Egypt comes one of the most spectacular, which tells of extremely ingenious robberies from the treasure-house of Rampsinitus, who is Ramses III, and it is not only breathlessly exciting but ends with the thief receiving the Pharaoh's daughter in marriage for being 'the most intelligent of mankind'.[12] Another story comes from Persia and tells how, when the three main Persian conspirators had to choose which of them should become king, they agreed that it should be he whose horse neighed first after sunrise. This was arranged for Darius by his groom, who gave his master's stallion the scent of a mare and tethered her where they were to meet in the morning. The stallion neighed, and Darius became king. Such stories belong to all countries, but Herodotus tells them with a brilliant ease and liveliness, never making too much of them but bringing out their essential points with the right emphasis. He could also find them in Greece, and such must be the source of his account of a famous wedding. Cleisthenes, tyrant of Sicyon, summoned suitors from all over Greece for the hand of his daughter Agariste. Among them was the Athenian Hippocleides, whom Cleisthenes favoured. When the day came for the betrothal, the suitors competed in music and talking. Hippocleides began to dance, and ended up by dancing on a table and then standing on his head and beating time with his legs in the air. Cleisthenes was horrified and told him that he had danced away his wife, to which he answered: 'What does Hippocleides care for that?'[13] This is an ancient story which has a parallel in an Indian tale of a dancing peacock. It is hardly historical and looks as if it came from the market-place. Herodotus uses such tales to vary the tone of his work and to introduce popular elements which everyone could enjoy.

A second model, which he undoubtedly had in mind, even though it called for considerable adaptation, was tragedy. He must often have seen tragedies performed at Athens, and he was a personal friend of Sophocles, who wrote a poem, now lost, to him. Herodotus shows such influence early in his work when he tells how Croesus, king of Lydia, tries to avoid an oracle which says that his son will be killed by an iron weapon. He keeps the boy from all manly pursuits in the hope of saving him. A man, Adrastus, comes and begs asylum from Croesus, who gives it him, and soon after this he persuades the king to let the son go on a hunting expedition against a monstrous boar. The boar is killed, but Adrastus accidentally kills the son, and the oracle is fulfilled. It is possible that in this case Herodotus followed an actual tragedy, but in other cases we can see the example of tragedy shaping his narrative. In a not dissimilar way he gives a pattern to the story of Cambyses, the Persian king who conquered Egypt. He defied the Egyptian gods and began to go mad, killing his brother and heir, and hoping to hide it. But he accidentally wounded himself on his sword, and asking in what place he was, was told it was Ecbatana. He recalled an oracle which told that he would die at Ecbatana, but he had assumed it would be his capital in Persia, not an obscure Egyptian town. He now saw that the oracle was right, and died. This is very much the kind of oracle which Heracles recalls in his dying moments in Sophocles' *Women of Trachis* and, though such a theme was common enough in narrative, it was part of the mechanism of tragedy, and Herodotus' treatment suggests that this was where he found it.

Thirdly, Herodotus had been brought up on the epic, and his own uncle, Panyassis, had tried to keep the old art alive by telling of the labours of Heracles. Herodotus recalls the epic in the size and scope of his main themes, and especially in his structure. Like the *Iliad*, his *History* begins with a series of separate episodes, but, as it advances, various threads are brought together in the uniting theme of the Persian Wars. Like the epic, it has many digressions and some of these are told simply for their own sake and interest. Epic calls for striking characters, simply built on a large scale, and these appear on every page of Herodotus. His noble Persians, like Darius and his satraps, must have been largely Herodotus' own invention, but he formed them, not on current Greek notions of Persians, but on his own intuition of what characters men of such power and enterprise must have had. In his own country local legends, which often contain acute conceptions of personality, must have guided him in such vigorous figures as Cleomenes, king of Sparta, who after a career of unceasing action, goes mad from drinking his wine neat and mutilates himself to death, or Miltiades, who by sheer force of will dominates the strategy and tactics of Marathon but, after it, overreaches himself and is discredited by the failure of his attack on Paros, or of Themistocles, whom he does not admire without qualification but whose cunning and foresight he appreciates at their epic value. Above all in the easy flow of his narrative, his eye for the telling detail, his sense of surprise, and his majestic handling of large themes in speeches by the leading characters before decisions are taken, he shows how the technique of the epic can be transferred to historical narrative and add much to its liveliness and reality. Just as Homer shows no bias in dealing with Greeks and Trojans, so Herodotus in dealing with Greeks and Persians does his best to be fair to both sides and to present the main figures in the round. His 'great and wonderful actions' are not after all very different from the 'glorious doings of men' of which Achilles sings in his tent.

Herodotus sees the doings of men as inexorably governed by the will of the gods. His attitude towards them is on the surface ambivalent and even contradictory, but that is not uncommon in most religions at most times, and certainly it was common enough in the fifth century, when the new criticism of theology had made some mark but had neither discredited the old beliefs nor come to a compromise with them. It was all the easier because Greek religion had no creeds or sacred books and left plenty of room for speculation. Herodotus shows his traditional allegiance to the Olympian gods in many ways. He accepts their existence, respects their rites and shrines, and says not a word against them. He does not question the utterances of the Delphic Oracle and takes pains to point out that, even when they were thought to have been falsified by events, they turned out to be true. He reports but need not necessarily believe that when the Persians came to Delphi they were repelled, with much loss, by strokes of lightning and the fall of huge rocks from Parnassus. He repeats the charming stories of Pan's appearance to the runner Pheidippides when he was taking the news of the Persian invasion to Sparta and of Helen's appearance to a Spartan woman. Such tales would have been accepted by his audience, and there is no need to think that he did not accept them himself. Yet, as Gibbon observed, he 'sometimes writes for children and sometimes for philosophers'. Herodotus' credulity was matched by moments of a quiet, ironical incredulity. He allows that a ravine in Thessaly may have been made by Poseidon, because Poseidon is said to produce earthquakes, and the ravine looks like the result of an earthquake. He allows that the Athenians believe a great snake to live on the Acropolis, but he leaves the question open when he says: 'They present a honey-cake every month as to a creature existing.'[14] He accepted the existence of the gods of Egypt and liked to find points of similarity between them and Greek gods, notably Heracles, and he was in this respect a pioneer of comparative religion. The religion of Herodotus was in many ways what we should expect from a man living in the middle of the fifth century, when religion was still a reality in public life but was being modified and re-modelled in many directions.

In one respect Herodotus might seem to be more superstitious than we should expect. He speaks often of the *phthonos* which the gods feel against any man who is more than usually successful. The word means 'envy' or 'resentment', and we assume that for Herodotus 'the divine', as he calls it, is a jealous god, and indeed he says explicitly that 'the divine is resentful and disturbs us.'[15] He applies this doctrine almost schematically to Croesus, king of Lydia, and to Polycrates, tyrant of Samos. Croesus is the richest man of his time, but doom falls on him and he is defeated and dethroned by Cyrus. His case is the more striking because he is unusually devout and makes generous gifts to the god of Delphi, whose ambiguous oracle, wrongly interpreted, brings him to defeat. Polycrates is a more brilliant and more engaging figure, who combines piracy and command of the sea with patronage of art and science, but ends by falling a victim to treachery and is crucified by the Persians. Herodotus admires and likes both, but that does not affect his theory of their fall. Taken literally, this theory means that the gods suffer from jealousy like men and vent their resentment on those who are too successful. But we need not take Herodotus literally. He uses the language of theology for a fact about the universe, and his theory of divine envy has close relations to views held by poets and philosophers. Just as Sophocles found the origin of a tragic situation in some breach in the ordered system of the world, so physicists and philosophers found that the whole scheme of things depended on the maintenance of a balance or harmony, and that, if this were destroyed, nature asserted herself to put it right. So Anaximander said that the balance was kept in the universe 'for things make reparation and satisfaction to one another according to the appointed time'[16], and Heraclitus is not far from him when he says: 'The sun will not overstep his measures; if he does, the Erinyes, the handmaids of Justice, will find him out.'[17] Herodotus applies to the affairs of men a theory which distinguished thinkers had applied to the physical universe and, though his language is traditional, so also is theirs. The vocabulary of myth is turned to a new purpose and applied to subjects for which it was not originally fashioned. This was inevitable at a time when thinkers had to forge their instruments of speech for the first time and naturally picked up images and phrases which with a little adjustment could be made to suit unprecedented ends.

Herodotus, without any inconsistency, combines this theory with another, with the traditional belief that some men are so intoxicated by vanity that they work their own destruction. This is hardly to be found in Homer, but it is at least as old as Solon and was favoured by Pindar, who used it in tactful warnings to his princely patrons against wanting too much or going too far. It is based on sound psychology. Some kinds of success breed a pride which is blind to its limitations and attempts to do what is beyond its reach. In applying such a theory there is no real need to introduce the gods, but for a Greek it was natural to do so, since it was they who set before men the temptations which they could not always resist, and in this infatuated mood men were liable to disregard the gods. Herodotus applies this above all to Persian ambitions. He had a fine poetical precedent for this in the *Persians* of Aeschylus, in which Xerxes in his self-confidence and lust for success tries to get more than is possible, and is greatly humiliated. It is a special application of the Greek doctrine of the Mean and it provides a dramatic and reasonably convincing explanation of many human actions. Herodotus takes it up for Xerxes on a large scale. He admires Cyrus and Darius, though he thinks that both of them sometimes went too far, but in Xerxes he shows how the scheme really works. He gives Xerxes many royal and even impressive traits. He is generous to those who disagree with him and, though he is a stern master who punishes shirkers and cowards, he has good reasons of state for doing so. His infatuation lies in his belief that he can conquer the Greeks. To us it seems almost incredible that with his vast resources in men and money he failed to do so, but this was not how Herodotus saw it. He believed that the Greeks, fortified by their belief in liberty guaranteed by law, could not fail to defeat the subjects of the Great King, who were no better than slaves. In this there is an element of truth, for after all Greece defeated Persia because she had something to fight for, whereas most of Persia's other victims merely changed one autocracy for another.

Though Herodotus owes much to popular tales, to epic, and to tragedy the form which he created was his own. He was concerned with a narrative of varied actions in prose, and these actions belonged to the historical past. He assumed that history must be interesting for its own sake, but he also saw that truth was indispensable if we are to trust it, and, without trust, enjoyment is worse than incomplete. There is no reason to think that he said a single thing in which he did not believe and, although we may think that we know better, it is remarkable how sane and balanced he is. He has the essential virtues of a historian who thinks that he has to tell a story. He does not mean it to be technically useful for students of politics, but, like Homer and the Attic tragedians, he means to instruct while he gives delight. In this he succeeds triumphantly. As a teller of tales he is in the first class. He varies his scale, his manner, his tone, from tale to tale, and in each he secures some striking, often unique effect. He catches the attention at once by a bold stroke, as when he says of a Lydian king: 'This Candaules fell in love with his own wife and thought her by far the most beautiful of all women';[18] or starts his account of a Persian king who has just come to the throne: 'Astyages had a daughter called Mandane and he dreamed one night that she made water in such enormous quantities that it filled the city and swamped the whole of Asia';[19] or prepares the way for the turning of the Greek rear at Thermopylae by telling about the traitor Ephialtes, who came to Xerxes, 'in hope of a rich reward, to tell the king about the track which led over the hills to Thermopylae – and the information he gave was to prove the death of the Greeks who held the pass'.[20] In each case the start rivets our notice and is entirely relevant to what follows.

This instinctive feeling for a situation comes out in many unexpected ways. Arion, a famous poet of Corinth, has made a large fortune in the west, but on his way home he is thrown into the sea by robbers who want his money. He acts with great calm, puts on his best clothes, sings a famous song, and then leaps into the sea, where he is picked up by a dolphin, on whose back he comes to land. It is entirely unaffected and unforced and not even beyond the bounds of possibility. An impostor makes himself king of Persia by pretending to be Smerdis, who has been murdered by Cambyses, but he does not dare to appear in public. He is unmasked by one of his wives who finds out in the dark that his ears have been cut off, and this proves that he is not Smerdis. When the Ionian rebel Histiaeus, who is detained forcibly at the court of Darius, wishes to send a message to his nephew Aristagoras, he shaves the head of a slave, pricks the message on the scalp, and, when his hair has grown, sends him off to Miletus. Polycrates of Samos throws a valuable ring into the sea, perhaps a foretaste of a ceremony like the wedding of Venice with the Adriatic, and thinks that by doing so he will avert misfortune. But a fisherman catches a large fish, brings it to Polycrates, who thanks him and rewards him, but then finds the ring inside and knows that his exorcism has failed. When Cyrus was killed fighting the Massagetae, their queen, Tomyris, found his body, took his head, and flung it into a skin filled with human blood – to give him his fill of blood for treacherously killing her son. Periander, tyrant of Corinth, mislaid a valuable possession. So he sent messengers to enquire in a remote shrine by the river Acheron from the ghost of his wife, Melissa, where it was. She refused to tell, since she was cold and naked for her clothes had not been burned with her. Periander then stripped all the women of Corinth, burned their clothes, and prayed to the spirit of Melissa, who on the next enquiry told him where to look. All such stories are of course closer to legend than to history, but they have a peculiar verisimilitude. Because Herodotus believes in them, he sees them with a vivid imagination and sets them out with a delightful sense of human behaviour in strange circumstances. His range of effects is far wider than Homer's just because he is not confined to heroic effects. He can be grotesque, macabre, brutal, ingenious, and, when he has to be, heroic.

Herodotus need not have taken part in war to know what it is. Among those with whom he consorted there must have been many who had been or still were soldiers, and from them he could learn about war as soldiers see it, when it often has little relation to the plans of the higher command or the theories of tacticians. In fact Herodotus' account of battles in the Persian War is usually more convincing than many modern reconstructions of them. He knew the battlefields and men who had fought on them, and it is pedantry to disbelieve his main accounts. But what catches his imagination is the give-and-take of warfare, the unforeseen episodes which account for much of the excitement and glamour of war. He marks how at Marathon the Greeks, for the first time known to him, advance at the double, how the weakening of their centre draws the Persians on and makes it easier to cut off part of their force from the rest, how Cynegirus, brother of Aeschylus, had his hand cut off with an axe as he was catching hold of a ship's stern and so lost his life. He describes at length the different uniforms and weapons of Xerxes' multi-racial army and, whether he got his information from a picture or from an eye-witness, the result is of a brilliant variety. When, at Thermopylae, Xerxes sent a horseman forward to report on the Greek troops, he found some of the Spartans stripped for exercise and others combing their hair, and none took any notice of him. When his troops failed to break the Greek line Xerxes leapt three times from his throne in fear for them. When the Greek ships were lying in the Bay of Salamis and some of the leaders wished to take them away, Themistocles forced the issue. He sent an agent, Sicinnus, in a boat to the Persian fleet, who told them that the Greeks were planning a withdrawal. The trick worked, and the Persians attacked, to their own disastrous loss. At Plataea, when the Greek troops were asleep at night, Alexander, king of Macedon, rode over from the Persian lines and informed the Greeks that the Persians intended to attack in the morning. In the actual struggle the Persians joined fight at close quarters, catching hold of the Spartan spears and breaking them, while their general, Mardonius, surrounded by his personal bodyguard, rode into battle on his white horse, and it was his death that took the heart out of the Persians and led to their defeat.

Herodotus' sense of a dramatic tale is matched by a variety of comments which he gives to others or even contributes in his own person. They come from the storehouse of popular wisdom and have a charming aptness and freshness. So the Persian Otanes sums up what is in fact the common Greek objection to a tyrant in that 'he breaks up the structure of ancient tradition and law, forces women to serve his pleasure, and puts men to death without trial'.[21] The exiled Spartan king Demaratus says to Xerxes of the Spartans: 'Being free, they are not free in all things, but the law is over them for master, which they fear in their hearts much more than your people fear you.'[22] Periander, tyrant of Corinth, tries to win over a recalcitrant son by speaking of his own position and says: 'It is better to be envied than pitied',[23] in words very like those in which Pindar addresses Hieron of Syracuse. When Darius offers the wife of Intaphrenes to save the life of one of her family, much to his surprise she chooses, not her husband, but her brother and argues: 'God willing, I may get another husband, and other children when these are gone. But as my father and mother are dead, I can never possibly have another brother.'[24] Sophocles gives the same argument to Antigone, and it reaches very far back into primitive beliefs about blood-kinship. When Gelon of Syracuse finds that he cannot help the Greeks because it would be demeaning himself to take orders from anyone else, he tells their messengers that they must 'tell Greece that the spring of the year, the fairest of the four seasons, is lost to her'.[25] The image seems to have been borrowed by Herodotus from a speech by Pericles on the Athenian dead, but it makes its mark in its context. These remarks are not historical in the sense that they were spoken by those to whom they are attributed, but they are material for history in that they show how the Greeks judged conduct and events and shaped their theories into neat aphorisms. Herodotus' own personal comments have the same terseness. He notices that 'the Egyptians in their manners and customs seem to have reversed the ordinary practices of mankind';[26] that the Persians teach their boys three things only, 'to ride, to use the bow, and to speak the truth';[27] that in practising circumcision the Egyptians prefer 'to be clean rather than comely';[28] that 'the misery arising in a country torn by internal strife is worse than united war in the same proportion as war itself is worse than peace'.[29] Herodotus addressed himself to the common man, whose wisdom and insight he appreciated and shared. He makes no attempt to inflate his thoughts but leaves them to make their impact by their easy and graceful wisdom.

Though his home at Halicarnassus was a Dorian foundation and, though he himself spent only a part of his time at Athens, he is very much its spokesman and conveys its spirit as Sophocles does, but on a much wider scale and with a far greater knowledge of the general Greek world. He dates the importance of Athens from the expulsion of the tyrants and, when he says 'Athens had been great before; now, her liberty won, she grew greater still',[30] he shows his understanding of her. This was the age of high confidence and huge enterprises but, though Herodotus admired and loved Athens and felt that she was superior to Sparta or Corinth or Thebes, he did not absorb the narrow view of her which came with her increase of power. He was born into the Ionian enlightenment, but he gave depth and strength to this by what he learned at Athens, and especially by the Athenian curiosity about all human matters. He shared the Athenians' admiration for their own past, but probably saw their enemies as more formidable and more interesting than they did. His preference for the 'middle state', which he does not conceal, indicates that he was not of the advanced democratic wing, but that he saw something formidable in Pericles is clear from his single reference to him, when he records that 'Agariste dreamed during her pregnancy that she gave birth to a lion, and a few days later she became the mother of Pericles'.[31] In this his great successor in the art and science of history would have agreed with him.

A generation separates Thucydides (*c* 455–*c* 400 BC) from Herodotus, but it was a generation so rich in change that it is hard to imagine that the two men could have met in Athens. If Herodotus derives his inspiration from the rise of Athens after the Persian Wars, Thucydides was, in his first manhood, carried away by the ideals of Pericles and lived to see them depraved by demagogues and end in the fall of Athens to Sparta in 404 BC. Thucydides came from a good family, which owned mines in Thrace, and was related to Miltiades. His origins suggest that he would belong to the party which opposed Pericles, and his admiration for him is that of a convert who has no doubts that he is right.When the Peloponnesian War broke out in 431 BC, he was actively involved in it. He caught the plague at some date between 430 and 427 BC, but, unlike many others, recovered. In 424 BC he was in command of a small squadron of ships in the Thracian war-zone, but failed to reach Amphipolis in time to save it from the Spartan general Brasidas. For this he was exiled and did not return until twenty years later, when the war was over, and died a few years afterwards. He spent his exile in collecting material for his History and working at it, but left it unfinished at his death.

The words with which Thucydides opens his History reveal his intention and his determination:

I began my history at the very outbreak of the war, in the belief that it was going to be a great war and more worth writing about than any of those which have taken place in the past.[32]

This judgment is founded on solid facts and inspired by a remarkable foresight. The facts are that in this war the whole of Greece was divided into two sides as it had never been before and that the war also affected a large part of the non-Hellenic world; the foresight was that the war did indeed ruin classical Greece by exhausting, not only Athens, which had played the leading part in the fifth century, but also Sparta, which was left unable to take over the place left vacant by the fall of Athens. After 404 BC Greece was never the same again. Something had vanished for ever, the old confidence and courage, the conviction that no success was beyond the reach of human effort, the trust that the Greeks had something to teach the rest of the world. Thucydides' forecast was fulfilled in a way that he may not himself have anticipated, but he was right to mark the unique importance of the war which he studied with such care. His purpose was not like that of Herodotus. He was not interested in the war simply as a chapter of human affairs; he expected his researches to be useful to future generations:

It will be enough for me if these words of mine are judged useful by those who want to understand clearly the events which happened in the past and which (human nature being what it is) will, at some time or other and in much the same ways, be repeated in the future.[33]

Without mentioning them by name he disclaims the precedents both of Herodotus, because he admitted 'an element of storytelling', and of Hellanicus, who, in attempting to create a chronology, did not make sure of his essential facts. From the start Thucydides limited the scope of his history in three directions. First, he was concerned primarily with a war between two Greek confederacies and confined himself to it. Secondly, he was not interested in facts which he could not himself verify, and he took great trouble not merely to interview eye-witnesses but to get a cross-check on them whenever he could. Thirdly, he saw that chronology was an essential framework and, though it was difficult to fix, he did his best to do so. Working within these rules, he intended his work to be as good as it possibly could, and proudly proclaims that 'it is composed as a possession for ever rather than a prize-performance for the moment'.[34]

This practical purpose and the high intellectual standards which accompany it are the fruit of the scientific and philosophic movements of the fifth century. As a historian Thucydides relies not on ordinary tales or tragedy or epic but on the livelier sciences of his time. He shares their belief that truth is the first aim and that no pains must be spared in finding it, but his notion of them is less capacious than that of Herodotus. Anthropology lay outside his scope and, though he examined the battlefields, his conception of geography was essentially specialized in that it helped to explain certain limited events, and it is possible that he himself was not well acquainted with its methods, since he makes serious mistakes on the size of the island of Sphacteria, where an important action between Spartans and Athenians took place in 425 BC. On the other hand he was deeply influenced by the flourishing sciences of politics and medicine. The first had made a shy, innocent appearance in Herodotus, but in Thucydides it is fully mature and underlies some of his most important judgments. For him politics is enough of a science to allow a general study of recurring phenomena and to enable men to examine them with knowledge and prudence. Yet though Thucydides believes this, and has behind him a substantial body of hard study, he is very careful in his own application of lessons from history. He gives them abundantly to his main figures in their speeches, but these are not always his own views and are not put forward as such. He shows his hand more in what he does not say than in what he does, and in this he reveals his clear-cut convictions and his absence of current superstitions. For instance, Herodotus, and indeed most other Greeks, would put down much to mere luck, and leave it at that. With the notion of luck Thucydides will have nothing to do. For him it is not interference from outside by super-natural forces but simply what cannot be foreseen or foretold. In this he follows the new theories of the scientists, notably Democritus, who says: 'Chance is an idol which men fashioned to excuse their own mental incapacity.'[38] That is why Thucydides avoids any words which suggest doom or fate or nemesis. For him the fortunes of men are determined by natural causes and especially by their own decisions. Though the plague, which did such destruction at Athens, might be regarded as a stroke of bad luck, it was only because it was not to be foreseen. Even though he thought that it is in the nature of things to decline, he did not presuppose some mysterious, supernatural process, but knew that in a world of change this is what happens.

Though Thucydides was deeply stirred by the spirit of scientific enquiry, he was essentially a man of action who expected his enquiries to produce practical results. In his time the most conspicuous science which did this was medicine. Hippocrates of Cos (469–399 BC) was slightly older than Thucydides, and new methods which he and his school instituted influenced the historian more decisively than any other science. From them he learned to treat the body politic as analogous to the human body and to accept the corollary that it is impossible to understand the parts without understanding the whole. In treating disease Hippocrates insisted first on a precise and complete observation of all symptoms, next on a classification of them and comparison with other observed cases, and finally on a diagnosis. Once the diagnosis was established, a tentative cure could be prescribed. This was a truly scientific process, and how fully Thucydides understood it is clear from his account of the plague at Athens, from which he himself suffered. He records all the symptoms, but finds that the plague is unique in modern experience. Hence it was impossible to cure it, or indeed to explain it. But, since he is after all a political writer, what interests him most in the plague are its psychological consequences, the futility of oracles and prayers to abate it, and the consequent refusal to pay attention to either, the despair into which it drove its victims, thereby weakening their resistance, and the contempt for religion and law which it engendered. The methods with which Thucy-

dides examined the plague were equally applicable to a formidable
political phenomenon, the growth of civil strife in Greek cities and its
evil results for all. Though he dissects this in Corcyra, where he could
examine it in detail, his analysis applies to most Greek cities. He groups the
symptoms under a general heading and says that war, which makes it
difficult to supply daily wants, brings men's minds down to the level of
their actual circumstances. A specially acute symptom of this political
disease is the growth of parties and of the qualities which the partisan
spirit creates and encourages. He then analyses what this means:

> To fit in with the change of events, words, too, had to change their usual
> meanings. What used to be described as a thoughtless act of aggression was now
> regarded as the courage one would expect to find in a party member; to think
> of the future and wait was merely another way of saying one was a coward;
> any idea of moderation was just an attempt to disguise one's unmanly character;
> ability to understand a question from all sides meant that one was totally un-
> fitted for action. Fanatical enthusiasm was the mark of a real man, and to plot
> against an enemy behind his back was perfectly legitimate self-defence.[36]

In this searching analysis, as in his account of the plague, Thucydides
describes the symptoms and the results, gives his diagnosis of the cause,
but suggests no cure. Though this is the only occasion in which Thucydides sets out his own views at some length, this careful examination of
facts was fundamental to his whole work and, though he seldom delivers
praise or blame or shows where his own sympathies lie, there is no doubt
that he had deep convictions which he cannot altogether conceal and which
shape the outlook from which he describes events.

Thucydides writes about events from an exclusively political point of
view. No doubt he thought that political history must be treated in this
way, but equally this was the way in which his own mind worked. He
was much narrower than Herodotus, but he was also more searching,
more critical, and more intensely concerned. The quality which he most
admired was intelligence, and those who possessed it in political matters
are singled out for praise. Thus, Themistocles, 'through force of genius
and by rapidity of action, was supreme at doing precisely the right things
at the right moment';[37] Pericles saw the right strategy for defeating the
Spartans, and when this was abandoned by his successors, Athens was
defeated; Hermocrates, who led the Syracusan resistance to Athens, is
described as 'a remarkably intelligent man'.[38] On the other hand Thucydides thinks less well of those men who lacked this kind of intelligence.
Cleon, who was by no means wanting in courage and was responsible for
the final stroke by which the Athenians forced the Spartans on Sphacteria

to surrender, gets harsh treatment, being accused of violence of character and credited with no judgment. Nor can we fail to detect a note of damning irony in the verdict which Thucydides passes on the virtuous and beloved Nicias, who was largely responsible for the failure of the Sicilian expedition and was in the end captured and killed by the Syracusans – 'a man who, of all the Hellenes of my time, least deserved to come to so miserable an end, since the whole of his life had been devoted to the study and the practice of virtue'.³⁹ Intelligence was what Thucydides valued, and he was willing to grant it to Alcibiades, despite his dangerous character and the harm which he did to Athens. Thucydides has been compared with Machiavelli, and the comparison is fair, in so far as both thought that in a politician the first and most important quality was practical wisdom.

With Machiavelli the important consequence follows that 'a statesman is often compelled to act against faith, humanity, and religion', and we inevitably ask how far this is true of Thucydides. He certainly was not unconcerned with morality, nor did he preach any doctrine of 'might is right' in ordinary life. He sees the advantage of honesty and trustworthiness in public affairs, praising them in Pericles and deploring their lack in Cleon. The decline in religious faith which came with the plague and the deterioration of moral standards bred by civil strife both earned his explicit disapproval. Yet, though he genuinely applied high moral standards, he seems to have justified them by claiming that they benefited the state. A man like Pericles was more likely to take right decisions than Cleon; civil strife by causing disorder weakened a state's power to resist enemies. Moreover, when it came to international politics, in the sense of the relations of one Greek state with another, Thucydides applied with ruthless logic his doctrine that the first task of a state is to be powerful even at the expense of moral considerations. In discussing the Sicilian expedition, he says not a word about the iniquity of Athens attacking a city which had not provoked or threatened her, but dwells entirely on the incompetence and indecision with which the actual expedition was conducted. When the Athenians are unable to persuade the inhabitants of Melos to join them, they argue consistently from the point of view of expediency, and when the Melians think that the gods will look after them, the Athenians answer:

Our aims and our actions are perfectly consistent with the beliefs men hold about the gods and with the principles which govern their own conduct. Our opinion of the gods and our knowledge of men lead us to conclude that it is a general and necessary law of nature to rule wherever one can.⁴⁰

We cannot be certain that these are Thucydides' own views, but they are perfectly in accord with his attitude towards the power and policy of Athens.

Yet, though Thucydides relates private morality to public expediency in this ambiguous way, it is not the most important thing in his outlook. He clearly wished Athens to be great, not merely because she was his own city, but because she stood for much that he valued very highly, and which he associated with the personality of Pericles. He sets in the mouth of Pericles three speeches, each of which must owe something to what Pericles actually said but has at the same time been organized by Thucydides to make important points. The first speech concerns the conduct of the war, and on this Thucydides thinks that Pericles was right, and that his critics were wrong. This is of course based on considerations of expediency. The second speech is the famous funeral speech, which Thucydides places in the first winter of the war. This was the time for Pericles to remind the Athenians of what they were fighting for, and the right place for Thucydides to record the speech, since it explains much that took place. It may contain themes that Pericles advanced on other occasions, but we cannot doubt that it represents what he believed and contains his ideal of Athens. It is presented so fully and is itself so rich and powerful that in the structure of the History it has a special place, which Thucydides must have deliberately chosen for it. From it we know what Athens was believed to be by Pericles, and we may conclude that this is very much what it meant also to Thucydides. Though there are certain elements in it which Thucydides in his more cautious moments might not have accepted, it stands out in his work as his interpretation of Athens. It was for such a city that he thought that every effort of intelligence and foresight should be made to extend its power.

This notion of extending power may itself have been derived from natural science. The philosopher and biologist, Anaxagoras, who was patronized by Pericles, advanced a theory of Mind as a primal, efficient cause but also contended that it was continually expanding its control of phenomena, and it is possible that Pericles applied this idea to politics and used it to justify his conception of imperial Athens. But, if he accepted this, Thucydides knew very well what it cost, and in the third speech which he gives to Pericles he sets this out. In this Pericles defends his policy against sharp criticisms from his own people. He insists that they must be ready to face disasters and never sacrifice their glory, and to those who do not agree with him he imputes cowardice. This time he does not praise the great achievements of Athens but admits that the empire is a tyranny which they cannot now surrender. He recognizes that the Athenians are hated because of it, and he drives home his lesson:

All who have taken it upon themselves to rule over others have incurred hatred and unpopularity for a time; but if one has a great aim to pursue, this burden of envy must be accepted, and it is wise to accept it. Hatred does not last for long; but the brilliance of the present is the glory of the future stored up for ever in the memory of men. It is for you to safeguard that future glory, and to do nothing now that is dishonourable.[41]

This perhaps is what Thucydides also thought. Before his death, or indeed before finishing his History, he knew that the Periclean policy had failed, and this he set out to examine. His explanation was that the policy was itself right and that its failure was due to the mistakes and miscalculations of men who did not really understand it. He seems indeed to have idealized Pericles beyond what we might expect from his critical temper. Instead of blaming his general strategy, which certainly asked too much of the Athenian people in expecting them to sit within their walls while the enemy devastated their land, he insisted that it was right; and, though he himself valued some kind of modified democracy, he accepted the Periclean ideal of a sovereign people, if only because 'it was he who led them, rather than they who led him'.[42]

Thucydides' subject, which is a single war, is handled with restraint and severity. He treats it strictly for what it is and avoids even matters which we might think relevant to it, such as party politics in Athens, the personalities of leading characters, intellectual and artistic achievements which are mentioned only once, and the economic history of the time, which is confined to the superior financial resources of Athens. This sense of relevance makes Thucydides much less informative on many matters than Herodotus, but, at the same time, his devouring curiosity about the events of which he writes forces him to go beyond his strict limits, and what he does in this way is revealing about his art. Before he really gets started on his chosen theme he has two long, closely related digressions, the first on the beginnings of Greek civilization, and the second on the history of Greece between the finish of the Persian Wars and the outbreak of the Peloponnesian War. The first is by any standards a most impressive piece of work. Thucydides accepts ancient stories like that of the Siege of Troy but examines them with a critical insight and applies modern methods, including archaeological discovery, to substantiate theories about them. His aim is to prove that Greece has grown from humble beginnings and this is why the Peloponnesian War is greater than any previous war, but he also stresses other matters which still influence the present – the growth of sea-power, the foundation of colonies, the archaic character of Spartan government, the birth of the Athenian Empire and of the Spartan League. Though he deals with these matters at no great length, he abounds in strokes of piercing insight and keeps to a single thread of argument. Not long afterwards he has a second, long digression on Greek history in the fifty years before the outbreak of war. It is in outline a summary of events, but it shows how the war between Athens and Sparta came and confirms his view, stated earlier, that 'what made war inevitable was the growth of Athenian power and the fear which this caused in Sparta'.[43] Later in his work he has other digressions, not indeed so long or so fundamental as these, but his use of this device shows that his vision of history was, despite his self-restraint, large and sweeping and that he saw present events in a vast perspective going back into the legendary past.

To Thucydides' concentration on relating historical facts there is one apparently great exception. His narrative abounds in full-dress speeches delivered, often in debate, by the leading characters and concerned with the main issues at stake. Herodotus of course did much the same thing, but his speeches are clearly his own invention and give both his idea of what his characters were and his own commentary on them. We might suspect that in his own much more modern spirit Thucydides did something of the same kind, but he himself says that this is not so and that he treated speeches in his own way:

I have found it difficult to remember the precise words used in the speeches which I listened to myself and my various informants have experienced the same difficulty; so my method has been, while keeping as closely as possible to the general sense of the words that were actually used, to make the speakers say what, in my opinion, was called for by each situation.[44]

In other words, though the speeches in Thucydides are based on what was actually said, they have been modified and altered by him to make them more illuminating. They are both records of fact, even if not very exact, and a kind of commentary from the inside on what happens. In general they reflect the personalities of the speakers. Before the outbreak of war the old Spartan king Archidamus openly expresses his doubts and misgivings about it. The three speeches of Pericles show his policy from three different angles, but in each we see the air of authority with which he spoke to his Athenian audience and his ability to chide them for their mistakes. The speeches of Cleon reveal his arrogance and violence, and those of Alcibiades his vanity, ambition, and skill in twisting an argument in his own interest. This general temper finds concrete shape in some phrases of such idiosyncrasy that we cannot but assume that these at least are literally reported. Before the war the Corinthians say of the Athenians: 'They are by nature incapable of either living a quiet life themselves or of allowing anyone else to do so',[45] and this must be just what their opponents said of them. We hear the authentic voice of Pericles when he says: 'What I fear is not the enemy's strategy but our own mistakes'[46] or 'Our love of what is beautiful does not lead to extravagance: our love of things of the mind does not make us soft',[47] or 'The whole earth is the sepulchre of famous men.'[48] The gallant Spartan Brasidas exposes Athenian pretences to the people of Acanthus: 'It is more disgraceful . . . to gain one's end by deceit which pretends to be morality than by open violence.'[49] The sophistry and the vanity of Alcibiades are manifest when he is busy betraying his country to the Spartans: 'The country that I am attacking does not seem to be mine any longer; it is rather that I am trying to recover a country that has ceased to be mine.'[50] When he has lost all hope at Syracuse, Nicias makes his last appeal to his men and concludes it by saying: 'It is men who make the city, and not walls or ships with no men inside them.'[51] Phrases of this kind suggest the authentic utterance of the speakers to whom they are attributed, and catch the spirit of some dramatic occasion when words count for a great deal.

Yet, though there is always some genuine element in the speeches of Thucydides, there is equally another element, probably stronger, of adaptation by him. From the mass of speeches available to him he has clearly chosen those which best suit his purpose, and in a few we may suspect his own inventing hand. The dialogue between the Athenians and the Melians before the destruction of the latter can hardly have taken place in this form and smacks too much of a rhetorical exercise on one side and of fierce, individual convictions on the other. Though the speeches are spoken in character and represent personal views, they are so arranged as to give different angles on a single situation. Thus, before the Peloponnesian War breaks out, Corinthian envoys at Sparta denounce the aggressive designs of Athens and call for action against her. They are answered by Athenians, who happen to be at Sparta 'on other business', and warn the Spartans about the dangers of attacking Athens. Then, the Spartan king, Archidamus, calls for prudence and moderation, and finally the ephor Sthenelaidas in a very short speech brushes aside the king's advice and calls for war with Athens. Just as the Athenian speech counters the Corinthian, so the ephor's counters the king's. All that is said is relevant to the occasion and many matters of general principle are introduced. The result is certainly a debate, but a debate more organic and more to the point than it may have been in actual fact. On other occasions, before events take a new turn, Thucydides stages a debate, and it is always used to throw light on the main issues from more than one angle. When Mytilene revolts, Cleon urges the Athenian Assembly to put the Mytilenaeans to death, and wins the day, but the next day Diodotus, on grounds of simple prudence, gets the decision cancelled. In the debate on the Sicilian expedition Nicias opens by pointing out the risks and the difficulties but is answered by Alcibiades, who stresses the enormous advantages to be gained and the means of gaining them. Nicias then speaks again, pointing out the large forces needed, but his hope that this will deter Athens from the expedition is foiled because he gets all that he asks for. In Syracuse the imminence of an Athenian invasion provokes a full discussion. Hermocrates, whom Thucydides admires, points out that the danger really exists and suggests a full programme to meet it. Against him the democratic leader, Athenagoras, throws doubts on the expedition and at the same time claims that Syracuse can defeat it unaided. He ends by an excursion into party politics which is not relevant to the main debate but shows his own disgruntled attitude. The two debates on the Syracusan expedition display contending political parties at work and throw light on the problems involved. In no case are they purely intellectual. Thucydides is well aware of the power of passion in politics and displays it at work in the arguments advanced. His speeches are consciously dramatic in that they precede events of great significance and set in high relief their main controversies.

The language of the speeches is remarkable. Not only is it quite different from the language of the main narrative, but it has surprising idiosyncrasies, which have little in common with the free and easy manner of Herodotus on the one hand and the subtle and musical clarity of Plato on the other. Yet it is at least probable that the style of these speeches was normal in the latter part of the fifth century. It is never easy; it delights in antithesis, in the rigid balance of clauses, in emphasis secured by assonance and even by rhyme; it is notably condensed and at the same time it seems to put even quite familiar matters in a complex shape. If we need an extreme example of this style it is to be found in the fragments of the Sicilian rhetorician Gorgias (*c* 483–*c* 376 BC) who came to Athens in 427 BC and made a powerful impression. But we need not assume that Thucydides imitated him. Gorgias was rather a practitioner of an existing style who took it almost to the point of absurdity by his advanced mannerisms. A simpler but still formidable example of the style can be seen in the lawyer Antiphon (*c* 480–411 BC) who wrote exemplary pieces on how to conduct certain kinds of case, and these have much in common with the speeches of Thucydides, who praises him on the grounds that 'he had a most powerful intellect and was well able to express his thoughts in words'.[52] But behind even Antiphon we can see the dominating manner of Pericles. To those who think that Thucydides imposed his own style on Pericles, we can quote words of his from another source. In 440 BC he delivered a speech on the fallen of the Samian War and in it he compared the dead to the gods: 'For we do not see them in their persons, but from the honours that they receive and the benefits that they give, we infer that they are immortal.'[53] This is in the manner, not only of the Funeral Speech reported by Thucydides, but of many other speeches in his History. We may perhaps conclude that Thucydides wrote his speeches as he did because this was the style of oratory in his time and that he conformed to it as a model to be followed. Despite its difficulty it has certain advantages. Its very complexity gives it an intensity, and its avoidance of standard phrases makes things look more interesting than they are commonly thought. It is an instrument to probe the less obvious movements of the mind, and to this degree it owes something to poetry. At times it is capable of a most moving eloquence and it always keeps the intelligence hard at work to grasp its implications. In using it Thucydides shows his half-concealed passion for his subject and his understanding of the emotions which are always at work in politics and call for powerful words to express them.

On the whole the style of Thucydides' speeches is different from that of his narrative, and the one real exception serves to emphasize the difference. In describing the character of party-strife in Corcyra and formulating the shapes which it took in many parts of Greece he writes very much as if he were composing a speech on a technical question of politics, and this indicates that this was the style which he thought appropriate to abstract analysis and general considerations. In dealing with particular facts he is much more straightforward, but he still lacks the fluent ease of Herodotus, partly because he packs his sentences with a fuller weight of meaning, partly because, even in human actions, he finds occasional paradoxes and surprises. He eschews alike metaphor, perhaps as being too inexact, and asyndeton, perhaps as being too histrionic. He likes the concise phrase, which does its full work in a few words and is well fitted to the technicalities of warfare in which he is entirely at home. On a few occasions something unusual may stir him to emphasize its paradox by an unusual choice of ideas. So the confused amphibious fighting at Pylos appeals to him by its oddity.

The Spartans, in their desperate excitement, were actually fighting a sea-battle on land, and the victorious Athenians, in their anxiety to take the fullest advantage of their successes were fighting an infantry battle from their ships.[54]

This is highly exceptional, and could only have been written by a soldier, who was also a sailor, as most Athenians were and as Thucydides himself had been. Normally he keeps to the plain facts, and only when something has to be summed up in a general conclusion does he allow his rhetorical training to take command. Even so he uses it with great restraint and makes it his instrument to speak of something which has deeply disturbed him and which he sees in its wider implications, as when he sums up the failure of the Syracusan expedition:

This was the greatest Hellenic action that took place during the war, and, in my opinion, the greatest action that we know of in Hellenic history – to the victors the most brilliant of successes, to the vanquished the most calamitous of defeats; for they were utterly and entirely defeated; their sufferings were on an enormous scale; their losses were, as they say, total; army, navy, everything was destroyed, and, out of many, only few returned. So ended the events in Sicily.[55]

Even here he keeps to a statement of fact, but through it we can see a powerful emotion at work, though not a single word is used to evoke pity or horror. Thucydides' intellect is so in control of its material that he does not need to state more than the extent of the disaster, but this he does with a fine piece of dramatic speech, which is his epitaph on the whole expedition.

Thucydides never allows his general considerations of war and politics to interfere with his precise, detailed account of events. Among these battles take first place, and there is no doubt that he had a more than professional interest in the art of war. His accounts of fights on land and sea are always intelligible and even easy to follow, though he can have achieved such results only by a most careful examination of the evidence. He understands the importance of small points and their effect on military actions. When the Thebans get into Plataea by night, the inhabitants, who know the streets and houses better than their enemies do, manage to divide them and corner them. Later, when Plataea is besieged by the Spartans and Boeotians, a party gets out of the town across the wall which the enemy has built round their own, and at one moment a falling tile almost betrays them. When the Spartans are blockaded on the island of Sphacteria, divers try to provision them by swimming under water and trailing bladders filled with poppy-seed, honey, and pounded linseed. In advancing to battle at Mantinea the Spartans march slowly to the music of many flute-players in their ranks, and this enables them to move steadily without breaking their line. The seafights in the harbour of Syracuse are won by the Syracusans because they are more inventive than the Athenians, whether in feigning to retreat and then advancing when the enemy has gone back to base, or by covering their bulwarks with ox-hides so that grappling hides can get no grip on them, or by building a barrier in the harbour which the Athenians cannot break. This love of details gives body to the large-scale accounts of battles. Thucydides knows enough about tactics to see that Cleon lost the battle at Amphipolis by exposing his right flank to the enemy, that once the Athenians had failed to encircle Syracuse they could never win the campaign, that nothing is so contagious as good morale when things are going well or bad morale when they are going badly, that once an army believes that it is defeated it will cease to fight. These lessons he does not underline, but he presents them in forms so clear and convincing that they tell their own tale without comment.

If Thucydides achieves much of his effect by a sheer professional interest, he also does much more. He sees the events of the war as parts of a vast human drama, and he writes of them with a passion which is partly concealed by his objective manner of narrative but forces itself on us as we read what he tells. This is a real concern for all the actors in war, from the men on ships or battlefields to the people of Athens hideously crowded within the walls and shattered by a devastating plague. He conveys alike the thrill of victory and the melancholy of defeat, the zest with which men fling themselves into a fight and the suddenness with which they find that they have won or lost. If his major debates set the psychological background for great events, he gives also shorter speeches delivered by commanders just before action, in which they encourage their men by reminding them of what they are fighting for or of their advantages over the enemy. He understands the intimate relation between war and politics and, though he may have overrated the strategy of Pericles and underrated some of the contributory causes of the war, he still astonishes us in that he, who was so close to the actual events, was able to judge them so impartially and with so keen a sense of their significance. He belonged to the generation which had learned much from the Sophists, professional teachers who talked about all matters physical and political and were sometimes too given to hair-splitting and scepticism, but from them he learned how hard it is to discover the truth, which is for a historian the first and indispensable duty. He established history as a science by his insistence on examining all the available evidence, but he also maintained it as an art which makes the actions of men live again for us and seem as real as they did to those who took part in them.

Thucydides left his History unfinished, and its unique quality is the more clearly evident when we compare it with the continuation written by Xenophon (*c* 430–*c* 354 BC), who carried the story from 411 BC, through the fall of Athens in 404 BC, to the battle of Mantinea in 362 BC. Xenophon was a man of action, who as a young man joined an expedition under a Persian claimant against the Persian king. The claimant was killed, and Xenophon, finding himself in command, conducted a masterly retreat from Persia to the Black Sea. This he recorded in his *Anabasis*, which keeps all the freshness of a personal experience and reveals a simple, friendly, loyal personality. He can depict a scene and make a character live, and he knows military tactics from the inside, especially if they are performed by cavalry. But his qualities were not enough to make a serious historian of him. His *Hellenica*, which carries on the tale of Athens, has indeed some notable moments, as when he speaks of the wailing which passed along the Long Walls from the Peiraeus to Athens, when the news came that the Athenian fleet had been destroyed at Arginusae and every-one saw that Athens was now doomed. He has a sense of a dramatic situation and writes with an agreeable ease, which is occasionally varied by attempts to do something more impressive but usually failing to do so. He must have enjoyed literary composition because in addition to his chief works he composed several tracts and also a *Cyropaedia*, which is an idealized biography of Cyrus the Great and serves many purposes of a manual of education. Xenophon suffers from complacency and senten-tiousness, and draws too many morals which are obvious or not worth drawing. As a serious historian he has few claims. He took little trouble to make sure of his facts, and, though he follows Thucydides in giving speeches to his characters, they perform no very useful function and lack the intellectual intensity of his master. Though Xenophon knew Athens before its fall and must have fought in the Peloponnesian War, he does not seem to take any great pride in it and rather preferred Sparta to Athens. Though too he knew Socrates and recorded conversations with him in his *Memorabilia*, it is hard to believe that the philosopher who so inspired Plato can really have been so platitudinous as this. In Xenophon the Periclean spirit has disappeared, and its place has been taken by a commonplace morality which offers cheap remedies for evils but lacks both imagination and passion. After him there were many historians, whose works survive in fragments, but none of them shows any sign that he could begin to approach the high standards of Thucydides. The fifth

7*

century was the zenith of Greek historiography, and when Athens failed, history failed with it. Stern conviction and passionate curiosity were not easy to find in the impoverished intellectual world of the fourth century, and even the prodigious exploits of Alexander failed to inspire anything that approached the strength of Thucydides. His only worthy successor was Polybius (*c* 203–*c* 120 BC), who applied some of his methods to the history of republican Rome. In Thucydides a strict scientific sense of truth, a deep conviction of the seriousness of the Athenian mission, and a philosophic outlook on history were matched by a mind of most unusual power and penetration and by the artist's passion to present conclusions in a shapely and impressive way.

7

THE ANTIDOTE OF COMEDY

THERE is no doubt about the origin of the word 'comedy'. It comes from the Greek *kômôidia*, which means 'song of a band of revellers', but this does not tell very much, since a *kômos* might appear in almost any convivial or exhilarating conditions and was certainly not confined to comedy even in the broadest sense. What emerges is that comedy was connected with revelling bands and must have kept some of their characteristics even when it became an accepted form of poetry. In Athens it received official recognition in 486 BC and was thenceforward, like tragedy, performed annually in the spring. But before this very little is known of it, and it has no pioneer comparable to Thespis. Yet something of the kind seems to have had a long pre-history in several parts of Greece. In Sparta and in Corinth there existed in the sixth century, as we can see fom pictures on vases, bands of dancers grotesquely dressed, sometimes as animals, and performing wild antics. Since they are often provided with a phallus, they can be recognized as conducting a fertility-rite and encouraging living things to reproduce after their kind. Their virility is emphasized by padded clothing and salacious gestures. Moreover these dances contained a small element of acting and introduced such obviously comic characters as quack doctors, stealers of food, and robbers of orchards. But, though such performances were lively and popular and played a part in social life, there is no evidence that they did anything for the art of words or, even if they contained songs or interchange of speech, that these were of any lasting interest. Something of the same kind certainly existed in the sixth century at Athens and, though it may have arrived by way of Megara, it was fully established as an Athenian custom when the dancers could be dressed as various kinds of men, birds, insects, animals, fishes, riders on horseback, and the like. The elements of dance and impersonation were already present; what was needed was something to bring them into a wider context and add substance to their performance.

At the same time something quite different was happening in Sicily.

Epicharmus of Syracuse (*c* 530–440 BC) wrote short plays which had some kind of plot. Since they had no chorus and presumably no dancing, they were quite different from the *kômoi* of the mainland, and indeed their titles and the remaining fragments suggest that they were lively farces which dealt with various kinds of subjects. In *Odysseus the Deserter* Odysseus, who has been sent as a spy to Troy, has grave misgivings and wonders how he can get out of it. In *The Marriage of Hebe* Poseidon appears as a fishmonger, and in *Busiris* a main topic was the greed of Heracles. So far Epicharmus must have burlesqued old stories and not been afraid to make fun of gods and heroes. But he seems also to have introduced controversial topics and to have made his plays vehicles for arguments. His *Earth and Sea* discussed which of them gave the more blessings to men; his *Hope and Wealth* forecasts later comedies about money; his *Male and Female Reasons* suggests argumentative possibilities, which unfortunately we cannot unravel; his *Persians* may conceivably be a parody of Aeschylus. He seems also to have introduced stock characters like the parasite and the country bumpkin. Epicharmus catered for an intelligent audience and wrote not in a local dialect but in a literary language. He liked both parodies and philosophical discussions and, if he really was the first to compose plays in this way, he is rightly regarded as the father of comedy. He was certainly known in Athens in the fifth century, and we can hardly doubt that when Attic comedy, as we know it, came into existence, it was the combination of two quite disparate elements, the old *kômos* or ribald and comic dance, and the short, literary farce of Epicharmus. The result is a unique art-form, which has no parallels anywhere in the world. Attic comedy is indeed boisterous and outspoken and reckless, but it is also capable of discussions on politics, literature, and philosophy and is, in its own extraordinary way, a criticism of life. By a strange paradox its primitive side owed something to the cult of Dionysus just as tragedy did, but in the result it is as different as possible from tragedy and looks at life from an antithetical point of view.

There was indeed a third kind of dramatic performance which we might expect to have influenced comedy, but it does not seem to have done so. When tragedies were performed, each triad was followed by a Satyric play, in which the Chorus seems always to have been composed of Satyrs under the leadership of Silenus. This surely would provide ample opportunities for boisterous fun and give a complete contrast to the tragedies which had preceded it. Of such plays one survives, the *Cyclops* of Euripides, and some substantial fragments of the *Trackers* of Sophocles. The first deals with Odysseus' adventure with Polyphemus, the second with the theft of Apollo's cattle by the young Hermes, as it is told in the Homeric Hymn to Hermes, and it gets its title from the Satyrs who set out to find the stolen beasts. In both these plays there is a good deal of humour, and there is nothing that approximates to the tragic spirit. But they are much closer to tragedy than to any Greek comedy known to us. They keep the stately language, the formal interchange of speeches, the choral songs. They are not boisterous or rowdy, and they do not touch on living affairs. Whatever the first Satyric plays may have been, the surviving examples suggest that they have been accommodated to the tone of the tragedies which preceded them and, though they do much to lessen the tragic tension and to provide a contrast with it, they are much too decorous to upset the solemnity of the occasion. Yet the presence of Silenus and his Satyrs indicates that in the beginning such plays could have been developed into an exuberant kind of comedy which might have provided a real antithesis to tragedy. We may guess that they were made to follow tragedies because they also had some relation to the cult of Dionysus and the performance of the dithyramb, but their place was settled for them at an early date and they were kept to it. Authentic comedy grew to maturity quite independently of them and appealed to a much richer range of tastes. The original dances from which Greek drama grew must have been of many kinds. If one was the father of authentic tragedy, another, less dignified and specially concerned with Silenus and his Satyrs, ended up in Satyric drama. Comedy itself was born of a more complex ancestry and contained some remarkable characteristics.

The combination of two quite different elements in *kômos* and farce meant that Attic comedy fortified some sort of plot with a Chorus, which might be clothed in a fantastic manner, and indulged an extraordinary freedom of speech hindered by no laws either of libel or of indecency. The main outlines of this form were settled already by Cratinus (*c* 484– *c* 419 BC), who followed Epicharmus in his burlesques of mythological stories, but also dealt with current matters in a bold, outspoken way. His fragments suggest that he had a remarkable vitality, and Aristophanes compared him with a winter torrent which carries all before it. He made fun in various ways of Odysseus and the Cyclops, of the Golden Age, of the arrival of Perseus as a baby on the island of Seriphos, of the birth of Helen from an egg. In contemporary affairs he ridiculed the Sophists, Pericles, and even himself, presented as a drunkard, whom his true wife, Comedy, tries to persuade to abandon his mistress, Drunkenness. This assertion of his own personality was not so much a novelty as a return to the age of Archilochus, whose work Cratinus knew and who provided him with precedents for ridiculing himself. With him the Greeks coupled Eupolis, whose heyday of creation was from 429 to 410 BC. He was a more elegant and more delicate artist than Cratinus, but his chief interests seem to have been political. He looked back with admiration to the generation of Marathon and compared his own contemporaries unfavourably with it. His chief targets were the demagogues who directed Athenian policy. In 422 BC his *Cities* seems to have been a plea for a more generous treatment of the Athenian allies. His *Maricas* is an attack on Hyperbolus, whom Thucydides calls 'a bad man',[1] and his *Generation of Gold* on Cleon. There is no need to assume with him, any more than with Cratinus, that he looked at politics from any fixed angle or belonged to an established party. His task was to evoke laughter, and this he certainly did. Nor was politics his only theme. He also derided contemporary figures, whether war-shirkers in his *Men-women*, whose title explains itself, or his *Friends*, which mocked the cult of a handsome young man called Demos, who was famous for keeping peacocks. In the bursting life of Athens he had much to deride and seems to have done so with confidence and success.

Cratinus and Eupolis are known to us only from fragments, but from Aristophanes (*c* 450–*c* 385 BC) we have eleven complete plays, and to him we may turn with confidence for a full knowledge of Attic comedy. He seems to have done very much what Cratinus and Eupolis did in his choice of subjects, but he reinforced this with his own remarkable genius, a reckless and magnificent fancy, a consummate lyrical gift, and a temper less violent than that of Cratinus and less devastating than that of Eupolis. He outlived the form of the Old Comedy of which he was such a master, but in his hands it took a more or less fixed shape, which at once throws light on its origins and illustrates the Greek talent for giving life to a form which might seem to have few claims except that it was traditional. A character appears with a bold or brilliant idea of putting some large trouble right; a chorus, which needs by no means consist of human beings, comes into conflict with him or is converted to his schemes; much dispute and horse-play follows, which quietens down into a formal debate; the chorus then turns to the audience with addresses combining absurd and serious elements and interspersed with magical hymns to the gods. Behind this must lie the original form of Attic comedy, consisting of a *kômos*, which made a dramatic and voluble entry, incited a struggle or debate, addressed the audience and sang hymns, and ended with a riotous scene such as a marriage or other exuberant celebration. Into this were introduced the old phallic gaieties of the Dorian mime and character-types, who may have started with Epicharmus. Aristophanes picks up all these elements and transforms them into homogeneous works of art by the power of his personality and his poetry. Even at his most earthy and most comic he remains a poet, in his exuberance, his concentration of power, his inimitable fancy. The complex form allowed him many liberties, and he took advantage of them all and, though his plots have seldom a complex coherence, they are undeniably plots, which begin with a striking situation, pass through wonderful adventures, and end in uncontrolled delight. The tone varies with every moment and, though laughter governs the whole design, it is not the only response evoked.

Aristophanes sets out to amuse, not sedately and quietly but hilariously and uproariously. The world of his creation lives by its absurdity and, though it is based on actual life, its great strength is that it defies its rules and its limitations. For him laughter is an end in itself, an absolute, which cannot be countered or defied. To the Greeks, who saw themselves severely limited by human nature and divine control, Aristophanes offered an imaginative escape from such restrictions and displayed in action men of unquestionably human capacities and appetites triumphing impossibly over circumstances. There is no limit to what they can do. In the *Acharnians* (425 BC) the chief character succeeds in making peace with Sparta in defiance of generals and public opinion. In the *Peace* (421 BC) Trygaeus ascends to Olympus on a dung-beetle, in a parody of Bellerophon ascending on Pegasus, but meets with no such untimely end. In the *Birds* (414 BC) two adventurers co-operate with the birds in building a city in the air and not only keep out gods and men but end by taking over dominion from the gods. In the *Lysistrata* (411 BC) the women stop the war by refusing to sleep with their husbands. Such conclusions were just what the Greeks knew that they could not have in actual life, and even in other plays, where the themes are less wildly improbable, there is the same assumption that nothing is beyond the power of the gay adventurer. The comedy of Aristophanes is a defiance of the Mean as Greek morality so diligently inculcated it, and it finds its characters in men and women of an abundant, almost overpowering normality. They have a full share of physical instincts and appetites; they respond to events with immediate, strong reactions; they have no scruples about getting what they want; they have a vitality which never fails and an ingenuity which surmounts every obstacle. The women, no less than the men, are 'cards', who do the most preposterous things with an instinctive confidence. They fit beautifully into their absurd situations, and we cannot but believe that they are responsible for them. Even in their complaints and quarrels they are delighted to be alive. They are not full characters in the modern sense but in their own world they do all that can be asked of them.

The world of wild fantasy in which Aristophanes moves has close relations with the familiar world of Athens in the last quarter of the fifth century BC. Otherwise it would lack flesh and blood, and these it has in abundance. Aristophanes exploits real circumstances, not only to make his characters convincing, but to provide their talk and their plots with material. Their talk is full of topical references of every kind, to politics, philosophy, literature, war, to recent events, to well known personalities with their mannerisms and foibles and absurdities. It is in turns scurrilous, indecent, imaginative, paradoxical, and always crisp, pointed, and full of zest. It conveys the reality of Athenian life even in a world of fantasy. In all this Aristophanes is not a comedian in the sense that he exaggerates the real; he lifts it into another sphere and gives it a greater degree of reality by his uninhibited invention. But, at the same time, he is concerned with issues which concern his audience very closely and towards which he must define his attitude. This he does, usually through his Chorus, which speaks at length on contemporary matters and often outlines a point of view towards them. This is no doubt his own point of view, and to this extent Aristophanes tempers his comedy with serious reflections. It is true that these reflections are richly interspersed with wit and fancy, but their main purport is usually clear enough. But beyond this it is risky to treat Aristophanes as a man with a message, who uses comic fancy to dress up some serious purpose. Often enough he wishes to be comic and nothing else, and even if he has some more serious purpose in reserve, it is not always easy to extract it. He is not a satirist who writes from an established morality or a comedian of manners whose characters stand for various 'humours' or virtues or vices. In dealing with present issues his first weapon and first aim is laughter, and this after all can be directed with equal justice against what he likes and what he dislikes, and he may not expect us to distinguish between them. It is wrong to assume that Aristophanes uses his art to tilt against persons and causes of which he disapproves. He certainly does so, but it is by no means all that he does.

Aristophanes' most creative years coincided with the Peloponnesian war and, though it did not provide him with all his themes, it was never far from his mind and at times occupied it with nagging insistence. We do not know that he fought on either land or sea, but he knew the war from first-hand because in the first years Attica was annually invaded by the Spartans and Athens itself, crowded with refugees far beyond its ability to contain them, was for parts of the year a beleaguered city.

Aristophanes writes about war from the inside, and of course he disliked it, marked its privations and its absurdities, and made riotous fun of its advocates. The *Acharnians* (425 BC) is a play of unflagging brilliance, which mocks the behaviour of many characters, both public and private. The hero, Dicaeopolis, who may have been played by Aristophanes himself, makes a private peace with Sparta, and, having done so, has first to convince his own villagers that he is right, and then to rout the fire-breathing general Lamachus. He is then free to start trading with the enemy, first with a starving Megarian who offers his two small children as sucking-pigs, then with a Boeotian, who offers vast quantities of food and is paid, in the absence of cash, with an Informer, who is stuffed into a bag. The play ends with a riotous feast, the triumph of Dicaeopolis, and a general scene of wild conviviality. The greater part of the play is concerned with the war, with such absurdities as a Persian envoy who is more eager to receive than to give bribes, with Thracians who offer highly improbable help, with generals who look magnificently ferocious but are humiliated by ridiculous accidents, with plain country people who are torn by the issues of the war. Aristophanes has been thought to have written the *Acharnians* as a pacifist tract, and to have been lucky not to have been punished for it. It is certainly true that he makes great fun of the more bellicose patriots, of the causes of the war as presented by Pericles, of the graft and corruption and fat jobs which it bred. But these are just the jokes which men make who really know about war, and in 425 BC all Athenians did, and even if Aristophanes instils a stiff dose of 'common-sense about the war', he would find many to agree with him who would not in the least wish to capitulate to Sparta or shirk their duty to Athens. In the same way anyone involved in war thinks often and eagerly how agreeable it will be when peace comes and how he will enjoy himself. Aristophanes appeals to this feeling and has every right to do so. There is no reason to think that he was regarded as a dangerous pacifist. He was not a pacifist at all, but an ordinary man who released all the complaints and fancies which soldiers on active service indulge. His triumph is that he makes them all hilariously funny, and for that reason alone he must not be treated as a solemn advocate of peace at all costs. His strength is that in the middle of war he can treat it with these high spirits, and the strength of the Athenians was that they could share his feelings and enjoy what he said and yet continue to fight with the same persistence as before.

The *Knights* (424 BC) is less fanciful than the *Acharnians* and reveals a new facet of Aristophanes' genius when he takes prominent men of his time and makes them figures of comedy. He makes their impact more forcible by reducing the plot to fewer and simpler elements and giving to his characters a richer elaboration. He presents two generals, Demosthenes and Nicias, and makes them the slaves of an old man, Demos, who stands for the Athenian people, and the victims of the prominent demogogue Cleon, disliked by Thucydides for his violence. The two generals and Cleon are firmly characterized. Demosthenes is impulsive, pleasure-loving, and not shy of the bottle; Nicias is timid, respectable and careful; Cleon is a loud, boisterous, and offensive bully. No doubt all three are caricatured, but no caricature is worth anything unless it resembles its original in essential points. The *Knights*, even more than the *Acharnians*, shows how far an Athenian comedian was allowed to go in dealing with contemporary personalities. The plot turns on the discomfiture of Cleon by a man who excels him at all his own faults. This Offal-Monger takes Cleon's place in the regard of Demos, but when he is installed becomes a reformed character and promises to clean up Athens. The conclusion of course is a flight of wishful thinking, and adds much to the fun, but it must not be taken as referring to any individual who has won Aristophanes' trust. The *Knights* is, despite its fancy, closer to reality than the *Acharnians*, but it remains a pure comedy because the fun is concentrated on individuals. Both Demosthenes and Nicias are ridiculous, and so is Cleon in a more odious way, but he comes to a comic end, when he is outclassed and humiliated by the Offal-Seller. In dealing with him, Aristophanes allows himself a nice degree of savagery, but that is in accord with Cleon's character and would be accepted as such. Once again the driving power is the absurdity of the situations in which real figures are placed. There is no likelihood that Cleon saw the joke himself or that Nicias and Demosthenes were at all pleased, but the Athenian audience liked the play and saw it for what it was – a vivid mockery of powerful public men and their ways.

In 421 BC Nicias negotiated a peace with Sparta. It was indeed precarious, and did not in fact last long, but just before it was concluded Aristophanes appropriately celebrated it in his *Peace*. Cleon was dead at Amphipolis, and receives only a passing mention, and the plot has again taken a new direction. The hero, Trygaeus, is of the earth earthy, but in his way wise, enterprising, and inventive. He flies to Olympus on a dung-beetle, but when he gets there finds that there is a food-shortage as on earth and that the gods have left and handed things over to War. He has buried the maiden Peace in a deep pit, and is about to pound the cities of Greece in a mortar. Fortunately he has broken his pestle and gone out to get a new one. Trygaeus promptly summons all the Greeks to drag

Peace out of her pit, and, when she emerges there follows a scene of revelry and song and Trygaeus is married to her. The *Peace* is the first extant play of Aristophanes which treats gods with the same levity as men, and uses myth to enhance the absurdity. The war is present everywhere, and those who profit from it make brief, laughable appearances, in the forms of an armament-seller, a general, a slave who plans to run away. But the strength of the play is the way in which Aristophanes is able to make vivid, individual poetry out of abstractions and large units such as cities. In pulling Peace out of her hole the Argives are found not to be doing their share – they are too busy selling food to both sides, while the Megarians are too starved to be of any use, and the Athenians are so busy with litigation with each other that they do not really exert themselves. When Peace at last appears, the various cities, wounded and bandaged and disfigured by black eyes, dance around her and laugh for joy. When he wrote the play, Aristophanes knew that peace was near, and into the hope of it he throws a delighted poetry of the good life, but he keeps a wary eye open for opponents and hints at one moment that Cleon, 'the infernal Cerberus', may rise from the dead. The actual peace was signed a few days after the first performance of the play, and Aristophanes could feel for a moment that all was well. He has raised the issues of peace and war beyond local phenomena to a cosmic level, which is none the less comic because it involves gods and peoples, each of whom behaves according to its kind.

In treating the war in these very diverse ways Aristophanes by no means exhausted his creative ingenuity. At the same period he assailed other themes, which might have some relation to politics but were primarily concerned with a different issue – the differences between the older and the younger generation. This is of course a perennial theme for comedy, and usually it is the younger generation which is put in the wrong. Of this we cannot quite acquit Aristophanes, but he sets about his subject with his usual independence. The *Clouds* (423 BC) is concerned with the different attitudes of the father, Strepsiades, and his son, Pheidippides, to what may be called the 'new thought'. Strepsiades is the usual 'card', who stands for no nonsense, while his son is the victim of fashion and takes to new ideas, which are embodied in no less a person than Socrates. For us Socrates has been so sanctified by Plato that we can scarcely believe that Aristophanes presented him as he did, and when Plato, in his *Symposium*, shows Aristophanes and Socrates as being on excellent terms, he clearly wishes it to be thought that they really were. In the *Clouds* Aristophanes gets a lot of fun out of Socrates, to whom he attributes all the absurdities, and more, of the Sophists, but the nub of the play is much simpler than this. Strepsiades is in debt and wants to be taught how to make the worse appear the better reason and so defeat his creditors. This is why he goes to study with Socrates, but he is so inept that he is turned out. He sends his son, Pheidippides, in his place, who goes very unwillingly, but is completely converted to his teacher and shows his new knowledge by beating his father. This is sheer knockabout fun, but the treatment of Socrates is more subtle. He certainly has much in common with his historical self. He and his disciples live in austere poverty, study physics, as Socrates once did, enquire how many of its own feet a flea can jump, how a gnat makes its noise, what causes rain and thunder. These are of course travesties but they are based on solid enough fact. Socrates is made to ascribe spiritual objects to a thin layer of air, and certainly does not respect the usual gods. His mannerism of looking sideways under his brows is marked, as are his habit of walking barefoot, his objection to music at meals, and his theory that the production of thoughts is to be compared with midwifery. This is legitimate fun, and does not fail to amuse. Nor is Socrates accused of anything worse than being dirty. Yet the play is weighted against him in two obvious ways. First, there is an ingenious debate between the Just Cause and the Unjust Cause, of which the latter speaks for Socrates and his works, and the Just triumphs over him. In the debate there is much drollery, but also a strain of seriousness which cannot be quite dismissed. Worse than this, the play ends with the destruction of Socrates' 'Thinking-shop', and cries of triumph over his discomfiture. This is of course a legitimate end to a boisterous comedy, but it is hard on Socrates. It is possible that both these passages come from a later, revised edition of the play, and were put in to catch a public which had begun to distrust him, but even then Aristophanes must have agreed with them. The *Clouds* is not a defence of the older generation, since Strepsiades is a twister and a cheat, nor an attack on the younger generation, but it is certainly an attack on the growth of new beliefs and a new scepticism in Athens. Perhaps this is not to be held against Aristophanes. The war called for great efforts and the spirit which questioned every assumption was full of danger, especially if it was not combined with Socrates' own kind of private religion, of which Aristophanes says and may have known nothing.

In the year after the *Clouds* Aristophanes produced the *Wasps* (422 BC), which also deals with the contrast between two generations. The father, Bdelycleon, is an addict of the law-courts, and likes not only the fees which he receives for being a juror but the sense of power which he gets from taking part in trials; his son is totally opposed to him and keeps him from attending them. Feeling that he must do something to keep the old man busy he stages the trial of a dog, which is accused of stealing some Sicilian cheese. The trial follows the right pattern, and though the dog cannot speak, his accuser can, and Philocleon acts like a bullying judge clamouring for a verdict of 'Guilty', only to find that he has been tricked into acquitting the prisoner. He then tries to follow his son's advice and reform his ways but, after going to a smart party, comes back highly exhilarated with a girl whom he wishes to make his mistress. And so the play ends. Here the main field of comedy is the conduct of the law-courts, in which Aristophanes saw much that was highly laughable but, though there is a difference between father and son, Aristophanes does not take sides between them. He is amused by their different attitudes, just as in depicting the father's old friends as Wasps he is amused by their inconsistencies, their mixture of cunning and old-fashioned simplicity. He sees the poetry of this rustic life and treats it handsomely, but that does not mean that he is unreservedly in its favour. The Athenians are litigious because they like money, and, though this is part of their simplicity, he does not pretend that it is admirable. The clash between two generations is equally balanced and what emerges is the comic element in both, but its main function in the play is to make fun of the Athenian passion for litigation and its remarkable effect on the simple countrymen who are engaged in it.

In the spring of 414 BC Aristophanes produced the *Birds* and once again struck in a new direction. Though it may have some slight resemblance to the *Peace* with its adventures on Olympus, the *Birds* sets all its action in the air and maintains its brilliant fantasy throughout. Though it was contemporary with the great expedition to Sicily, it does not mention it, nor need we assume that Aristophanes has it in mind. It is certainly not a consolation for failure, for the expedition had not yet failed; nor need we assume that it reflects the vaulting hopes which inspired and accompanied the sailing of the huge armada. It certainly indulges hopes, but not of an imperial or military kind. It looks rather as if Aristophanes sought to create a work of art which moved of its own right in its own world, and in which even satire is given a subordinate place. The plot of the *Birds* reveals its primary intention, which is to amaze and to amuse. Two enterprising characters, Euelpides and Pisthetaerus, seek a place where they can live more or less in peace, and find it by uniting with the birds to build it in the sky, safe alike from gods and men. But of course both try to enter into it. A rich assortment of dubious human characters try to sell their wares or their talents, and the gods are furious because they are cut off from the sacrifices offered to them on earth. But the two pioneers triumph and bring even Olympus into their dominion. The *Birds* is a flight of fancy, and nothing else. Even when the Chorus talks about human affairs, it draws attention to minor, comic ailments and suggests no policy or bias. The gay vitality of the *Birds* carries it through a series of brief, brilliant situations, each of which is as absurd as the rest, and derives its absurdity from familiar human foibles. If Aristophanes introduces the famous mathematician Meton and the poet Cinesias as well as such low characters as an oracle-monger, a son who attacks his father, and an informer, he is perfectly entitled to treat them all in the same spirit and extract his fun from each. The *Birds* is an imaginary world, free from many human limitations and to be enjoyed because it is free from them. The comic hero has found his full scope and enjoys himself to the utmost in defiance of men and gods.

Though the Athenian expedition to Sicily ended in total disaster, Athens held on for another nine years and not till the very end was it clear that she was beaten. Chances of a good peace were indeed fragile, but a grim determination held her to her task. In this period Aristophanes lost none of his brilliant ebullience, but turned his gifts to new and surprising inventions. In 411 BC he produced the *Lysistrata*. The plot turns on the women of Athens and Sparta refusing to sleep with their husbands until peace is made. They come to this decision with comic reluctance, but, once they have come to it, they are obdurate, and it works. The husbands are in such a state of desire for their wives, who have maliciously and provocatively put on their best clothes and adorned themselves to the utmost, that they cannot go without them and agree to make peace, and the play ends with two choruses, one of Athenian, the other of Spartan women, singing songs of delight and merriment. The play is constructed with considerable care and has a real development, and each scene provides its own hilarious pleasure. Such a subject can be treated only with complete frankness, and of this Aristophanes takes full advantage. The reluctance of his women and the physical agonies of his men are depicted with abundant realism, and the relief of both sides when at last agreement is reached is sheer joy. The *Lysistrata* is one of Aristophanes' boldest flights of fancy, but all its action takes place in a familiar world, and it has the strength that belongs to it. His first aim is to amuse, and this he does throughout, but we feel more in the *Lysistrata* than in the early plays about the war that Aristophanes is really eager to end it. His chief character is a woman, and her predominance gives the lie to any views that the

Athenians kept their women locked up at home. Lysistrata conducts the proceedings with skill and eloquence and keeps her more fragile sisters in control but, though we admire her brilliant resource, we cannot fail to be touched by the way in which she speaks of the deprivations of women in war, especially in their separation from their husbands, whom they see only at rare intervals. Aristophanes makes this point with poignancy and pathos, and he means it to be taken seriously. The war strikes at the roots of family life and affection and security. When he makes Lysistrata say that the women would manage things better than men, he does not mean it to be taken literally, but he stresses the harm done by war to what matters most for human beings. Lysistrata is also concerned with the corruption and intrigue bred by war and calls for them to be purified, and among these she classes the harsh treatment of her allies by Athens, which could easily be brought together into an equal and just union. Aristophanes certainly has much to say about the war, and this provides the background of his fantasy, but the fantasy is not damaged or diminished by it. The imaginary situation into which it takes us is all the stronger because of its consciousness of unpleasant facts and its real desire to get rid of them.

The *Lysistrata* is Aristophanes' last full excursion into politics, and for the rest of the war he contented himself with matters less painfully immediate. They may indeed be called plays of escape, but they do not show any abatement in his vigorous interest in all contemporary matters, nor are they an attempt to shirk serious issues. Aristophanes was a poet passionately interested in poetry, and in the last, dark years of the war he turned the minds of his audience to it as a consolation but in no sense as an anodyne. In the same year as the *Lysistrata* he produced the *Thesmophoriazusae*, which is concerned primarily with poetry and incidentally shows how well educated an Athenian audience must have been to take all its allusions. The play turns on the personality and the poetry of Euripides and is both a keen criticism and a farce which makes full use of them. The criticism comes through the farce, since Aristophanes, not only misuses or parodies many lines of Euripides, but makes him appear on the stage to rescue his friend, Mnesilochus, who is being mauled by the women at their special feast, arrive in the role of Perseus rescuing Andromeda, and contrive a getaway by the use of arguments from the *Helen* between Helen and Menelaus. All ends happily, when Euripides escapes with Mnesilochus from the women who wish to punish him for giving them a bad name. Euripides is treated throughout as a figure of fun. His language, his interest in philosophic speculation, his plots, his personal remoteness are all turned to ingenious uses, and the basis of the plot is that women hate him. Here, as in the *Lysistrata*, Aristophanes gives women a prominent place, but for quite different reasons. They provide a stick with which to beat Euripides, and that is good enough. Aristophanes is no champion of women's rights, but women help him here with his unusual plot. His attitude towards Euripides is in some ways ambiguous. For the man he seems to have little liking, and that is perhaps understandable, for Euripides was thought to be a crank and a recluse, and Aristophanes was neither. Moreover, though the Athenians were fascinated by Euripides' poetry, they may by this time have liked him less for his opinions. Soon after this he retired to Macedonia, where he died, and this was surely because he felt himself no longer at home in Athens. The poetry is a different matter. Though Aristophanes makes every kind of fun of it, he knows it incredibly well, and this is at least a kind of admiration. He stresses its more sensational sides – its fallen women, its criminals, its neglect of the gods, its vague metaphysics, its touches of science, but these were novelties which called for attention and were legitimate objects of jest. Aristophanes seems to be both fascinated and shocked by them. In his enormous knowledge of Greek poetry he seems to have felt that Euripides was not quite right, but he could not get him out of his system and plainly enjoyed him hugely. Moreover Euripides provided him with just the right means to create a new world of fantasy. By transferring to actual Athens the devices of Euripidean drama he could achieve a series of unprecedented effects and at the same time make them move at that level between reality and nonsense which parody provides.

A year before Athens surrendered to Sparta, Aristophanes produced his last play in his grand manner. The *Frogs* (405 BC) followed in some respects the precedent of the *Thesmophoriazusae* and dealt mainly with literary topics, and especially with Euripides. Even more than in the earlier play we feel that Aristophanes is trying to cheer his countrymen in a dark time with his most brilliant and enlivening art. But, whereas the *Thesmophoriazusae* mocks Euripides for his plots and his thought, the *Frogs* is concerned with the worth of his poetry. The plot is that Dionysus, the god of the festivals at which comedies and tragedies were performed, goes down to Hades to fetch Euripides, who has just died, back to earth. Athens is short of poets, and Dionysus is convinced that Euripides is his man. The god is himself a comic figure with a comic slave, and tries to make himself impressive in the underworld by dressing himself as Heracles with lion-skin and club. He has little dignity but great resilience and is alike the author and the victim of much knockabout fun. After an adventurous journey under the earth, in which he and his slave are accompanied by Initiates of the Eleusinian mysteries on their way to the afterlife, Dionysus finds a literary crisis in full blast. Euripides has displaced Aeschylus as the enthroned poet of Hades, and there is much dispute about it. This provides the main action of the play. Dionysus is called upon to judge between the two poets, and the struggle, which is the centre of the comedy, is the competition between Aeschylus and Euripides for the throne of poetry. It falls into four stages. In the first the two poets attack one another's subjects, and Dionysus scores off both by his apt comments. In the second their actual lines are set against each other, and, while Euripides accuses Aeschylus of being tautological, Aeschylus accuses Euripides for the flatness of his prologues. In the third their lyrical art is compared, and in the forth selected lines from each are weighed in a scale, and those from Aeschylus always win. In the end Pluto, the god of the dead, confirms Dionysus' judgment that Aeschylus has won, and sends him back to earth. The contest is extraordinarily varied and perceptive. Joke after joke makes an excellent point, and parody and apt quotation on both sides build up perceptive pictures of two different kinds of poetry. Behind the dazzling exterior Aristophanes shows himself to be an excellent critic and, though he couches his criticisms in absurd forms and aims mainly at the faults of the two poets, his shafts go home. In the end Euripides is certainly humiliated and resents it, but that after all is how many comedies end, and we must not take it too seriously. When Aristophanes sends Aeschylus back to earth, it is because he thinks that it is his spirit, more than that of Euripides, which Athens needs in her vast calamities.

With the *Frogs* the great period of Aristophanes' achievement comes to an end, and we can pause to look at some of its more striking qualities. The comic invention is limitless and covers every kind of absurdity, but it is at intervals varied and exalted by outbursts of the purest song. Aristophanes does not often indulge his lyrical gift, but when he does it is in the great Greek tradition and has an effortless ease and melody which are all his own. He much admired Phrynichus, who was an elder contemporary of Aeschylus, and may have learned something from him but the fragments of Phrynichus are too scanty to afford any comparison. Aristophanes puts his finest songs in the *Clouds*, the *Birds*, and the *Frogs*, no doubt because these plays belong to an order of fancy where the lyrical spirit can move at ease. Through it he gives quite a new direction to his themes. The Clouds, who form a Chorus, are chosen because they suit Socrates' new ideas about the Air and what it really means, but, though Aristophanes makes full use of this, he presents them also from another angle in a charming song:

> Clouds, ever drifting in air,
> Rise, O dewy anatomies, shine to the world in splendour.
> Upward from thundering Ocean who fathered us
> rise, make way to the forested pinnacles.
> There let us gaze upon
> summits aerial opening under us;
> Earth, most holy, and fruits of our watering;
> rivers, melodious, rich in divinity;
> sea, deep-throated, of echo reverberant.
> Rise, for his Eye, many-splendoured, unwearying
> burns in the front of Heaven.
> Shake as a cloak from our heavenly essences
> vapour and rain, and at Earth in our purity
> with far-seeing eye let us wonder.[2]

Here is the authentic genius of song, the rapturous surrender to a moment of enchanting joy, and the free movement of the spirit in its own world. In the *Birds*, where the birds themselves are all fierceness and foibles, and join the human adventurers only after a sharp tussle, Aristophanes shows a remarkable and intimate knowledge of ornithology, but also creates an airy poetry suited to these creatures of the air. When the Hoopoe summons the other birds to join him, he first speaks in bird-notes and then bursts into his detailed call:

> Marshy dyke
> leave you now
> all who snap
> piercing gnats.
> Water-fowl,
> leave the moist
> meadow-lands;
> seek no more
> heart's delight
> deep in green
> Marathon.
> Hither come all,
> hither come *you*
> speckled and splashed
> francolin,
> francolin.[3]

In the *Frogs* Aristophanes, not only gives the frogs themselves their own songs of marsh and mere, but makes the Initiates on their way to Hades sing a Hymn which tells of all that they hope for beyond in the grave, where the sun shines on roses and sprits dance out the hours. Though Aristophanes uses song most in these three plays, it belongs to his poetical endowment and casts sudden lights on even his most boisterous passages. It adds a special dimension to his plays and accentuates the high imagination which goes to their making.

Aristophanes was also a master of parody. He applies it to all kinds of styles, including oracles, laws, physics, philosophy and public speeches. Some kinds of pomposity may be legitimately punctured by imitation, and Aristophanes has a great gift for it. So in the *Knights* he fashions an oracle to foretell the fall of Cleon, the Paphlagonian, before the Offal-Seller, and it is in the true Delphic tradition of obscurity and bombast:

> Nay, but if once the Eagle, the black-tanned mandible-curver,
> Seize with his beak the Serpent, the dullard, the drinker of life-blood,
> Then shall the sharp sour brine of the Paphlagon-tribe be extinguished,
> Then to the entrail-sellers shall God great glory and honour
> Render, unless they elect to continue the sale of the sausage.[4]

This is of course no more than fun, but parody, aptly and ingeniously applied, can be an authentic form of literary criticism, and this is the use which Aristophanes makes of it in dealing with Aeschylus and Euripides. Though he makes Aeschylus win the contest, he is quite as sharp with him as with Euripides. If he demonstrates how the cleverness of Euripides falls into silliness, he no less demonstrates how the majesty of Aeschylus falls into bombast. His parodies are not merely imitations with a comic purpose; they are based on a clear estimate of the different gifts of the two poets and of the lapses into which each was likely to fall. He could not have done them half so well if he had not been intimately acquainted with their work and in his own way loved it, even for its faults. He was himself so consummate a craftsman in poetry, so at home with its elaborate techniques that even in parody he displays many touches of authentic art.

The fall of Athens in 404 BC brought an end to Old Comedy. Nobody was rich enough to supply the Choruses with the rich dresses which made them so attractive, and, more seriously, the old high independence of spirit, the willingness to hear anything, however outrageous, and the ability to say it, consorted ill with the depressed spirit of Athens. Aristophanes survived for nearly twenty years, and, though we know nothing of his personal fortunes in this time, two plays survive from it, the *Ecclesiazusae*, which means 'Women in Parliament', and the *Plutus*, or *Wealth*. Circumstances forced him to adapt himself to impoverished conditions, and in both plays the Chorus on the old model is missing, with all that it meant in action and song. The *Ecclesiazusae* (391 BC) is based on philosophic ideas of communal ownership of property and wives, such as Plato was to advocate in his *Republic*. From early versions of this, known from talk or from some other philosopher, such as Antisthenes, Aristophanes picked up an idea with great comic potentialities. But, though he has good moments, and in his chief character, Praxagora, creates a successor to Lysistrata in enterprise and ingenuity, the play lacks his old vitality. The plot turns on the establishment of communism by the women and has many possibilities, but the jokes are a little forced and the old gay bawdry has become calculated and cold-blooded, even at times depressing. The *Plutus*, produced in 388 BC, is a new kind of comedy altogether and points forward to what was to come. It has very little fantasy and absurdity, few topical allusions, and no songs. Its theme is that Wealth is blind and helps the wrong people, and in a nice way its chief character, Chremylus, sets out to put this right. Sight is restored to Wealth, and then a series of agreeable results follows. An Honest Man becomes prosperous; a bankrupt Informer is denounced but puts up a good defence for his trade; an Old Woman, who keeps a young lover, is ruined, but manages to keep him all the same; Hermes finds himself almost out of a job and has to be content to be the god of games. Nobody frequents the temples now that money is justly distributed, and the priest of Zeus leaves his master's service, to find that Zeus himself has already departed. The play ends in a great procession and all seems well. The *Plutus* has many good points, some clearly defined characters and some admirable comments on life. But here too something has gone—the enormous zest, the creative drive, the infusion of irresistible song. The play illustrates what has happened to Athens after its collapse, and even hints at what has happened to Aristophanes. It harps on the theme of poverty, and we can hardly doubt that this was appropriate to a hardstricken time, but, more than this, it indicates a decline of confidence, of imaginative vigour, which we can attribute to the collapse of a society which has believed almost too greatly in itself and was able up to its last agonies to temper this belief with laughter.

In the *Plutus* Aristophanes marked out the lines on which comedy was to develop. The New Comedy, of which it is a forerunner, is quite a different art from the Old. Political and literary criticism are out; the observation of manners and types is in. The main interest belongs to a more or less realistic presentation of human situations, which have a humorous but seldom uproarious side. Of this the great master was Menander (342–291 BC), from whose works survive a large number of fragments and one complete play, *The Curmudgeon*. Menander probably owed more to Euripides than to Aristophanes, but avoided mythological subjects in favour of contemporary themes. In general his theme is love, but he manipulated this with endless variety, putting many obstacles in the way of lovers' union and ending sometimes with two or three marriages. He is not a mere creator of types. His miser, swaggering soldier, and slave have other human and engaging characteristics. Menander writes smoothly and easily, more in the manner of Euripides than of Aristophanes and makes the words suit the personalities of those who speak them. He uses comic irony and farcical humour but hardly any verbal display. He much enjoys pithy remarks, and many of them were much quoted in later antiquity, even by St Paul, when he says: 'Evil communications corrupt good manners.'[5] *The Curmudgeon*, which was recently discovered more or less intact, is, it must be admitted, disappointing. It is an early play, and this may account for its short supply in that kind of humanity for which Menander was respected. But it had, like other plays of Menander, an enormous progeny. Adapted into Latin by Plautus and Terence, and taken over from them by masters like Ben Jonson and Molière, the comedy of manners has long been established in our own world. It reflects a civilized, not very adventurous and not very speculative society, curious about its members and fond of improbable situations which illuminate the paradoxes of human character. From it our own idea of comedy is derived, but the boisterous spirits of Aristophanes have no place in its sentimental attractions.

8

THE DRAMA OF PHILOSOPHY

In the fifth century Athens, surprisingly, did not produce any very distinguished scientists. The best of them was Archelaus (fl. 441 BC), who was concerned with the physical importance of air and was reputed to have taught Socrates. But to make up for its lack of indigenous thinkers Athens attracted distinguished men from other places, and among them were Protagoras of Abdera (c 500–c 432 BC), Anaxagoras of Clazomenae (c 500–c 428 BC), and Gorgias of Leontini (c 483–c 376 BC). Though Anaxagoras was interested in biology and made experiments in it, the tendency was to forsake natural science for more strictly philosophical subjects, notably the theory of knowledge and the study of ethics. In both of these pursuits new methods of strict argument were employed and great efforts were made to find first principles by coherent thinking, but in the absence of accepted basic assumptions a searching scepticism was the result. Protagoras said: 'Man is the measure of all things, of things that are that they are, and of things that are not that they are not,'[1] and this must mean that things are to me as they appear to me, and to you as they appear to you. All knowledge is thus reduced to subjectivity and even to solipsism. Gorgias, who was a less serious thinker and may be suspected of talking for effect, went even further and sought to prove three propositions:

1 That there is nothing,
2 that, even if there is anything, we cannot know it, and
3 that even if we could know it, we could not communicate our knowledge to anyone else.[2]

This scepticism was a natural consequence of the view of Heraclitus that all things are in a state of flux and that nothing really *is*. It discredited both mathematics and any kind of positive philosophy, and its results extended into ethics and led to the theory that what was called right was really might and that what was called justice was really the 'interest of the stronger'. This was the view of Thrasymachus of Chalcedon (fl. 430–400 BC) and may be seen at work in the arguments given by Thucydides to the Athenians in their debate with the Melians. It could claim ample precedents in the actions of the gods and was naturally popular during the Peloponnesian War when the struggle for power and even for existence was present to every combatant. This scepticism covered religious beliefs, and Protagoras said:

> With regard to the gods, I cannot feel sure either that they are or that they are not, nor what they are like in shape; for there are many things that hinder sure knowledge, the obscurity of the subject and the shortness of human life.[3]

These destructive tendencies were partly enhanced and partly countered by the remarkable figure of Socrates (469–399 BC). We hear of him from Aristophanes in the *Clouds*, from the fragments of his pupil Aeschines of Sphettus, from Xenophon in his *Memorabilia* and other works, and on an enormous scale from Plato (428/7–347 BC). Though on the surface these accounts differ on many points, a consistent notion of Socrates can be found if we assume first that Xenophon was not much interested in philosophy and therefore records the least important parts of Socrates' conversation, and even then with no real accuracy, and secondly that Aristophanes exaggerates, as a comedian must, but does not really falsify. What then emerges fits in with the fragments of Aeschines and the main lines of Plato's extensive portrait. Socrates wrote nothing, and his doctrines were delivered in talk. In some respects he resembled other philosophers of the time. If he began with an interest in physics and is displayed as such in the *Clouds*, he lost it and pursued knowledge by looking into first principles and trying to find out what people meant in asserting their convictions, and this took him to ask what is meant by knowledge and by virtue. This apparently sceptical and endless pursuit, which he applied to all and sundry, was matched by a religious temperament of an unusual kind. Socrates had at times what may be called mystical experiences. During the campaign of Potidaea in 430 BC, when he was not quite forty years old, he stood without moving from one morning to the next dawn and then said a prayer and went about his business. He had, even as a boy, a 'divine sign', which manifested itself quite unexpectedly, always in a negative sense, telling him not to do something. He seems to have believed in popular notions of rewards and punishments after death and in reminiscence from a previous existence, and to have thought that the soul cannot attain perfect purity until it is released from the body.

This personal religion was closely connected with a strong social conscience. Socrates had a great respect for the laws and refused to act against them. In 406 BC, when it was proposed illegally to try together all the generals who had failed to recover the dead after the naval battle of Arginusae, he refused to put the matter to the meeting, and in 403 BC when, during the brutal rule of the Thirty tyrants imposed by Sparta, he was sent to arrest Leon of Salamis that he might be put to death, he did nothing about it but quietly went home. Yet in 399 B C he was prosecuted on the ground that he did not believe in the gods worshipped by the state but introduced other new divinities and that he corrupted the young by teaching them accordingly. After a trial in which he did little to appease or conciliate his prosecutors, he was condemned to death, and even then he might have got off with a lighter sentence if he had not treated the whole matter with a provocative irony. Hemlock was administered to him, and he died in the presence of his friends. The execution of Socrates has often been regarded as one of the most odious crimes in history and taken to illustrate the decay into which the Athenians fell after their defeat by Sparta. Yet, despite the intolerance which it presupposes, the actual charge may have had something in it. Socrates had once believed in strange gods, and the memory of this was still strong in the *Clouds*, where he worships Air. Nor is it at all clear that he accepted the official gods of Athens with any conviction. He had, moreover, a powerful influence on rich and handsome young aristocrats who, no doubt, exaggerated his views and made too great a show of their destructive side. But behind the actual charge, which was not entirely implausible, we may discern more forcible reasons for prosecution. Among his ardent followers were some men who had won an evil name in the last years of the war and afterwards. Alcibiades, who had after all betrayed Athens to Sparta, had an affection for him, which was amply returned, and other disciples were Charmides and Critias, both of whom had been members of the Thirty and executed when its tyranny came to an end. These were reputable reasons for thinking that Socrates was not a lover of democracy and that his teaching produced unscrupulous enemies of law and liberty, and such accusations would carry great weight when Athens was laboriously trying to recover its dignity after the humiliating end of the war. At such a time even his habit of questioning first principles to their damage without putting anything in their place might seem to confirm the view that he was a danger to society.

Socrates would not be of no great importance if he had not caught the imagination of Plato, who was twenty-eight years old at the time of his execution and had been a member of his inner circle. Plato devoted a large part of his long life partly to justifying Socrates, and partly to developing views which he attributed to him. The first task was fulfilled in four dialogues which concern the last days of Socrates. In the *Euthypro* Socrates is about to attend his trial and before it discusses the true nature of piety; and this is Plato's version, presumably based on fact, of what Socrates thought on this fundamental matter. The *Apology* purports to be the actual defence made by Socrates in the court, and is likely to embody much that he really said, which is more than can be said for Xenophon's account of the same speech. Indeed it is hard to believe that Plato could have invented the last words, which ring with the strange combination of irony and conviction which have learned to think Socratic:

The hour of departure has arrived, and we go our ways – I to die, and you to live. Which is better, only God knows.[4]

In the *Crito*, when Socrates is in prison and receives offers to secure his escape, he refuses on the grounds that the laws must be kept because they are the foundation of civic order and he himself owes everything to them and will on no account break them. The much longer *Phaedo* describes the last hours of Socrates and ends with his actual death as he drinks the hemlock. Before this there is a long discussion on immortality, which is so skilfully constructed and presents its problems from such different angles that it cannot be a literal record of what was said, but no doubt Socrates talked in very much this way, and the whole work is designed to show him as he was and to justify the narrator's closing words:

Such, Echecrates, was the end of our companion, a man, as we should say, the best and the wisest and most righteous of our time.[5]

These are Plato's monuments to the trial and death of Socrates and, though we do not know how soon after the event they were written, and the *Phaedo* may have been written a good deal later, they present what Plato saw in Socrates and are a corner-stone of a much larger achievement.

Plato was obsessed and inspired by the memory of Socrates, not merely of his career, but of his personality, his methods and topics of discussion, his moral and religious convictions, his frugality and simplicity of life. By this example Plato was convinced that philosophy was not a pastime but a way of life, which imposed heavy obligations, and perhaps it was this that drove him to make a disastrous incursion into politics when he tried to instruct the young tyrant of Syracuse, Dionysius II, in the duties of a philosopher-king. Plato is one of the few Greek writers whose works survive intact, and have been increased by a suppositious apocrypha but, though this great mass of writing is primarily concerned with philosophical questions, Plato seldom speaks in his own person. The marvellous style is indeed his own, but the ideas which he discusses may often have come in the last resort from Socrates. A letter, attributed to Plato, which may not be authentic but seems to be based on genuine material, contains the remarkable statement: 'There is no systematic writing of Plato, nor will there ever be. What go by the name really belong to Socrates turned young and handsome.'[6] There is in this a certain sly irony, but it indicates that Plato did not regard his writings as an expression of his own views. Though the merest hint dropped by Socrates might expand and develop beyond all probability in Plato's powerful and imaginative mind, it looks as if the first elements and the first impulse came from the master. Socrates made a very strong impression on this extremely intelligent and impressionable man in his early manhood, and Socrates' death, which showed him at his noblest, set a final seal on his ideas as a gospel calling for elaboration and discussion. In the disillusionment and depression of the post-war years Plato found in Socrates an ideal to engage all his powers both as a thinker and as an artist, and however much he added to it from his own resources, it remained the centre of his intellectual and moral being. In his last years the vision receded, and Plato began to speak more freely in his own person, but through his most creative period he used the Socratic spirit as a starting-point and a guide in his discussion of philosophy.

However devoted Plato's respect for the ideas of Socrates was, he was not prepared to speak dogmatically about them or about his own deductions from them. He was convinced that the pursuit of truth is best conducted by question and counter-question and that the actual pursuit matters more than the conclusion, for the first keeps the mind in full play and the second can never be truly final. What was needed was not discourse but dialectic, as Socrates had practised it, and as it was developed by Zeno of Elea (*c.* 490–? BC), who was a master of puzzling paradoxes. Dialectic is conversation governed by strict rules, in which question and answer must be stated in the fewest possible words. It then becomes an attempt to define concepts in current use but which are shown on examination to be full of contradictions. It assumes that thought, to be true, must be self-consistent and, though this was not a new idea, it had never before received such prominence. Dialectic became Socrates' chief interest in his later years when he was disillusioned with science and even with Anaxagoras' attempt to show that all things had been ordered by Mind. Plato turns it into a literary form. For this he had some faint precedents. The Greeks were much too fond of argument not to make literature out of it, and it is possible that the plays of Epicharmus discussed, not very seriously, matters of general or philosophic interest. Herodotus' discussion of the three kinds of government suggests a simple form of such literature, and from the end of the fifth century there survives a small collection called *The Double Arguments*, which, though not cast in the form of a dialogue, contains nine short articles on the opposite meanings which words can have in common discussion on matters such as good and bad, true and false, justice and injustice, and the like. Plato made from these not very promising beginnings a new form of literature. His development of the philosophic dialogue enabled him to display the pursuit of truth in its actual processes and to make full use of dialectic as he had learned it from Socrates, but it also opened opportunities of creating a work of art from what might have seemed to be rather a narrow and restricted form. Before Plato philosophers had by no means lacked style and distinction, but now philosophy was given an entirely different shape, much closer to what Plato thought that it ought to be.

In his dialogues Plato shows a keen eye for the characters of those who take part in them. The scheme is usually that Socrates starts asking someone about his life and opinions and then ties him up in knots with a series of questions until he is forced to admit that he does not know what he is saying. Socrates dominates the scene and is a far more vivid and more familiar figure than any other in Greek literature. He is courteous and even friendly to his victims, some of whom he clearly likes, but he exerts a strange hold on them. Meno, who admires him with some reluctance, compares him with a torpedo-fish, not merely because he looks like one, but because he numbs anyone who comes near him, and leaves him speechless. Alcibiades compares him first with Silens equipped with pipes and flutes and then with the satyr Marsyas, who looks grotesque but charms everyone by his music. Socrates speaks with great simplicity, drawing his examples from the humble pursuits of every day and enlivening his argument with many personal touches. Plato depicts his adversaries with equal skill, whether it is the young Charmides, who is modestly shy of his remarkable and much admired looks, or the rhapsode Ion, who is passionately occupied with his recitations and interpretation of Homer, or the brilliant, not very scrupulous Callicles, who argues that might really is right, or the old Cephalus, who embodies the wisdom and the calm of old age, or the noisy Thrasymachus, who does not like being questioned and is not very good at defending himself, or the revered Protagoras, whose urbanity and self-possession take some of the edge off Socrates' attacks. Plato's art lies in his ability to conjure up a personality not merely through a few mannerisms but by making him talk in character and showing that his views, which are subjected to so careful a scrutiny, are an essential part of himself. Plato's characters resemble neither the broad, simple creations of the tragedians nor the blithe caricatures of Aristophanes. They are domestic and almost intimate and they reveal how keenly the Greeks observed one another. No doubt this was common enough in the leisured, aristocratic circles in which Plato was bred, but it gives a new range and depth to his art because he finds the clue to a man's personality in his opinions and in the seriousness with which he is prepared to discuss them.

This convincing realism is an ingredient in a more complex unity. Plato's dialogues are works of art in every sense, and, since their material is talk, it is on this that he relies for his effects. His language has almost no parallel anywhere for lucidity, grace, variety, and ease. The rippling sentences make their way almost without our noticing how strong they are and how easily they deal with any matter, however abstruse or abstract. Whatever his predecessors may have done to find a proper medium for philosophy, Plato surpassed them in his astonishing creation of a language which is in some ways close to conversation but never fails in grip and clarity and is always surprising us by new effects. He was treating ideas of which many were quite unfamiliar and for which there can have been no standard vocabulary, but, though his thought grew increasingly more subtle, his use of words is remarkably consistent in all his writings. From the start he saw that bold speculations needed a lucid and coherent vocabulary, and this he found and developed for them. He is unlikely to have learned this from Socrates, and it is more probably the reflection of Plato's own mind when it got to work on ideas in its own strength. Yet this style, so admirably fitted to precise discussion, has other remarkable qualities. When Aristotle says that it is midway between prose and poetry,[7] he makes a just comment. For its intellectual structure is continually enlivened by flights of fancy and imagination, by metaphor and myth, which show that he is half a poet. As a young man he wrote some charming short poems, and even in old age, when he heard of the death of his friend, Dion of Syracuse, he wrote an elegiac lament of six lines, which shows how deeply he was affected. But his poetical gift was throughout controlled by his philosophic temperament, which it aids and completes and enriches but which it never completely dominates. We may doubt whether this reflects Socrates, who is indeed known to have written verses but does not seem to have any characteristics of a poet. In this respect Plato's genius took command and transformed the hearsay and the experience of his youth into a world whose characters talked as few men can ever have talked in practice, and discussed the deepest issues of philosophy with a consummate precision and delicacy and charm.

Plato's mind was fixed not only on Socrates but, through him, on the circle in which he moved, and found in the recollection and reconstruction of an age just before his own a setting for his dialogues. Though in the bitterness of Athens' fall he felt no enthusiasm for the adventurous exploits of the Periclean age, he passed much of his inner life in imagination with its more intellectual representatives. Just as his few surviving poems deal with people whom he can hardly have known and treat them as contemporaries despite the gap of years between them and himself, so, in his dialogues, he sets his imaginary scenes at various imprecise dates from before the outbreak of the Peloponnesian War in 431 BC to the Syracusan expedition of 415 BC, when he was a boy of fourteen years. His works on the trial and death of Socrates are based on a later date, when he was old enough to know what happened, but most of his other dialogues are set in a past of which Plato might know much from hearsay but directly no more than he could have picked up in a precocious and receptive boyhood. His mind and his imagination are both busy with the past, but we are not very conscious of it and may be right to think that he has to some degree adapted its problems to his own age and by adroit use of hindsight so restated its problems that they are still relevant. To look back to a vanished world was perhaps natural for an Athenian aristocrat whose family cannot fail to have suffered from the economic decline of Athens in and after the Peloponnesian War, and his unusual attitude gives to Plato's outlook a certain nostalgia for the past. But he does not praise it; on the contrary, he has many harsh things to say of it, especially of those consummate achievements in action and the arts which posterity has most admired. Yet he is imaginatively at home in it, as if, having grown up before the fall of Athens, his mind was set in this period and he found it difficult to adapt himself to new circumstances. Such an outlook may lead to serious defects in understanding actual events, but artistically it has the advantage that the past is seen with an affectionate clarity and is simpler and more vivid than the confused present. The problems with which Plato deals were certainly lively in the fifth century but in his distance from them he sees that they are also relevant to his own time.

Plato's first experiments in his new art were made on a small scale without any great pretensions. He composed short conversation-pieces, in which Socrates himself is usually the narrator and retails talks, in which he himself has taken a dominant part. In each the conversation turns more or less on a single theme, on temperance in the *Charmides*, friendship in the *Lysis*, courage in the *Laches*, and poetical inspiration in the *Ion*. The caste is always small, not more than four or five, and in some respects the dialogues read like one-act plays with a very high conversational content. A handsome young man, a devoted friend, two famous generals, and a Homeric reciter are asked questions on a theme which touches their lives very closely, and easily shown by Socrates to be quite inconsistent in what they say. In the end Socrates, having tied them up in knots by not very scrupulous or always flawless arguments, drives them to admit that neither they nor he know what the subject discussed really is. The discussions are enlivened by many deft personal touches, such as the differences between the two generals, Laches and Nicias, or the all-absorbing passion which Ion has for Homer. These dialogues are accomplished literary performances, and their interest lies in the give-and-take of argument, though Socrates is always made to get the best of it, partly by wearing out his opponents by the obstinate persistence of his criticisms, partly because he is really eager to know what they are talking about, and the others, who practise some activity, are not very much troubled about its definition. No doubt this kind of thing happened often in Socrates' long career of talk, and the sketches look as if they were based on fact. But, though they are vivid records of the Socratic method at work, they are not in the least constructive. Socrates destroys reputable and reasonable convictions and offers no alternatives to them. Plato seems to admire Socrates for his dexterity in argument and to be happy that negative conclusions are better than wrong conclusions, but he is not yet ready to attribute to him views of any positive kind, though at times he suggests that behind the light-hearted play with words there lurk deep convictions. As yet Plato's work belongs to literature rather than to philosophy, and if this literature finds its substance in discussion, that is after all natural in a society like that of Athens, where ideas were daily meat and drink.

Before long Plato transformed this unpretentious and tentative art into something much richer and more serious. He extends the scale of his dialogues, and with more space at his disposal he gives a larger treatment to his characters and the points of view which they represent. At the same time his arguments are more carefully considered and more sustained. From a sequence of them he builds an artistic whole, at the end of which a whole process of thought is revealed on a single main theme and brought to some sort of conclusion. In these works of his first maturity Plato has expanded his conception of Socrates and found much more in him than a dexterous inquisitor. No doubt he is still true to his memory of Socrates,

218

but this memory has been deepened and strengthened by his own thoughts and experience. The fundamental subject of the *Protagoras* was to occupy Plato for a large part of his life—can goodness be taught? Socrates has grave doubts, based on actual examples, whether it can, but the case for it is made with skill and eloquence by the old and skilful Protagoras. He is quite sincere in claiming that he can make men better by instruction, and in a long parable explains that men can be taught to take a responsible part in society and that any comparison with savages will show how well this is done at Athens. This is a commonsense point of view and entirely legitimate for Protagoras, whose idea of goodness is relative to a man's social usefulness. But this does not satisfy Socrates, who demands not a relative but an absolute good and argues, quite correctly, that in Protagoras' system this is not properly considered. The argument takes many turns and varies its tone and temper, as when a poem by Simonides on the difficulty of being a good man receives a somewhat fantastic and amusing discussion, which is an implicit commentary on the Greek view of poetry as a repository of inspired wisdom. The real development of the dialogue lies in its discussion on the nature of goodness, and, since Protagoras and Socrates hold diametrically opposite views, nothing in the end is decided, though perhaps we are meant to conclude that Protagoras has attacked the problem on false assumptions. The human element is fully at play, but underneath it we see Plato struggling with the difficulty of establishing that goodness is an absolute value. Socrates cannot prove this, but that does not make it unworthy of full attention.

The *Gorgias* takes its name from another famous teacher, though Gorgias cannot have been so serious or so candid as Protagoras. He is present throughout the dialogue but plays a part only at the beginning, when he states his case for teaching the art of rhetoric or persuasion. Since rhetoric played an enormous part in Greek political and public life, it was of first importance in considering basic problems of government. Gorgias puts up a poor defence of it, and soon falls out of the conversation, which takes on a much more serious tone as first a young man called Polus and then a far more formidable figure, Callicles, take up the case on a broad basis and try to maintain that in general the 'good' is what satisfies a man's desires and appetites and that in politics might is really right, since this is what happens in nature and all attempts to reverse the situation are merely human conventions. Callicles is almost certainly a real person, though nothing else is known of him, and he stands for a point of view which was common enough in the late fifth century and has of course had advocates in later times like Nietzsche. Callicles argues his case with brilliant skill and, though he has some unattractive traits such as fits of patronage, rudeness, and the sulks, Socrates seems to like him and to respect his honesty in 'saying frankly what other people think but will not say.'[8] Plato may well have seen in him qualities which he himself would have admired if he had not come under the influence of Socrates and indeed almost what he himself might have thought about *Machtpolitik* in his disgust with the failure of Athens. As in the *Protagoras*, the argument between Callicles and Socrates cannot end in any agreement because they use the word 'good' in quite different senses and draw widely different conclusions from it. Callicles admires Archelaus, king of Macedon, and tells with admiring gusto how, by a series of crimes, he made his way to power and, though he is 'the greatest criminal of all the Macedonians',[9] he is what everyone would like to be. He cannot be refuted on his own assumptions, and in the end Socrates has to set against this ideal of happiness his own ideal of goodness. He is indeed able to show that the life given entirely to pleasure may in some cases disgust even Callicles, but his real strength lies in his appeal to the moral consciousness, partly in a myth, but more especially in his remarkable conclusion when he says that we must return good for evil and practise justice and virtue:

> This way let us go; and let us exhort all men to follow in it, not in the way to which you trust and in which you exhort me to follow you; for that way, Callicles, is worth nothing.[10]

Plato sets up one system of values against another, and appeals to the human conviction that in the end his is the only right one.

What the *Gorgias* presents as a matter of moral principle, the *Phaedo* embodies in the last hours and death of Socrates. The economy and restraint with which these are related show how consummate an artist Plato is and how much he manages to make of what is on the surface a very simple narrative with no rhetoric or elaboration. Yet the record is instinct with a deep feeling for the nobility of Socrates and the calm dignity in which he faces his end. This is how a philosopher, who believes in the rule of reason, should meet injustice and death, and Plato leaves us in no doubt about his admiration, both personal and moral, for Socrates. But the *Phaedo* is much more than this. It tells of what Socrates and his inner circle of friends discussed in these last hours and, if the binding theme is the immortality of the soul, this takes them into other equally fundamental matters. The case for survival after death is argued with Pythagorean friends from Thebes, but Socrates finds that the first arguments have serious flaws. This indicates how seriously the matter is treated and shows that the Socratic belief in survival is not a matter for faith alone. Socrates then puts forward his final argument, which is based on what was to be a central point in Plato's philosophy, that reality consists of Forms, which are the only true objects of knowledge, and that all particular things, perceived by the senses, are but reflections of them. This doctrine may have been held by Socrates, and in the *Phaedo* provides a foundation for a belief in survival on the grounds that, since that which makes things live is in the soul, and death is incompatible with life, therefore death is incompatible with the soul, which must be immortal and indestructible. The long and careful argument is the climax of the dialogue and must be accepted as such. However, Socrates then fortifies it with a long myth about 'last things', and once again his appeal is more ethical than logical. What Plato in effect says is, that the soul alone really matters and is alone fully real; therefore it must survive. The idea was to be revived more than once later, but in the *Phaedo* it provides a religious backing to the emotions aroused by the death of Socrates.

Unfortunately we do not know in what order or at what date Plato's dialogues were written, but it seems likely that the three major dialogues which we have just considered belong to his early middle years. In each of them he develops a main theme which he may have learned from Socrates but makes very much his own. In the *Republic* he brings them together and composes on a much larger scale than before but without quite the same command of a general design. He begins by a lively conversation-piece in which, after the manner of the early dialogues, Socrates routs Thrasymachus, who is a noisy exponent of the theory that Justice is the interest of the stronger, and ends by a religious and cosmological revelation. Between these extremes he deals, at some length, with other matters, whose relative importance is revealed as we read the book. The *Republic* keeps the form of a dialogue, but after the first book, the exchange of arguments is perceptibly diminished and Socrates holds the field as he expounds his views to willing hearers. It is fundamentally a discussion of the ideal state. Such discussions seem to have been common enough in the fourth century and there are hints of them in Aristophanes' *Ecclesiazusae*, and of course they have been no less common in recent times from Thomas More and Campanella to William Morris. Such Utopias are not meant to be practicable; their purpose is to indicate lines on which political action may be taken towards reputable if never fully attainable goals. Plato is well aware that his ideal republic is not in the crude sense possible, but it can at least provide some sort of guidance to politicians and it asserts certain principles by which politics should be conducted. It thrives on the assumption that politics is concerned with goodness and the production of good men. For this Plato lays down a scheme of education and, though it seems unlikely in any conditions to produce the results that he wished, it emphasizes his belief that the practical life called for a stern discipline of mind and character and must not be left to private whims and fancies. In dealing with this main theme he gave much attention to other themes related to it and anticipated much that he was to discuss later.

In the *Republic* Plato picks up the subject of the ideal Forms which he describes in *Phaedo*. In the history of philosophy the Forms play an important part since they bridge what seemed to be an insuperable gap between the unchanging reality, as it was framed by Parmenides to be the only possible object of knowledge, and the mass of particulars which Heraclitus saw in a permanent state of flux. Plato's system makes sense of appearance because it partakes of reality, and allows at least opinions to be formed about it. But Plato was too much of an artist to be content with a purely logical scheme like this. He wished to make his system not merely intelligible but convincing, and to this he applied some of his more subtle arts. The theory of Forms caught his imagination and determined his whole sense of reality. What it meant to him can be seen from the remarkable passage in which he compares men in the common world with men in a cave. They have their backs to the light, and are so bound that they cannot look at it, and, since they have a fire behind them, what they see is the procession of shadows on a wall in front of them. The image recalls a cinema, and it is as if the only things that men can see and have acquaintance with are shadows on a screen, which they take to be the only reality. By this remarkable imagery Plato suggests the unreality of the visible world, and hints at a reality of which it is a faint reflection. He then argues that if these men are released and taken towards the light, they will find it very difficult to adjust themselves to it. But he thinks that it is possible, and that this is what education should do. He wishes to make it the instrument by which men's minds are turned towards the eternal Forms. But this is not a purely intellectual process. Plato hopes that this will bring men to understand the Form of the Good, but knowledge of the kind that he prescribes will not easily do this, unless it implies more than he suggests. This it does. He compares the Form of the Good with the sun, and through it knowledge is made possible. We cannot say that by this Plato identifies the Form of the Good with God, but at least it is what gives significance to reality and holds it together. In using for it the imagery of light he reveals his religious, even mystical attitude to it, and recalls Pindar who uses a like imagery to convey the magical moments when human life is transformed by the presence of the gods. Plato, like Pindar, thinks that divine things are the only real things, and, though for him the Forms are not gods, they are the reality behind the known world and any knowledge of them takes us away from appearance and guess-work to reality and knowledge, and, if we really *know*, we are on the way to being good. In the Forms Plato found something which at once satis-fied his need for a logical coherence in the theory of knowledge and pro-vided a significance to what happens in the familiar world. The paradox is that this world, which he saw so clearly and in many ways so enjoyed, is for him not merely a fleeting show, but never more than a shadow. In moments of disaster or defeat the heroes of Greek tragedy might think the same thing, but it was only a momentary mood. Plato set his whole philosophy to accord with it.

From this point of view Plato hopes to devise a scheme of education to make men what they ought to be, and such a scheme demands a system of government. Plato, with perfect consistency, demands that this govern-ment shall be by the wise, that is by men who study the Forms and are acquainted with the Good. His discussion of it has a negative and positive side. On the negative side he examines with much care and some moments of dazzling insight the different types of men produced by different types of government. He puts this schematically as a series of types, each worse than the preceding from which it arises, and in this he indulges a certain amount of playful satire. Timocracy, or rule by the most honoured men, declines into oligarchy or rule by the rich, which in its turn declines into democracy, and democracy destroys itself by reaching its culmination in tyranny. On each kind of government Plato makes telling points, and his account of democracy is a fierce satire on Athens of the fifth century, almost an answer, point by point, to what Pericles says on its behalf in his Funeral Speech. To Plato democracy means the state in which a man does what he likes, and to him this is deeply shocking. His mathematical mind called for an absolute order in which every man performed a function, and democracy of course is the antithesis to this. Moreover, in his account of schemes of government Plato tries to equate each with a type of man according to his own psychology. He believed in a tripartite soul, consist-ing of a reasonable element, a self-assertive element, and an appetitive element. For him the last is dangerous if it is undisciplined, and it has full opportunities in democracy. The second element can, if united with reason, be good, but it can also be too assertive, and this is the main feature in timocracy, or government by respected people. The ideal self is that in which reason reigns with self-assertion as an ally and with appetites well in control, and this is what Plato wishes to secure. The whole discussion, brilliant and amusing as it is, belongs to neither history nor logic and, though it may be an attempt at social psychology, it fails to convince. Not even in Greece did governments fall into so simple a classification.

As a positive alternative to these systems Plato offers his own scheme by which philosophers are kings and kings are philosophers. To suit his psychology he divides the rest of the population into soldiers, who stand for self-assertion, and workers, who stand for the appetites and are therefore firmly disciplined. Of course such a system of government has never existed, and those apologists for it who compare it with the Council of Ten at Venice or even with the British Monarchy are very wide of the mark. Though our own century has seen men in command who might in some sense be called philosophers, it is not likely that Plato would have approved of Woodrow Wilson or Lenin or Masaryk or Gandhi. Even though his sketch is meant to be no more than an ideal, it is too remote from reality to be tenable even as a model. Philosophers as he sees them are very unlikely to be men of action or to have that practical wisdom, which Aristotle wisely distinguished from the theoretical wisdom in which Plato put all his trust. There were many authoritarians before Plato, but his special contribution is to give to their authority a special claim based on special arguments. In this he denied and rejected that freedom of choice which made the grandeur of Athens in the Periclean age. He knows that he is doing this, and he does it after the fullest consideration. No doubt his upbringing in aristocratic circles taught him to distrust the demagogues of Athenian politics, but the real cause of his rejection lies deeper. In his early manhood he had witnessed the decline and fall of a proud and brilliant system, and instead of lamenting it, as he might have done, he found peace for himself by saying that it was all wrong and doomed to failure. Perhaps it was. Perhaps, if Alcibiades had succeeded in his ambitions and conquered Carthage, Athenian democracy might indeed have brought a new terror to the world, and come to a deservedly hideous end. But what troubles Plato is that brilliant success cannot last, and he desires above all a system that can last. He is prepared to sacrifice almost everything to permanence and security, and in the end it is clear that what most moves him is fear. It is this which makes him so distrustful of human nature and its ambitions and desires, of any kind of liberty personal or political, of variety and change, of the whole richness of life which Athens had done so much to discover and to sustain.

If Plato thought very lowly of Athenian politics, he was no less hard on what we regard as an almost equally great Athenian contribution—the fine arts, especially poetry, and painting, and, to a lesser degree, music. Here too Plato is concerned with the fifth century much more than with his own age, and, though this is natural enough in the case of poetry, it is more surprising with painting in the time of Apelles. In the arts, as in other matters, Plato formed his tastes young and did not see much in later work. His feeling for poetry is manifest in his own writing, for painting in his brief sketches of visible scenes, for music in the extreme care with which he discusses its effect on character. But he attacks all three and wishes to exclude them almost entirely from his ideal state. The attack has three prongs. First, he disapproves of poetry which sets the gods in an unfavourable light. In this he has distinguished precedents in Xenophanes and Pindar, and we need not quarrel with him for holding a reasonably established opinion. Secondly, he thinks that the arts encourage emotions which should be kept in control, and this applies equally to poetry, which depicts and presumably incites grief, and to music, which too often destroys a man's self-control by its release of passions. We might almost complain that the better the arts are, the more Plato disapproves of them, and this is confirmed by the examples which he takes from Homer and Aeschylus. Being himself an easy victim of the arts, he seems to have attributed his own responses to others and to have been afraid that they would not observe that temperance which he regarded as indispensable to the balanced self. He did not anticipate Aristotle in claiming that, by arousing pity and fear, poetry, in the form of tragedy, cleanses us of these emotions, and he did not see that in our enjoyment of the arts the final state is beyond any emotions and is in fact exalted delight. This objection was, so far as it went, moral. But thirdly, Plato develops a theory against the arts based on his belief in the ideal Forms. If the physical world is a reflection of the ideal, then works of art are reflections of the physical world and three times removed from the truth. Plato insists on this with some power, and it is useless to try to belittle his case by arguing that he is merely against 'representational' art and not against art as such. For he makes it clear that art is in itself dangerously far from the ideal. On the surface this seems perverse and unreasonable. No art is mere imitation and nothing else, and certainly Greek art has much more in it than imitation, of which it is not a very good example. Nor is it clear that Plato would have liked a strictly non-representational art like Persian carpets or Cubist painting. When he objects to art as imitation, what he has in mind but does not state very fully is the whole mythical manner of thought which the Greeks had pursued until the end of the fifth century and which stirred their emotions much more than Plato liked. Even when they had begun to think in abstract terms, they still thought also in myths and images and stated many important truths through them. It is this that Plato really condemns. When he committed himself to the pursuit of truth through dialectic, the mythical approach stood in his way, and he felt bound to attack it. The mathematician in him triumphed over the poet, but the victory was not complete, and Plato himself did not cease to make considerable concessions to the mythical manner, which he rejected.

Plato often varies his arguments with myths, that is with stories which stress a point or provide an emotional and imaginative conclusion to an argument as it begins to run dry. Some of these myths are little more than illustrative tales which could have been told in a straightforward factual way but are more engaging with a slight change of dress. Such is the myth which Protagoras tells in the dialogue called after him about the growth of civilization. This was a common theme, and Protagoras attributes it to the different parts played by Epimetheus and Prometheus in the beginning of history. While Prometheus plans excellently, he leaves the execution to Epimetheus, who botches it, and this accounts for both the success and the failure of men. So too, in the *Phaedrus*, Socrates explains the invention of letters as having happened in Egypt, when the inventor, the god Theuth, spoke of them as 'an elixir of memory and wisdom'[11] to another god, Thamus, who rejected them on the grounds that they would produce forgetfulness. But more often Plato uses myths for more serious purposes, notably in the *Gorgias*, *Phaedo*, and the *Republic*. The three myths are quite different from one another in details, but all are concerned with eschatological matters and especially with the judgment of good and evil actions after death. They are written in a more elaborate style than Plato's conversations and have their full share of poetical words, but their powerful appeal lies in the firm imagination with which Plato describes his different worlds beyond the grave, especially in the *Republic* when the soul of Er the Armenian leaves his body and is instructed, not only in rewards and punishments, but in the mystery of rebirth, when each soul chooses what form it is going to take on its return to earth. In these remarkable passages Plato uses doctrines which had been current for some time in Greece but had nothing to do with the Olympian religion. They may owe something to the mystical mathematician Pythagoras (*c*. 570– *c* 495 BC) and to Empedocles, and they were known to Pindar, but their real popularity seems to have been in certain mystery-cults which flourished in many parts of Greece at a not very high social level. Socrates must have known them and felt that there was something in them, even if he did not trust the details. These Plato picks up and elaborates with a detailed cosmology in the *Phaedo* and a whole scheme of reincarnation in the *Republic*. They are not the myths of poetry, but they bear a considerable resemblance to them.

The obvious use of these more serious myths is that they help to underline conclusions which cannot be settled by argument but can appeal to the moral feelings. In describing what happens to the wicked in the after-life, Plato does indeed, with some anticipations of Dante, show that their punishments are not merely what they deserve but almost part of themselves, states of suffering which are inseparable from their corrupt ways of life. Such myths are certainly not mattters of knowledge, nor are they matters of opinion, since they are not confirmed by any evidence of the senses. They are 'stories' which may contain an essential truth in a dress of imaginary detail. Their strength is that they appeal to deep convictions in us, not merely in their strong insistence on the difference between good and evil, but in the desire to survive after death which is inbred in many people. We might perhaps complain that by putting forward schemes of rewards and punishments for good and bad actions Plato debases the pursuit of good for its own sake and reduces it to a calculation of possible happiness or misery in the long run. Perhaps he does, but it does not diminish his actual sense of good and evil as they really are, and we might even think that their main use is to emphasize this. None the less, Plato's myths are essentially a kind of poetry. The concrete form which he gives to various hopes and fears and longings is just what poetry does, and nothing else does it so well or so satisfactorily. Plato might denounce poetry but he could not deliver himself from its influence or achieve his full results without it. The moralist might seem to win, but the quarrel between philosophy and poetry in Plato himself was never quite healed, however much he might need the second to support the first.

Plato's inner conflict with poetry is matched by something not entirely alien to it, his attitude towards love. The love which concerns him is not that between a man and a woman, though he is aware that this has its claims to respect, but that between one man and another, and, though this is a common form of Greek sentiment, it also reflects personal inclinations both of Socrates and of Plato. In the fourth century such love might be condemned if it led to physical action, but in the fifth even this was commonly accepted, and such love was freely spoken of and cultivated in aristocratic circles, as it had been for centuries in Athens and elsewhere. Plato's interest in it, as in so much else, comes from the fifth century and is fully at work in his early poems. In his *Lysis* and *Charmides*

he displays Socrates' attitude towards it and leaves no doubt that in handsome young men Socrates found something which greatly attracted him
and stirred his desire to talk to them about themselves. It is most unlikely
that he went beyond this, but he was candid about their fascination for
him and liked to engage their interest. In a society where young men
exercised themselves naked in the wrestling-ground and were watched by
a large crowd of their elders, the cult of youth was a common topic of
talk, and Socrates was no exception in indulging it. In the *Clouds* Aristophanes seems to have hinted obliquely that he or his disciples sometimes
went too far in the matter, but that is not suggested elsewhere and is
surely false for Socrates himself, but his influence on young men was
notorious enough to be mentioned in his indictment, and this, no doubt,
incited Plato to say something about it and to transform a psychological
inclination of his master into a system by which love plays a leading part
in the nurture of the soul.

Plato develops this theme in the *Symposium*, which is the most human
and least argumentative of his dialogues and is given a form which is well
suited to the emotional theme which it discusses. At a feast which lasts
till dawn, five friends agree to discuss love, and are later joined first by
Socrates, who has been standing in a trance at the door, and then by
Alcibiades. Each makes a speech in its praise, and, though these speeches
form a sequence which leads to something like a climax, individually they
look at love from various, different angles, and the result is a full picture of
it from several sides. The young Phaedrus begins the series by connecting
love with honour and shows how it calls for sacrifices even in women,
as Alcestis gave herself for her husband. Pausanias distinguishes between
two loves, one heavenly and the other popular, and comes down firmly on
the side of the first. Then Eryximachus relates the nobler kind to wider
issues and makes it the source of happiness. Then by an adroit move Plato
varies the steady advance of the theme by introducing Aristophanes, who
tells a delightful fable in which human beings are halves of what were
once composite creatures, and all the halves are looking for their lost
partners, which accounts for the many varieties of love and its overpowering influence. He is followed by the poet Agathon, who delivers a flowery
panegyric, and then comes Socrates, who relates how he once met
Diotima, a holy woman, at Mantinea, who taught him to rise above
beautiful bodies to the love of an eternal beauty and the world of immortal
things. This might seem to be a satisfactory culmination, but at this point
Alcibiades bursts in, half drunk, and talks with brilliant gaiety about his
love for Socrates. His enchanted admiration shows what the subject of the

abstract discussion means in actual life. It leaves us with the impression that, whatever may have been said, this is what love really is and we must relate the speeches to it, for it has something in common with all of them. The talk goes on, and some of the company go to sleep, until the dawn comes and Socrates goes about his business. If the *Symposium* rejects the lower forms of love, it states a powerful case for love as a source of inspiration and noble action and leaves no doubt about its paramount meaning for Plato.

The *Symposium* has a kind of sequel in the *Phaedrus*, which is set in the country and has no characters but Socrates and Phaedrus, who talk in the heat of the day under a plane-tree by a stream. They discuss both rhetoric and love, and, though the two themes are skilfully intermingled, the more important parts are those in which Socrates discourses about love. The *Phaedrus* supplements the theme of love at both ends, the lowest and the highest manifestations of it. The lowest side is provided by a tract of the orator Lysias (*c* 459–380 BC), who tries to prove that a beloved is wiser to give himself to someone who does not love him, since he will get more profit from it than from someone who does. It is a cheap, trashy affair, and Socrates has no trouble in demolishing it. He then advances to his own high view of love as a creative, spiritual force. He claims that the human soul is like a two-horsed chariot, of which one horse is uncontrolled and wilful, while the other seeks only the best and highest things. The soul is capable of this second course and is led to it by love. If it follows this lead, it is brought into an unseen world of reality and inspired to many noble actions in actual life. Love may indeed be a kind of madness, but it comes from the gods and finds its fulfilment in the highest exercise of the faculties. For Plato it is a power that sets the soul to work in the right way, and, without it, the search for the good life would be even more difficult than it is. Plato's conception of love is not what is known as 'Platonic'. This indeed is given to a single person in complete devotion and inspires to high ideals, but it is concentrated on that person alone, whereas with Plato it passes beyond and moves in the authentic world of the spirit.

The *Phaedrus* is perhaps the last of the Platonic dialogues, which still owes something, however remote, to Socrates. In his later work Plato sometimes uses Socrates and sometimes other characters, but his art takes a severer and less dramatic form. His intellectual power is, if anything, even stronger than before, and his command of words, even when turned to the most abstruse and difficult subjects, remains consummate. He seems to have felt more confidence in himself and less need to speak in the characters of other men, and, in consequence, his later dialogues derive their strength less from personal touches than from the severe search for truth through argument. They deal with the three main subjects which had always engaged him—knowledge, cosmology, and politics.

In the *Theaetetus* Plato, in the plenitude of his intellectual powers, faces the question: 'What is knowledge?' and attacks the old problem raised by Protagoras that it is sensation. This is dealt with on a far more convincing plan than in the *Protagoras*, and when it is settled, Plato moves to his next point, that knowledge is not the work of the mind. If sensation has no reality beyond itself, thought by itself merely yields combinations of words. What matters for knowledge is the distinction between true and false, and the literary claim of the *Theaetetus* is partly the grace and delicacy with which the argument is conducted and partly, and more impressively, the magnificent digression on the philosophic life, which argues that the wise man is the best judge of what benefits the community, but derives its power from its plea for a life of knowing which is not troubled by practical concerns. From his quarrel with himself Plato built this eloquent appeal, with its culmination in the claim that by cultivating holiness and wisdom the wise man will escape from an evil world and become like God. Plato followed this with the *Parmenides*, which is, in the first place, a searching criticism of the theory of Forms and, in the second place, a remarkable demonstration of what can happen to the dialectical method when it is applied to the nature of the One and the Many. By using the methods of the Eleatic school, Plato, after putting forward eight hypotheses each of which ends in self-contradiction, shows that the difficulties of relating the Forms to one another is as great as that of relating sensible things to them. The later part of the dialogue is an astonishing feat of verbal and mental dexterity, and as such it is meant to be taken. If we apply these eristic methods, these are the paradoxical results that we get. The *Sophist* deals with the foundations of logic and, though written as a sequel to the *Theaetetus*, lacks some of its brilliance. It is fundamentally a criticism of categories of thought, especially of that of 'not-being', and the very nature of its subject prevents it from enjoying the sprightly play of argument which we expect from Plato. But the power of its argument is such that most subsequent philosophy owes ultimately something to it. Humanly it is perhaps more attractive for the changed view of the physical world which Plato adumbrates in it. It is not clear that this is his own view, but he pays attention to it and hints that though the visible world consists of appearances, yet these appearances in some sense *are*.

If the physical world somehow *is*, there must be a reason for its being what it is, and this is the subject of the *Timaeus*. That Plato is very far from dogmatizing is clear from his making the main speaker, not Socrates, but a Pythagorean called Timaeus of Locri. He tells in some detail how the divine Artificer made the world that it might be a visible image of the knowable god, on the principle that he wishes everything to be as like himself as possible. In much that is powerful and penetrating, as in his account of space or his refusal to place the earth at the centre of the universe, Plato places much also that is obviously fanciful and not meant to be taken at all literally. When he describes how birds are what they are because it corresponds with their natures as light-hearted men before they were transformed, or explains the structure of the human body to be an ingenious series of analogies, he is really creating a myth, like his earlier myths in its disguised purpose—that the world must be rationally constructed—and in its use of various cosmogonies both old and new. The mythical content is enhanced by the style, which is far from conversational and has a certain hieratic dignity, the air of being in some sense a revelation, not from science, but from religion, and moves in majestic periods enriched by antithesis and imagery. That Plato intended to continue this summer of myth-making but for some reason gave it up follows from the unfinished *Critias*, which was meant to follow the *Timaeus*, but abandoned after Plato had begun to tell with much spirit the story of the lost continent of Atlantis, where, for a time, men enjoyed a golden age, until they forgot the gods, and the gods turned against them. At this point it stops.

The *Critias* presumably would have moved to political matters, which concerned Plato more than ever in his old age. In the *Statesman* he faces the difficulties inherent in his notion of the philosopher-king as he sketched it in the *Republic*. In a myth he tells how once God governed the world, but like the captain of a ship, left its navigation to look after itself, as he retired into a conning-tower. The notion of a theocratic paradise is thus politely dismissed, and we need not think that Plato hankered for it. He is content to ask what can best be done in existing circumstances, and he sketches his ruler, who is a good enough approximation in an imperfect world. The ideal system may still set the standard, but in the meanwhile it must be tempered by realistic considerations. Plato's own experience in Syracuse taught him that he must compromise, and he was prepared to do so provided that he did not lose sight of what he really thought best. In his long and detailed *Laws* he goes even further and tries to translate his modified ideals into practical regulations for a real city. His method is impeccable. He first establishes his main principles, and then lays down laws in accordance with them. In dealing with religious practice, he first discusses with notable power the case for the existence of God and in so doing recognizes that there is an incurable element of evil in the world. Against this he sets up what defences he can, and nothing is too unimportant for him. Yet the *Laws* is in some ways a gloomy work. Plato did not trust men to act well on their own volition and believed in heavy penalties, including death, not only for murder, but for embezzlement of public funds, sexual offences, treason, sacrilege, atheism, and heresy. He wishes to isolate his city from other cities and demands punishment for those who travel abroad without leave. He had no premonition of the huge changes which were to come to the Hellenic world and is more than content with the narrow bounds of a small society. Since some of his pupils became law-givers, his suggestions were not without fruit, and were incorporated into later law-codes, including that of Justinian, and there are elements in this system which Stalin followed, even if he did not know their source. The tone of the whole work indicates a low view of human nature, and Plato gives himself away when he says: 'The affairs of men are not serious, but we have to treat them seriously.'[12]

We cannot read Plato without feeling that he was one of the most gifted men who ever lived. No notion is too intricate for him to unravel, no state of mind too rare for him to understand. He moves with equal ease among philosophical abstractions and the notions of ordinary men, and for each he finds a wonderfully expressive and appropriate style. His passionate seriousness in seeking the truth was matched by a no less serious concern for good behaviour and a rational system of life. In his greatest days he proclaimed a world of vision inspired by deep affections, and this he offered as an alternative to the confused, depressed society in which he lived. For him this was not an escape from reality, but an entry into it, and he hoped that even a slight knowledge of it would make men wiser and better. Yet, in the last resort we suspect that he is shirking something, not indeed the life of action in which he tried all too unwisely to take a part, but a real understanding of human nature and its worth as it had been understood in the fifth century. His country's defeat and decline dealt him a wound, which never healed, and at no point, even when he was most at home in his imaginative re-creation of the fifth century, does he share the high confidence which carried Athens to her proudest achievements. If he had lived a generation earlier, he might have done anything in response to the immense zest of the Periclean age, but, as he himself is reported to have said, 'Plato was born late in the day for his country.'[13] This was his tragedy, and he knew it. From his conviction of defeat and failure he built the stupendous structure of his dialogues and showed that even from disaster Athens was still able to create something that was indeed her own and could have been built nowhere else.

9

DEBATE AND DISPLAY

FROM the beginnings of their known history the Greeks seem to have enjoyed oratory and welcomed any fine display of it. The young Achilles is expected to be 'a speaker of words and a doer of deeds',[1] and among the different kinds of excellence for which a man may be honoured Tyrtaeus includes a 'honey-voiced tongue'.[2] Words were needed in council to win acceptance for policies and in battle to inspire warriors to ever greater efforts. Though Herodotus follows epic precedent when he gives long speeches to his leading characters, he must also have been touched by the development of oratory in democratic Athens. In the fifth century it was still used for the old purposes and sometimes took over tasks, like the praise of the dead, which in an earlier age might have been left to poetry. But the special conditions of Athenian democracy called into prominence two other kinds of speech, each of which was highly regarded. First, since almost nothing could be done at a national level without a debate in the Assembly, the effective speaker tended to get his way, and political speaking was much admired and much cultivated. Themistocles won the approval of Thucydides for his ability in expounding his policy,[3] and what he himself thought may be seen from some words which he is alleged to have said to Xerxes:

The speech of man is like skilfully worked embroidery; for, like it, when it is unrolled it reveals its designs, but when folded up, hides and destroys them.[4]

His admirer, Pericles, was renowned for his ability at public speaking, and Eupolis said of him:

> He bound a spell,
> And had this power, alone of orators –
> To prick men's hearts, and leave behind the sting.[5]

The matter and the manner of Pericles' speeches are known from Thucydides, and we can understand why he had such a grip on the Athenian Assembly. In the fifth century public speaking seems to have been freely cultivated in many parts of Greece and to have been as important in Syracuse as in Athens.

A second, largely Athenian phenomenon was the development of oratory in the law-courts. In his *Wasps* Aristophanes mocks the contemporary passion for litigation but shows how deeply it appealed to many Athenians. [6] It calls for a special kind of persuasion capable of convincing juries, and it soon created a professional class of pleaders, who might use their talents for other occasions also, but made an income by writing speeches for parties in law-suits. They developed a marked technique which was thought to be basic to almost any legal activity, but it seems to have taken a special form in Sicily, when after the expulsion of the tyrants in 465 BC many families, whose property had been confiscated, tried to re-establish their claims through the courts. At this time Corax, who was later regarded as the founder of professional rhetoric, wrote a handbook on its principles, and was followed by his pupil, Teisias, with another, which was said to be even better. They introduced an elementary psychology into debate by establishing what was to be a notable feature of Greek speeches—the appeal to probabilities, as when Corax makes a man who has been accused of assault say in his own defence:

It is obvious to you that I am weak in body, while he is strong; it is therefore inherently improbable that I should have dared to attack him. [7]

This kind of thing soon became popular in Athens, and forensic rhetoric evolved many such tricks and devices. The foundations were set for what was to be a highly elaborate technique, and enabled it to develop its own show-pieces, which were regarded as models of their kind and, not only admired on their first delivery, but preserved for the instruction of later centuries.

Sicily also did something for the rhetoric of display. In 427 BC Gorgias of Leontini came on an embassy to Athens and created a powerful impression on students of public speech. Thucydides was perhaps influenced by him, and his deleterious effect on the young was later emphasized by Plato, who took him as an example of the dangers of rhetoric in public life. Gorgias was a conscious artist of a peculiar kind. He tried to give to prose an impressive formality, and this he secured by rare words, a pointed use of antithesis and parallelism, and internal assonances and rhymes. He was much more interested in his manner than in his matter, and a few lines from a funeral speech give an indication of his deadly ingenuity in handling an ancient and well-worn theme:

Though they have died, our longing for them has not died with them, but immortal over bodies not immortal it lives when they live not.[8]

This is hollow and ridiculous, and it is hard to see how Gorgias made such an impression. Perhaps the explanation is that, when prose was still in its infancy, the Greeks still felt that it should have some of the formality of poetry, and, in a time when poetry itself was passing through a revolutionary change, did not see that this kind of prose was no substitute for it. Plato saw the absurdity of the whole thing and was not far wrong when in the *Gorgias* he compared rhetoric with cookery, having Gorgias very much in mind.

A mass of Athenian speeches survives from the latter part of the fifth century to almost the end of the fourth. They include some political speeches which supply a postscript to the speeches in Thucydides and show how much public oratory still counted in Athens and of what eloquence it was still capable. The second class, of private speeches delivered in the law-courts, is more abundant, and, though at times it touches on public affairs, its main interest lies in the light which it throws on domestic life and personal feuds, and in the resourceful inventiveness with which almost any case is made to appear plausible. A third kind, not so well represented, is that of display on public occasions. All three kinds show much the same qualities and illustrate some characteristic Greek qualities. In all of them great care is taken, not merely with the marshalling of arguments, but with the actual choice of words; a speech is almost as serious a work of art as a poem. It presents a view of life which may well be limited by the requirements of the occasion and the conventional psychology of the law-courts, but engages strong feelings and convictions. Oratory shares with philosophy the literary honours of the fourth century, and the comparison shows how much it has been forced to abandon in its concentration on immediate, narrow ends, but it has still an extraordinary force and vitality and illustrates how, even when their greatest glories were departed, the Athenians kept their zest for affairs, their competitive spirit, and their ambition to succeed.

Speeches in law-courts were usually written by professionals to be delivered by the actual defendants and plaintiffs, and these professionals came to be known as orators. They took their work very seriously with the Greek love for any complex technique, and it is characteristic that one of the earliest of them, Antiphon (*c* 480–411 BC), composed for the benefit of his clients *Tetralogies*, which are oratorical exercises meant to show in outline how speeches should be constructed. Each contains four speeches:

1 The prosecutor's opening speech,
2 The first speech for the defence,
3 The prosecutor's reply, and
4 The defendant's conclusion.

Three such *Tetralogies* survive. The first deals with a murder-case tried before the court of the Areopagus, the second with a charge of murder against a boy who has accidentally killed another boy with a javelin in the gymnasium, the third with an old man who has died from a wound inflicted by a young man. These may be based on actual cases and are certainly of the kind that came before the Athenian courts. In construction and presentation they are very close to two actual speeches composed by Antiphon. The *Murder of Herodes* deals with the disappearance of a man and the defence of another who is accused of murdering him, while *On the Singer* is the defence of a choir-master, who has given a drug to a boy to improve his voice and accidentally killed him. That Antiphon was no mere arm-chair theorist is clear from his own career. In 411 BC he played a leading part in a plot to establish an oligarchical government in Athens. He failed and went into exile, and on his return in the next year was tried, condemned, and executed, but not before delivering in his own defence a speech, which Thucydides regarded as the best of its kind which had ever been heard. A man who could deserve such praise knew his business, and his instructions were worthy of study.

With Antiphon forensic oratory was still in an experimental stage, and in him we can mark a conflict which reflects the conditions in which he worked. On the one hand he was touched by the manner of Gorgias and eager to show his skill at rhetoric for its own sake; on the other hand he was no less eager to persuade the jury that he was a common man who thought and spoke as they did and did not in the least wish to bamboozle them by being too clever. As an artist, he is not afraid of the fine phrase, as when a man who has lost his only son says: 'I am buried alive',[9] or a defendant appeals for pity: 'An old man, an exile, and an outcast, I shall beg my bread in a foreign land,'[10] or an apparently innocent young man protests his ignorance of speech-making in elaborate, carefully balanced periods. But as an advocate he must get the jury on his side, and he tries to do this by certain pretences to tolerance and a refusal to think ill of anyone. Thus in the *Murder of Herodes* the accused says: 'Not that I wished to avoid a trial by your democracy' and 'Of course I could trust you entirely without bearing in mind the oath which you have taken.'[11] Antiphon appeals to beliefs in divine vengeance which the jury may well hold but which he himself is not likely to treat very seriously. Yet, despite these concessions to vulgar credulity, Antiphon maintains his dignity and neither indulges in the personal abuse which was to appeal to later orators nor plays very strongly on the emotions. His trust in psychological probabilities gives to his speeches an air almost of scientific detachment. This is of course fallacious, but his apparent seriousness and self-control reflect the spirit of the fifth century and show that, however strong its passions sometimes were, it still demanded a certain decorum in the law-courts. These speeches are a small backwater in the great flood of the fifth century, but they show that even on its shabby side it maintained some style and dignity.

Antiphon's peculiarities are not to be found in a younger orator who was involved in hardly less notorious affairs. Andocides (c 440–c 390 BC) is famous because he was connected with a huge scandal in 415 BC, when just before the great Athenian expedition sailed to Sicily the images of Hermes throughout the city were found to have been mutilated. This was not only grave sacrilege but an evil portent for the expedition and all the worse because at the same time a profane parody of the Eleusinian Mysteries was said to have been celebrated in certain private houses. There were also undertones of political conspiracy, which could not be disregarded. Alcibiades was thought to have taken part, and was recalled from Sicily for trial, but took refuge in Sparta and was condemned to death in his absence. Andocides also was accused of complicity, and, though he succeeded in clearing himself of the graver charges, he admitted that he knew something about the affair of the Hermae. He gave his information under a promise of immunity, but by a later decree lost his civic rights and went into exile. He had certainly been implicated to some small degree, for, in 410 BC, when he managed to come back to Athens and plead his case for restoration of rights in his speech *On his Return* before the Assembly, he asks pardon for 'a youthful folly'. He failed to make his case and was not allowed back again until the general amnesty of 403 BC. But the old trouble still pursued him, and in 399 BC he was accused of taking part illegally in the Mysteries and entering the temple at Eleusis, and answered in his speech *On the Mysteries*. Either offence brought the death-penalty, but Andocides convinced the jury of his innocence and was acquitted. He seems to have stayed in Athens and to have played some part in public affairs.

Andocides' career is inseparable from his more famous speeches and through them we can see him for what he was. He is not a professional writer of speeches for others, but an amateur who conducts his own cases.

He is concerned with matters of very great public interest, in which he has played some part. His speech *On his Return* turns on a purely political issue and is addressed, not to a jury, but to the Assembly. He was a man of action to whom speech-making was a not very agreeable necessity. The ancient critics were hard on him for his lack of rhetorical devices and his general disregard of order in presenting a case. But they wrote at a time when rhetoric was judged by a number of technical rules, and what counts with Andocides is precisely his ignorance of them. His language is not very distinguished, but it is natural and effective. He can tell a story with vivid skill, as befits a man who has witnessed some astonishing events, as when he relates how on the day after the mutilation of the Hermae, two of his neighbours came to him and said:

We have done it, Andocides, and it is all over. Now if you will agree to keep quiet and say nothing, you will find us just as good friends as before, but if you don't, we shall count much more as enemies than any new friends you will make by betraying us.[12]

Somehow this rings true, and such verisimilitude is Andocides' most impressive gift. His whole account of the episode is realistic and detailed and in no way made to serve rhetorical ends. That he was successful in making his speech *On the Mysteries* may have been partly due to his convincing air of candour.

Andocides was sufficiently a man of the world to know how to suit his manner to circumstances. He can play on the emotions in a way that Antiphon does not, and he can strike an agreeably human note, which may not be very dignified but warms us to him. So he claims that in giving away the names of some men who mutilated the Hermae he saved the lives of his family, and asks with an innocent air:

How would each of you have acted? If I had to choose between dying a noble death and saving my life at the cost of my honour, my behaviour might well have been considered base – though many would have made the same choice; they would rather have remained alive than have died nobly.[13]

He does not quite give himself away, but there is something endearing in his admission that he might not have behaved very heroically. So too he is not shy of using scurrilous abuse to present his opponents in the worst possible light. Such vituperation was common enough in Athens not merely in Aristophanes but presumably in the violent speeches which Cleon delivered before the Assembly. Even before 417 BC Andocides said of the demagogue Hyperbolus, who was disliked both by Aristophanes and by Thucydides:

I blush to mention the name of Hyperbolus; his father is a branded slave, who still works in the public mint; and he himself is a foreign interloper who makes lamps.[14]

This kind of thing was expected from Andocides, who was no friend of the advanced democrats and was brought up in an age when hard knocks were freely given and received. He deals with one of the witnesses brought against him by denouncing him as an 'informer and common blackguard' and brings up against him his past as 'making a living as a common informer under the democracy and being a slave of the Thirty that you might not be compelled to disgorge any money you got from informing'.[15] Yet, when Andocides had a serious part to play in public affairs, he could rise to the occasion with dignity. In 391 BC he had to defend before the Assembly his decision, as member of an embassy to Sparta, to make peace between her and Athens. In his speech *On the Peace* he answers his critics firmly and argues that peace, even on not very favourable terms, is better than war. He was in his way public-minded, but his whole manner of speaking on an important public occasion is that of the unprofessional man of affairs who knows what he has to say and does not attempt to make too much of it.

With Lysias (*c* 459–*c* 380 BC) we return to a professional writer of speeches like Antiphon. He was by origin a Syracusan and the son of Cephalus, whom Plato presents so charmingly in the opening scene of the *Republic*, though his admiration for the father's character did not extend to the son's art. Some thirty of Lysias' speeches survive, all short and nearly all dealing with private cases for other men. He himself comes to the front in his speech *Against Eratosthenes*, delivered in 403 BC soon after the collapse of the Thirty, under whom Eratosthenes had arrested Lysias' brother, Polemarchus, and sent him to death. The speech, coming so near the brutal events on which it touches, throws a remarkable light on the Thirty and their motives. The tyrants, says Lysias with bitter irony, 'avowed that they must purge the city of wrongdoers and turn the rest of the citizens to virtue and justice'.[16] In fact what they wanted was to kill anyone with any money, which they could then confiscate, and, as Lysias says, 'they thought nothing of taking life but thought a lot of making money'.[17] The quiet tone of the speech and its lack of overt violence might suggest that Lysias is not rising fully to his opportunity, but in fact his sober understatements are deadly to his opponent and far more damaging than any outbursts of abuse. At the time it may not have seemed very adventurous, but it has weathered the years and kept much of its merciless freshness.

Lysias' most interesting and useful gift was his ability to get inside the characters of those for whom he wrote speeches and to make them talk in harmony with their known personalities. In this he is a far more subtle artist than Antiphon. In *For Mantitheus* he adapts his words to a young Athenian of good birth, who is candid and sure of himself but careful not to boast, though he is proud of what his ancestors have done for the state and what he has himself done on the battlefield. In another speech a man who has been refused a public pension pleads for one and argues that he is the victim of personal envy; he is accused of insolence because he rides a horse and points out that, since he cannot afford a mule, he occasionally borrows a horse from a friend rather than hop about on two sticks. Conversely, in his speech against Aeschines the Socratic, Lysias makes fun of him for borrowing money which he never repays and says that the crowd of creditors round his doors at daybreak makes people think that they have come for a funeral. This neat adaptability is matched by a style of unusual limpidity and elegance, which may not indeed be the way in which Lysias' clients ordinarily spoke, but is well fitted to their quandaries. He is never pompous or inflated, never rough or obscure. He avoids metaphors and striking figures of speech and aims, above all, at smoothness and clarity. His account of the Thirty gains greatly from the quiet way in which it is told, and his accounts of action, especially domestic, have a quiet neatness and charm. He does not even let his own feelings take command, and he can tell a complicated story so that we follow every stage in it. Though he was a Syracusan by origin, he moved in well-to-do Athenian circles, and it is tempting to think that in these he learned the lightness and the elegance, which Plato used in a like way. His is a truly Attic grace, which has never been touched by Gorgias, and he formed an art of words on the principle that their first task is to communicate and that clarity does not in the end exclude power.

Lysias also composed a Funeral Speech for the Athenians who fell in the war against Corinth *c* 394 BC. The *genre* was well established and had notable precedents in speeches by Pericles and Gorgias. Lysias is certainly much less powerful than the first and much less meretricious than the second, but his speech is too conventional to be moving and suggests that a theme of this kind, which called for powerful emotions and bold ideas, was beyond his scope. But, though this is perhaps his only excursion into this kind of oratory, the show-piece was a well-known form and was highly popular in his time. Its greatest practitioner was Isocrates (436–338 BC), who composed his works in the shape of speeches but really intended them to be read as political pamphlets. Among the Attic orators, with whom he is inevitably classed, he is almost alone in his paramount concern with public affairs and his far-ranging and imaginative but not altogether impracticable ideas. His thought is of considerable importance, and we can understand why, in the *Phaedrus*, Socrates compares him very favourably with Lysias and says 'there really is philosophy in the man.'[18] Like Plato, Isocrates was deeply concerned with education and political theories. He differed from Plato in being far less theoretical and less interested in main principles. He worked for immediate results and took great pains to fashion a flawless style. His language does not flow rapidly like that of Lysias, but has its own grave and careful correctness and is well compared by an ancient critic with 'a picture in which the lights melt imperceptibly into shadows'.[19] He avoided the repetition of similar syllables in successive words and the combination of letters which are hard to pronounce together. He did not allow hiatus between the end of one word and the beginning of the next, and he thought that prose should have rhythms of its own, which he carefully worked out. Yet, with all this he kept the natural order of words. At times indeed his structure of sentence is too elaborate, and they seem to topple before they come to an end, and, despite all his ingenuity, he can be so regular as to be boring. But he was a conscious artist, who had something serious to say and evolved an impressive way of saying it. Plato's Socrates may have gone too far in his hope that all speech-writers might seem to be children compared with him, but he speaks well for some of the best influences in the fourth century and deserves the high opinion which later antiquity held of him.

Though Isocrates wrote speeches for others to deliver in the law-courts, his important work lay in his long tracts on two subjects very near his heart, education and the condition of Greece. He had seen the rise of the Sophists, who claimed to make men wise for pay, and the corruption to which this had led, and he set out to discredit them and to offer something more honest and less pretentious. In the fragmentary *Against the Sophists* he does his work of destruction and attacks those teachers who claim to teach more than they know, especially a full knowledge of right conduct and all virtue. He dislikes their 'eristic' method, which is a kind of logic-chopping practised by the lesser disciples of Socrates, and his real complaint is that they care nothing for the truth. Isocrates in fact deals with the corruption of philosophy by the love of argument for its own sake. This tract was written in 390 BC when Plato was just getting to work, and it shows how two very different men distrusted the arrogant claims of the new education. Some years later in *c* 355 BC Isocrates followed it up with *On the Antidosis* which gives his positive views. By education he means culture in a broad sense, the training of a man in youth and manhood to play a full part in the state. In his general aim he is much closer to Protagoras than to Plato. Education must strengthen the character and help to form the gift of right judgment, and for this it must pay great attention to the highest of human powers, which is language. He does not believe in the pursuit of knowledge for its own sake, and, though he approves of philosophy, it is on the principle that 'philosophy is for the soul what gymnastic is for the body'.[20] He admits that we cannot obtain absolute knowledge, but we can make successful guesses, and that is what matters. Compared with the strict theoretical education advocated in the *Republic* the ideal of Isocrates is certainly modest, but behind it lies a clear conviction: the well educated are superior to other Greeks just as men are superior to animals and Greeks to barbarians. Isocrates reverts to the old ideal of the full man and bases it on his belief in practical wisdom.

Isocrates had a great love for his country, but to him it was much less Athens than Greece. He saw, as very few men of his time did, that the internecine struggles between Greek cities were not only ruinous to them but prevented Greece from civilizing the world. To this theme he remained faithful through his long life and was ready with one solution after another. In 380 BC he composed the *Panegyricus* for recitation at the Olympic festival. He saw that only some common cause could unite the Greeks and make them conscious of being a single nation. He began by proposing that Sparta and Athens should join and head a union of Greeks against Persia, but Thebes unexpectedly rose to power, and the design fell flat. In 368 BC he suggested to Dionysius I of Syracuse that he should be the Panhellenic champion, but this too came to nothing. In 356 BC Isocrates appealed to Archidamus, king of Sparta, to put an end to war between Greeks and curb the menace of the barbarians. In all these appeals Isocrates was unsuccessful, partly because his chosen champions were not up to what he asked of them, largely because the Greeks themselves did not wish to follow his policy. But then events took command from an unexpected quarter. Philip II, king of Macedon, had not only turned his own country into a formidable power, but was moving southwards to extend his dominions. Many Greeks were against him, but Isocrates saw in him the deliverer whom he sought, and in 346 BC appealed to him to unite the four chief states of Greece in an expedition to conquer the East. In 338 BC Philip defeated the united Athenians and Thebans at Chaeronea, and Isocrates, aged ninety-eight, heard the news and died. Legend said that he died of grief, but Philip's victory might have cheered him by bringing what he had always wished, and in fact he saw the first stage in the fulfilment of a grand design which was to take Alexander to India and to unite Greece under the Macedonian monarchy. The cause for which he argued so steadfastly was to be debated with much acrimony by others. It meant the end of the old Greek system and the city-state, which Plato regarded as a permanent element in the scheme of things. Isocrates saw beyond his time and lived long enough to see the beginnings of a vast change.

In the history of literature Isocrates holds a special place. To him more than to any other man we owe our notion of what prose is. Before him it had indeed been fashioned for narrative with supreme success by Herodotus and Thucydides, but neither paid regard to its more mundane purposes and each had in him a quiet spring of poetry. Plato was at least half a poet and, when he gave his gifts to strictly technical writing, he was a specialist of consummate ability. On the other hand, the orators sought methods to exploit the emotions as much as possible and to present cases on narrow lines to convince juries. Isocrates alone writes in a quiet, reasoning manner to convince his readers of the truth of his arguments. Even his noble or moving moments rise out of his argument and are not independent of it. His temper is so well matched by his style that he is a model for all writers who have something to say and wish to say it clearly and carefully and at its full worth. This temper matched his educational ideal, which was no more and no less than what we mean by Humanism. He believed that men become wiser by studying the great works of other men, and these are to be found chiefly in literature. He had none of Plato's hankering for mathematics, and this limited his educational ideal, which was perhaps even more severely limited by the conditions in which his Humanism could be studied. For him it was only the Greek past that mattered, whereas for the modern world it is a much richer and more varied past, which can always be extended with the birth of new masterpieces. Isocrates' Humanism has something inbred in it, and that is perhaps why it does not inflame us. It was indeed to have an enormous influence in the Hellenization of large parts of Asia with the conquest of Alexander and afterwards. In his conviction that the Greeks are vastly superior to all Barbarians Isocrates set the tone for the mixed world which was to rise so strangely from the chaos of Alexander's successors, and few men of letters can have had so enormous an influence either in space or in time, from Athens to the Indus, and from Alexander to the Renaissance and beyond.

The ideal of a united Greece which Isocrates advocated with such persistence became a matter of urgent and immediate politics with the rise of

Philip and aroused the blackest passions and enmities. What Isocrates asked for as a voluntary act from the divided Greeks was imposed on them by Philip, who was in the opinion of many not a Greek at all and not a supporter of their traditional liberties. To accept his suzerainty seemed to be not wisdom but gross treachery to their native cities. Philip's supporters might argue the case for peace and unity, but others saw them as corrupt sycophants bribed to secure his aims. The result was a deep cleavage in public opinion, and the parties were so nicely divided that they played into his hands, since he was an astute manipulator of men and knew how to profit from local feuds. The situation which he created and which was no less serious under his son Alexander is fully illustrated by the long-drawn hostility between two Athenian public men, who engaged in a fierce war of words and are still vivid from it. Aeschines (c 390–after 330 BC) and Demosthenes (384–322 BC) were shaped by circumstances and character to oppose one another on the main issues of Athenian foreign policy for nearly twenty years, and in their legal battles we see what discords rent Athens and other Greek cities. In general, Aeschines was for co-operation with Philip, Demosthenes for opposing him by force. It is quite possible that Aeschines took money from Philip, but in the strange regulations of Greek bribery it does not follow that he was dishonest in the political course which he took. In 348 BC, after believing in a policy of opposition, he saw that it was impossible, and to this conviction he adhered. The result was a series of actions which engaged him and Demosthenes and provoked a remarkable interchange of speeches. In 346 BC Demosthenes prepared to prosecute Aeschines for taking bribes and used a man called Timocrates as his colleague, but Aeschines was too quick for him and prosecuted Timocrates for sexual depravity. He seems to have won the case and for the moment to have silenced Demosthenes, but in 344 BC Demosthenes prosecuted again. Each party made a speech called *On the False Embassy*, and Aeschines was acquitted by a small majority. In 337 BC a certain Ctesiphon proposed to confer a crown on Demosthenes. Aeschines impeached him for illegality, and, when after a long delay the case was tried in 330 BC, and Demosthenes answered with his speech *On the Crown* Aeschines failed to get a fifth of the votes and was fined a thousand drachmas. He left Athens, and nothing more is known of him.

The speeches of these two opponents are composed on a generous scale, and, though they were delivered before law-courts, they have many qualities of public speeches and were no doubt heard as such by many Athenians. They deal with matters which affected very greatly the place of Athens in Greek politics and indeed her survival as an independent city.

Of the two men Demosthenes was by far the more gifted and the more formidable. Though he made himself a speaker by a great effort of will in subduing disadvantages, he became a consummate master of the spoken word. All his mature works have survived, and throughout antiquity he was honoured as the foremost speaker of all time and the model for all others. The anonymous author of the tract *On the Sublime*, writing perhaps in the first century AD, says that 'in his vehemence he burns and carries away all before him, like a thunderbolt or flash of lightning'.[21] Even when he deals with quite trivial affairs Demosthenes makes every word strike its target. He hammers everything home, but with economy and concentrated power. His closely knit sentences indicate hard thought which has mastered all possible intricacies and reduced them to a lucid and pungent form. He continually varies their length and pattern and is a more conscious artist in prose than any Greek writer except Plato. If he completely lacks Plato's imaginative brilliance, he has a strong sense of drama, as when he tells of the almost paralysing effect produced in Athens by the news that Philip had taken the town of Elatea:

It was evening, and someone had come to the committee of the Council with the news that Elatea had been taken. Upon this they got up from supper without waiting; some of them drove the occupants out of the booths in the marketplace and set fire to the wicker-work; others sent for the generals and summoned the trumpeter; and the city was full of commotion.[22]

Demosthenes' powerful mind is always in full control of its subject and, though it moves on narrow lines, its vision is all the sharper within them. He lacks the exalted tone and the generous range of the fifth century, but in his limits he is not ultimately the less forceful, and it is this hard, unyielding power which carries him to the end and is his very self.

The murky flame that is never absent from Demosthenes' public speeches is his love of Athens and his passionate eagerness to see her asserting herself against grave perils. This was the main theme not only of his interchanges with Aeschines but of public speeches, such as the *Philippics* and *Olynthiacs*, in which he emphasized the growth of Philip's power and the urgent need to stop him. In his fear of Philip he saw the more sharply the tricks and the treacheries by which Philip extended his dominions, but his denunciations are the more powerful because he controls their language as when he says:

As a house and ship must be strongest at the lowest parts, so must the bases and foundations of a policy be true and honest; which they are not in the diplomatic gains of Macedon.[23]

Without doubt or misgiving, Demosthenes believed in the essential greatness of Athens and, like other devoted patriots, had no difficulty in combining a high ideal of her with a conviction that she seldom lived up to it. His ideal was not far from the Periclean, but lacked its intellectual foundation and took too much for granted in the capacity of Athens to make herself felt. For his country he was ready to do anything, and in the end he sacrificed himself when in 322 BC he took poison rather than submit to the Macedonian general Antipater and his agent Demades. For those who, in his opinion, worked against Athens he kept his hardest words and, though he might pray for their change of heart, he can hardly have believed in it, and what he really desired was their defeat and destruction. So he ends *On the Crown* with a ringing paragraph on them:

Never, O all ye gods, may any of you yield to their desire! If it is possible, may you implant even in these men a better mind and heart. But if they are indeed beyond cure, then bring them and them alone to utter and early destruction, by land and sea. And to us that remain grant the speediest release from the fears that hang over us, and safety that cannot be shaken![24]

Demosthenes was driven by a fierce, unabating passion for his country, and this he turned into masterful words which convey the force of his convictions and his refusal to compromise about them. However narrow he may have been, he understood fully his own case and gave to it the whole force of his driving personality.

In so monolithic a character it is easy to find defects. Demosthenes made mistakes and miscalculations. Though he was a master at playing on all the more turbulent emotions, he was not at home with subtle and delicate effects. The ancient critics were particularly hard on the badness of his jokes, and indeed they are less jokes than scurrilous abuse, as when he unjustly taunts Aeschines with his low origin and mocks him for having been a third-class actor who lived on the grapes and olives thrown at him by his outraged audiences.[25] His inability to see the other side is sometimes an advantage, but not when he overstates his own case as he often does. He had little insight into character or interest in it. In his world everything was black or white, and there were no half-tones. He is most human when he indulges a bitter irony and talks of men 'who measure happiness by their belly and their basest pleasures'[26] or asserts a rude common sense as when he dismisses the common notion that Philip will not march against the next victim on his list. He has every technical trick at his command, from specious arguments based on probability to ingenious irrelevance and avoidance of the real issues. His defects are the other side of his virtues. He was obsessed by a vision of an independent Athens and by the memory of her former greatness. It was this that governed his actions and his words, and he believed that just as Athens had saved Greece from the Persians, so she could again save it from the no less deadly aggression of Macedon.

The long wrangle between Demosthenes and Aeschines was made the more bitter by the great dissimilarity of their characters and their gifts. While Demosthenes, obsessed by a single purpose, has the hardness and obstinacy of his convictions, Aeschines was happy to secure what results he could and to make the best of a given situation. When he first appears in public life, it is as an opponent of Philip, but on the embassy to him two years later, he changed his mind in the middle of negotiations and so won the lasting hatred of Demosthenes, who assumed that this could only be the result of bribery. But Philip seems to have been able to convince men of sterling worth like Isocrates, and Aeschines may well have fallen a victim to his wiles. But, more importantly, he decided that it was wiser to be with Philip than against him, and stated his position clearly:

Both individual and state must shift their ground according to change of circumstances and aim at what is best for the time.[27]

This does not mean that he was necessarily a traitor, and indeed there is no reason to think that he was. Philip, and Alexander after him, both admired Athens and were, within limits, prepared to treat her well. Aeschines took these intentions at their face-value and was not quite wrong to do so. Demosthenes adopted the policy of resistance at all costs to Macedon and naturally thought the worst of Aeschines. The conflict is between the man of the fixed idea and the supple, compromising man of the world, and it comes out in the difference of their characters. Aeschines does not indulge in abuse of Demosthenes; he is content to make him look absurd, as in his behaviour on the embassy to Philip:

When everybody was thus prepared to listen to him, the brute gave utterance to some sort of obscure, half-dead exordium, and having made a little progress over the surface of the subject he suddenly halted and hesitated, and at last completely lost his way.[28]

When Demosthenes accuses him of insulting an Olynthian lady, Aeschines is able to counter with dignity and detachment. He keeps his temper when Demosthenes loses his, and he has light touches of irony and sarcasm, which suit his air of a well-bred and well-educated man.

Aeschines was in his own way a patriot but he thought that Athens could maintain a dignified independence by keeping on good terms with Macedon. Of this he is not ashamed some years later:

I admit that I advised the people to come to terms with Philip, and make the peace which you, who have never drawn a sword, now say is disgraceful, though I say that it is far more honourable than war.[29]

When war came, Aeschines lamented not only that it had come but that it had brought a series of disasters, for all of which he blamed Demosthenes and his conduct of public policy. He deplored the collapse of Thebes and the humiliation of Sparta, and he saw the parlous state of Athens:

Our city, the common asylum of all Greeks, to whom formerly embassies used to come from Greece to obtain their safety from us, city by city, is struggling now not for the leadership of the Greeks but for the very soil of her fatherland.[30]

Aeschines does not lack moments of grandeur, and his humanity is warmer than that of Demosthenes. What he lacks is Demosthenes' daemonic drive and onslaught. He argues skilfully and persuasively, but he never overwhelms, and it is understandable that in the heated atmosphere of the late fourth century he should lose the last action in the long debate with Demosthenes and die in exile. Yet, in retrospect, we can see that the irony of history has proved both men wrong. Demosthenes strove against the rise of Macedon and failed completely to halt it. Before his death he knew of Alexander's vast conquests and must have seen that the city-state, which meant everything to him, was fated to be absorbed into some much larger unity. Even after the death of Alexander, when hope revived, he failed again and died as the victim of one of Alexander's generals. On the other hand Aeschines, who saw in Macedon an ally for Athens, was in the end no less wrong. For a time the triumph of Philip and Alexander seemed to mean the realization of his hopes, but after Alexander's death and the rise of the Successors, who disputed with one another for his empire by force of arms, there was little to be gained from Antipater and his agents. If Athens was not strong or determined enough to revive the glories of the Periclean past, she was equally unable to treat as an equal with the military dictators whom Alexander's early death brought to power over the Greek world. She was indeed to maintain for centuries a distinguished pre-eminence in the world of the spirit, but politically she ceased to count. It is hard not to be moved by the flaming patriotism of Demosthenes, but it came too late to have any chance of success, and, though we may admire the common sense of Aeschines, it was based on false assumptions and wrong forecasts.

While Demosthenes held the centre of the stage, other orators, challenged to emulation by his example, were at work and completed in the eyes of posterity the notion of the fourth century as the golden age of oratory. Hyperides (389–332 BC) was on the whole a staunch supporter of Demosthenes and was put to death at the same time on the orders of Antipater. Only fragments of his work survive, but he seems to have shown wisdom in cultivating the qualities which Demosthenes lacked, and, in antiquity, he was praised for his wit, his sense of humour, and his easy persuasiveness. That he could on occasion be both sharp and amusing is clear from a fragment:

> Orators are like snakes; all snakes are equally hated, but of them, the vipers injure men, while the big snakes eat the vipers.[31]

Lycurgus (?–324 BC), also an ally of Demosthenes, is known only from one speech *Against Leocrates*, against a man who fled after the battle of Chaeronea and about 332 BC returned to Athens, where he was prosecuted as a traitor. There is in Lycurgus something heated and inflated, apparent alike in his many appeals to divine justice and in the savagery of his prosecution. He aimed at a nobility and impressiveness which were beyond his grasp, and there is something not quite convincing in his assumption of high principles and his conscious effort to maintain a dignity of utterance. Perhaps a minor poet was lost in him. At least he makes an attempt to be something of the kind when he claims that the very land of Attica is calling for help:

> So imagine, Athenians, that the land and its trees are supplicating you; that the harbours, the dockyards, and the walls of the city are begging you; that the temples and holy places are urging you to come to their help.[32]

This is really more than Lycurgus can manage, and in the very effort to be impressive we detect a certain insecurity and lack of clear conviction. Greek oratory never excelled at this kind of appeal, and this was not the way to attempt it. The latest of these orators was Dinarchus (360–? BC), who came into fame after the death of Alexander when his more gifted rivals were dead. In him the beginnings of decline are manifest. He loots from his predecessors, and himself lacks originality. He prefers emotional appeals to argument and never fuses the two into a single effect. His abuse goes beyond the worst excesses of earlier speakers, and his lack of any clear principles is matched by his careless handling of words. It is symbolical that in a surviving speech, in which he attacks Demosthenes, he reveals all his opponent's faults but none of his virtues.

Greek oratory was largely a product of the fourth century and, as a living art, died with it. It reflects the spirit of an Athens reduced in wealth and power but still haunted by ambitions of greatness and at times displaying her old pride, even though the brutality of events was to show that she had little to be proud of. While Isocrates and even Aeschines tried to shape their ideas to suit new conditions, Demosthenes and his followers yearned for the revival of a splendid past, but over all of them there hangs an air of unreality. Their efforts to grasp the problems of their time were courageous and whole-hearted, but oratory was not the best medium for such an endeavour since it made problems look simpler than they were and led to unbalanced judgments on them. Oratory does not claim to pursue the truth in an undivided spirit, but great orators have usually some penetrating criticism of life to offer. The Greek orators were so occupied with immediate issues and with presenting them for public decisions, that in the end they had not very much of lasting importance to say. Isocrates' ideal of Hellenic culture is a little colourless and bloodless and accepts too easily the limitations of the human lot, while Demosthenes is too deeply sunk in the past to see the present as it really is or to have any solid comment to make on it. Hitherto the Greeks had treated literature as a means to interpret reality as they saw it, and this gave it a special integrity and strength, but now it became in oratory the instrument of political and personal designs aimed at immediate ends. In the fourth century the Greeks gave to this ultimately secondary art all the care and attention which they used to give to more objective and more universal studies. This is perhaps characteristic of the fourth century, which kept much of the old grand manner but lacked the authentic spirit to make it live. The passionate attention which the Greeks had given to their place in the world was now given to their personal squabbles, and, though at times the old dignity appears in noble forms, it is subjected to the distortion of persuasion and propaganda.

Yet rhetoric certainly answered a deep need in the Greek character. For centuries after the death of Demosthenes it was cultivated and studied with minute care. Rules were laid down for its proper guidance, and a skilful orator was honoured all over Greece. This lasted for centuries until the triumph of Christianity, and even later, and, though some of the surviving speeches are by no means without charm or ability, it is clear that in nearly all of them the manner is much more regarded than the matter, and the impression left is of an ultimate vacuity, in which even real convictions are smothered in a mass of words. Later Greek rhetoric lacks the dark passion of Demosthenes and tries to make up for it by a kind of poetry, by delicate phrases which have a certain evanescent charm but do not really reflect any vigour of mind or feeling. Unable to create poetry of any great worth, and perhaps equally unable to respond to it, the later

Greeks found a substitute in rhetoric. In it they instructed the Romans who governed them and the many Hellenized Asians who entered into the inheritance of Alexander. It was no doubt at the time an agreeable pastime, but today it rings like a hollow echo of an art which had once been at least an instrument for powerful controversy, even if it was already a confession of some failure at the heart of things.

THE SHRINKING HORIZON

THE disintegration of Alexander's gigantic empire immediately after his death at Babylon in 323 BC changed the whole pattern of Greek civilization. His successors aimed at maintaining military monarchies which had more than a semblance of oriental despotism, and, though after some troubled years Athens was left more or less to herself, she knew that power was no longer in her grasp and never again took a leading part in Greek politics. Her consciousness of decline did irreparable harm to her creative activities. She became a notable seat of education, but not of the fine arts. At the same time, while enterprising Greeks were infiltrating the new kingdoms of Asia and creating a Hellenism which was to have vast repercussions to India and beyond, the authentic Greek spirit could not fail to be weakened in the process. The years between the death of Alexander and the conquest of Greece by Rome, which culminated in the sack of Corinth in 146 BC, were not remarkable for their literature. New schools of philosophy flourished; mathematics reached unprecedented heights; natural science provided useful inventions. But literature, which had already shown signs of contracting its frontiers, continued to do so, and there is no reason to think that it produced masterpieces of which we know nothing. Hitherto it had been closely tied to political and religious life and derived much of its strength from them, but now politics was the monopoly of a few autocrats, and the Olympian religion, though maintained in all its outward forms, had been deeply corroded by philosophical scepticism. If literature was to exist, it must adapt itself to new, not very encouraging circumstances. It could not hope to have the old breadth or depth, or to deal with matters of universal urgency. Its prose-writers failed signally to rise even to the challenge of Alexander's exploits, but poets, bred on a tradition of artistic achievement, sought to do something new and suited to the time, and achieved at least some success which had both influence and renown.

In their restricted, often uprooted circumstances poets had to find their subjects in new fields of experience where they could expect little help from the precedents of a splendid past. One possibility was to make what they could of new ideas, notably in philosophy and, though this was inevitably rare, once at least it produced impressive results. Cleanthes (331–252 BC) was the head of the Stoic school from 263 BC to his death, and with the dry speculations of its founder were transfused with a religious ardour. Cleanthes believed that the universe was alive, with God as its soul and the sun as its heart. In this spirit he wrote a Hymn to his god. His vehicle is the hexameter as it had been used long before in the Homeric Hymns, but its contents and its spirit are very much his own. He has made Stoic doctrine so intimate a part of himself that he deals majestically with large conceptions and at the same time conveys his own devout and vivid faith in his otherwise remote and abstract god:

> So will I praise thee, ever singing of thy might
> By whom the whole wide firmament of heaven is swayed
> And guided in its wheeling journey round this earth
> In glad submission to thee: for in thine unconquered hands
> Thou hast a mighty servant, the thunderbolt of heaven
> Wrought with a double edge, and of never-dying fire –
> A pulse of life beating through all created things
> That walk in thy ways; and with this thou dost direct
> Thy Omnipresent Word that moves through all creation
> And mingles with the sun and the company of the stars.[1]

The god of Cleanthes is called Zeus, and his instrument is still the lightning, but in every other respect he is a far bolder conception than anything yet suggested by Greek religious thought. There is a remarkable imaginative power in this embracing vision, which is set out in majestic but not difficult words. Cleanthes does not, as earlier poets do, treat his god as a personal friend, but he feels his overmastering presence and his immanent control of all living things. Cleanthes is indeed unique at this time in his choice of a subject, but, if on one side he looked back to thinkers like Xenophanes who believed in the One, on the other he looked forward to a much later generation when the Neo-Platonists were to combine logic and mysticism in their attempts to comprehend the ultimate nature of being.

While Cleanthes explored the mysteries of time and place, other poets turned to the other extreme and, by paying an affectionate attention to humble sights and scenes, extracted from them a charming, unpretentious poetry which was true to their unadventurous but not unperceptive lives. Erinna, who lived on the island of Telos in the south-eastern corner of the Aegean, seems to have been active towards the end of the fourth century. She died when she was nineteen years old, but not before she had written a poem called *The Distaff*, which took its name from its references to her unmarried life as a 'spinster' but was primarily a lament for her friend Baucis, who also died at an early age. A fragment of a papyrus from Egypt suggests that it deserved the high opinion which antiquity held of it. In it Erinna recalls how she and Baucis used to play a game called 'Turtle-tortle', which was something like 'Prisoners' Base', how they clung to their dolls as they took the part of mothers, how they were frightened of a bogy called Mormo, which had huge ears and four feet, and kept on changing its shape. These memories are briefly and deftly touched upon, and then in contrast with them comes the end of girlhood with marriage:

> But when you came to marriage, you forgot all this
> That in your childish innocence your mother told you.
> Dear Baucis, Aphrodite made your heart forget.[2]

Erinna was no more than a girl, but her poem, with its homesickness for childhood and its bitter sense of loss, made a deep impression on other poets, who wrote prefatory lines to it and may have learned from it lessons in the poetry of the simple life. She was a pioneer in an art which was to have a long history, and her use of the hexameter proved that it could still assume new duties and give to them an easy flow. If the more complex metres of lyric song were beyond the scope of this age, the hexameter was ready to be used for more than one purpose, and perhaps the ancients were not quite wrong when they compared Erinna not unfavourably with Sappho.

Such new tendencies as poetry displayed found a centre and a focus in the city of Alexandria, which Alexander founded in 331 BC and where his body was buried. It was the capital of the kingdom of Egypt, which Alexander's friend and general, Ptolemy (*c* 376–282 BC), had with notable prescience seized immediately after his master's death. Egypt was a geographical unit, and Ptolemy and his descendants ruled it as successors of the Pharaohs until the death of the last and most famous of the line, Cleopatra, in 31 BC. Though she was the only one of them who spoke Egyptian, they assumed Egyptian airs in their absolute monarchy and their presentation of themselves as gods. But they remained Greeks in a foreign land, and around them fostered a form of Greek civilization whose members differed from the indigenous people in physique, colour, language, customs, and religion. The Alexandrian Greeks lived in a Greek city but in an alien society, and had all the characteristics of a conquering caste. Ptolemy I was no illiterate soldier of fortune but founded the famous Library, which was greatly extended by his successor and became a seat of learning on an unprecedented scale. The Library became the home of Alexandrian poetry in its heyday in the third century BC and of its three main poets Callimachus (310–*c* 240 BC) had a post on it and Apollonius (*c* 295–215 BC) was Librarian. As members of a small, highly educated class, which lived in a large city, they found much of their inspiration and material in books, and it was their admiration for literature that made them writers. They wrote, not for large, public audiences, but for their own social group, and, like other cliques and coteries, they developed marked signs of inbreeding, but in their different ways Callimachus, Apollonius, and their greater contemporary Theocritus (*c* 310–250 BC) shaped a school of poetry which has certain common characteristics and shows what happened when the Greeks were cut off from much that had hitherto inspired their literature. The Alexandrian age was an aftermath, which could not really hope to rival what had been done before, but at least it tried to demonstrate that it could make use of its opportunities and produce something that was undeniably its own.

The problem was what to do. In the Ptolemaic autocracy public occasions might sometimes call for choral song on the old model, but the model itself had long passed out of use at any respectable level and was at once too archaic and too complex to be capable of revival. The poets' aim was to combine something of tradition, for which they had a scholarly respect, with a pleasing novelty suited to the highly sophisticated circles in which they moved, but the combination could be made in more than one way, and it was easy to disagree about them. The divergence indeed was so sharp that it provoked a famous battle of the books between Apollonius and Callimachus. Apollonius believed in the long narrative-poem, which might be claimed as a successor to the epic, though it could not be handled in the old epic language, which was not so much out of place as impossible in a society which expected individual words to be chosen with a discriminating precision and each to do something new. Callimachus did not believe in the long poem, on the principle that 'a big book is a big evil'[3] and attacked Apollonius, who seems to have been so injured that he retired to Rhodes to nurse his wounds. Callimachus may of course have been inspired by personal animosity against him, but there is something to be said against the long poem, which was all too liable to have no more than an antiquarian interest. Callimachus sees it as a heavy wagon lumbering on a main road and prefers his own by-way; he even calls the epic poet a braying ass and himself a sweet cicada. His own gifts were for the brief effect, the sudden surprise, and he wished his own poetry to be rich but not heavy. He seems indeed to have been moved by an ideal of 'pure poetry' such as we have known in modern times and compared the long poem with the Assyrian river, which may have a powerful flood but carries all kinds of dirt and mess with it. He may even have felt that a long poem is a contradiction in terms, and in that case he anticipated Coleridge and Poe. In any case he was probably right in thinking that the short poem was much better fitted to his own age simply because it aimed at less ambitious effects and was well suited to the sharp sensibilities of scholars.

In the four books of his *Argonautica* Apollonius tells of the quest for the Golden Fleece and especially of Jason and Medea. The story was known to Homer, who makes a passing reference to it, and certainly belonged to the repertory of the old epic. It provided splendid opportunities for thrilling adventures and for those excursions into the unknown with which the epic varied its more straightforward episodes. But it demanded a heroic sense of human worth and of perilous action, such as Homer shows in every line, but this was just what Apollonius lacked. His Jason is the faintest of phantoms, and could hardly be otherwise, since Apollonius, living in the metropolitan society of Alexandria, had no conception of what a hero was. For this reason the poem from the start suffers from a deep defect. Nor was this the only one. Apollonius could not forget that he was an antiquarian and thought that he must garnish his poem with liberal titbits of recondite information. This is deadly, not only to the flow of the narrative, but to the actual poetry, which is stifled by it. It overloads his catalogue of heroes, and the geography of the unknown places where the Argonauts sail forfeits all interest through the accumulation of irrelevant details. The delight in learning for its own sake had hardly existed in earlier Greece and was a specially Alexandrian phenomenon. Since this learning was mainly literary, it seeped into poetry, without poets seeing how alien and hostile it really was. It was regarded as the sign of a cultivated man, and such every poet wished to be. Apollonius must have felt that it gave richness and dignity to his story, but in the end it makes it arid and pedantic. Moreover, though he admired the old epic and hoped to rival it, he had no conception of how to construct a long poem. His *Argonautica* is episodic in the worst sense, and moves by awkward jerks from one scene to another, without any real development in the process. What counts with him is the care taken on the separate episodes, and in this he resembles Callimachus, who in his *Aitia* strung quite different themes together in sequence. Apollonius may not have been entirely wrong in trying to write a long poem, but he certainly wrote it in the wrong way.

The quality of Apollonius' episodes varies enormously. At one end of the scale he indulges a frivolous prettiness, which recalls some of the less successful examples of Hellenistic sculpture. When Aphrodite looks for her son, Eros, she finds him in a garden playing at knucklebones with the child Ganymede, whom he defeats by cheating. She chides him for taking advantage of a small boy and offers him instead a nice ball to play with. The prettiness looks all the worse when we remember that, when Anacreon gives knucklebones to Eros, they are turmoil and madness, and as such sinister and terrifying. Eros, who was in his day a formidable god, has now been reduced to an ill-mannered boy. But this taste for prettiness can do better than this. When Apollonius tells how the beautiful youth Hylas is dragged down into a pool by a nymph who has fallen in love with him, he does it very well, since his dramatic economy avoids any kind of false pathos and we witness the nymph's ruthless determination as she puts her arms round the boy who is stooping to get water. Apollonius is also capable of doing much more impressive things than this. He was in some sense the first romantic. He wished to create a world very unlike that which he knew and to make it a setting for strange and wonderful events. Jason's voyage provided an excellent field for these, and, though Apollonius misses too many opportunities, he rises finely to his most exciting challenge, when he tells how Jason sows the dragon's teeth and from them sprouts a crop of armed warriors whom he engages in battle and destroys. He falls on them like a shooting-star and the furrows are filled with blood as runnels are with water. Apollonius presents the weird scene very vividly and catches the brilliant light shining from the armour and weapons. This struggle bears no resemblance to a Homeric battlefield, but in its unearthly strangeness it is convincing and complete. Homer places much of the *Odyssey* in even stranger settings, but always with a realistic, factual touch, but Apollonius glories in the strangeness for its own sake, and it is this that makes him a pioneer of that kind of poetry which deals with remote and unfamiliar themes just because they break the laws of being as we know them and have for this reason a special charm.

But Apollonius' genius really deserves the name when he deals with love. What engages all his powers is, not Jason's love for Medea, on which he leaves us uninstructed, but Medea's love for Jason, and it is this which makes Book 3 of the *Argonautica* shine out above the other three. Medea is still a girl, and she falls passionately in love at first sight. When she sees Jason, he seems to be like Sirius rising from the ocean, and Apollonius, not without reminiscences from Sappho, tells how a mist covers her eyes, her cheeks burn like fire, her knees are too weak to move, and she feels rooted to the earth. When a little later she helps him in his ordeals to win the Fleece, the light playing on his yellow hair makes her ready to tear the life out of her breast for him, and her heart melts like dew on roses in the morning. When their love is fulfilled, Medea is entirely absorbed in him and ready to do anything for him, but when he plans to return to Greece and in his callous indifference is ready to leave her behind, then the fierce side of her nature comes out and she bursts into bitter re-monstrances with him, chiding him with his ingratitude for all that she has done. If he really means to desert her, she invokes disaster and ven-geance on him and prays that the Furies will make him homeless. Apollo-nius in this part of his poem tells one of the first surviving love-stories in the world. Love was indeed a topic of Greek tragedy, but the poets dwelt less on its magical allurements than on its dire results. Apollonius dwells on both, and it is not surprising that, when Virgil wrote of the tragic love of Dido for Aeneas, he borrowed wholesale from Apollonius, though his great queen is no mere girl like Medea. Love had already dis-placed heroic exploits as a favourite theme in Alexandria, but it seldom rings so powerfully as in Apollonius. We may suspect that Callimachus did not quite understand love on this scale and preferred a more calculating approach to it, and in this respect Apollonius is very much his superior. The theme of love found an honoured place in serious literature, and nothing was now likely to displace it. From Alexandria it passed to Rome, and from Rome to the Middle Ages and the modern world.

Though Callimachus was so nasty about Apollonius, he shared some of his faults. His antiquarian allusions are even more recondite, and, though his contemporaries, like modern scholars, may have felt pride and satis-faction in deciphering them, they do not usually add to the poetry and may interfere with its progress by distracting attention from it. Calli-machus indeed goes much further than Apollonius in his love of un-familiar information. His *Aitia* was largely concerned with titbits of local history and legend, such as the origins of Sicilian cities, and in his *Iambi* he dilated on the early history of the olive-tree and its place in religious cults. His enormous reading did not interfere with his high productivity, and he turned what he read to some purpose or other. In the isolated world of Alexandria he tried to strengthen links with the past by studying it from many angles, feeling perhaps that this would bring him closer to earlier poets. Culturally no doubt it did, but poetically the gain was less obvious. Even when they dealt with remote myths, the earlier Greeks had made them relevant to their own time and spoke for it, but Callimachus likes them for their remoteness and their oddity, and has not even Apollonius' excuse that he is dealing with strange places and is entitled to enhance their strangeness. On the other hand Callimachus controls his material in the sense that he does not spend too much time on any single theme. He likes to say something in a few, choice, unexpected words, and then to move to something else. He is conscious that his highly educated readers are liable to be bored, and he takes trouble that they shall not be, if only because he never says anything as anyone else would, and in Greek literature, with its strong sense of precedent, this was a new departure. Callimachus is a stylist who is always making experiments with his style, and, though he usually works with traditional metres, he gives even to these a new balance and rhythm through the order of his words and the placing of his stops at various points in the line. In this he is vastly more ingenious than Apollonius, and perhaps it was this that made him feel so superior.

The longest surviving poems by Callimachus are six Hymns, written for special, high occasions and each celebrating a god or goddess in connection with some holy rite or place. Though five of them are composed in hexameters, they have nothing in common with the Homeric Hymns. Instead of a straightforward, unquestioning approach to a god we find a complex construction which looks at him from various angles and, in the end, leaves us in the dark on what Callimachus' beliefs were. For a moment he seems to be near the heart of the matter when he says that Apollo's shrine shakes as the god approaches it, but makes no more of the theme, and, though he connects both Zeus and Apollo with morality and order, and Demeter with crops, the connections do not mean very much to him. Callimachus seems to have seen the gods through literature and art and to have been less interested in their reality for the religious consciousness. What really engages him are stories about them which he can embellish with his own ingenious novelties. The childhood of Zeus, the birth of Apollo on Delos, the visit of Artemis to the workshop of the Cyclopes, are what he enjoys, and on these he expends his power to startle and to entertain. This is his undisputed talent, and the more unusual his theme is, the more care he takes to get unexpected effects from it. Into his *Hymn to Demeter* he inserts the tale of Erysichthon, who earns the wrath of the goddess by felling a poplar in her sacred grove and then making light of it. She dooms him to an insatiable appetite. He cannot eat enough and grows thinner all the time. Callimachus deals gaily and handsomely with this bizarre situation. The whole household tries to satisfy Erysichthon without success, and his father sees himself ruined as the boy eats up his sheep and his cattle, but the remorseless process goes on:

> But the great wains gave up their mules; and next
> His mother's ox went down, the fatted ox
> She kept for Hestia; down the horses went,
> Winner and war-horse both; and last of all
> The cat whom little creatures shook to see.
> Now while the house of Triopas could provide,
> Only its chambers knew the plague within;
> But when it failed of plenty, gnawed bone-dry,
> The king's son at the cross-road sat and begged,
> Craving his orts and scullions' table-scraps.[4]

This is a cautionary tale, and Callimachus stops neatly at this point without telling the end. Though the moral is that Erysichthon suffers because he has defied Demeter, the story is neither solemn nor horrifying but fanciful and amusing.

Callimachus' taste for the unusual takes different forms. At times he is content merely to play down an ancient theme by relating it to common life. In the *Hymn to Artemis* he does this with some subtlety when Artemis and her maidens visit the forge of Hepaestus. Callimachus sets the forge inside the volcano of Stromboli and tells how the din from it makes Sicily and Corsica cry aloud. The stage could hardly be vaster, but horrific though the Cyclopes are as they lift their hammers and strike in rhythm, Callimachus suddenly changes his direction and says that whenever any child of the immortals is disobedient, his mother summons the Cyclopes and Hermes, who plays bogy to the child until she runs, with her hands on her eyes, to her mother's lap. It is whimsical and charming, but the grand note is suddenly muted, as if Callimachus did not like to sustain it for long. Yet Callimachus' spirit is strangely unpredictable, and at times he is capable of an almost magical effect. In *The Bath of Pallas* he tells how Athene and a companion were bathing in a fountain on Helicon, 'and it was the noontide hour, and a great quiet held the hill'.[5] The young Teiresias, thirsty with hunting, comes to the fountain and sees them, and since this is an intolerable affront to her, Athene in sinister tones asks him what god can have led him, 'who shall never take your eyes from here'.[6] At once night seizes his eyes, and he stands speechless, his knees glued with pain and his voice silent with helplessness. It is all done in a very few words and yet it is poignantly dramatic. Despite all the care which he took

Callimachus was not a good critic of his own work and did not see clearly where his best gifts lay. He might claim that he had brought to the gods a pure and undefiled stream of poetry, but it contained just the same kind of impurities as he lamented in Apollonius.

The third Alexandrian poet of his age made a much wiser assessment of his gifts than either Apollonius or Callimachus. Theocritus agreed with Callimachus that the long poem should not be attempted in modern conditions and had no patience with 'those cocks of the Muses who waste their labour with crowing against the bard of Chios'.[7] He composed on a small scale, and when his poems were called 'idylls' or 'little pictures', it showed the limits of his ambition. Within them he was capable of a considerable variety of temper and theme. When he chooses mythical subjects, he is not above taking them from Apollonius, but his account of Hylas and the nymph has a greater richness and the boxing-match between Amycus and Polydeuces is more robust and more realistic. In other mythical themes, such as the marriage of Helen and the childhood of Heracles, he avoids alike the occasional pomposity of Apollonius and the circuitous cleverness of Callimachus. His language, melodious and vivid but also firm and economical, meets all needs, and the apparently effortless flow of his lines must conceal a considerable effort of art. His adjustments to different subjects may seem superficial in the general brilliance of his performance, but they are well calculated and do just what is needed of them. He shares with Callimachus a taste for small, familiar details, but he absorbs them more easily into his narrative and does not let them draw too much attention to themselves. Theocritus wishes simply to give pleasure, and his myths do not convey lessons but provide delightful scenes for the imagination. He has the wisdom to see that antiquarianism adds nothing to them and seldom indulges in it. In the quarrel of the librarians he got the best out of each side and was content with it. This was by no means his most important achievement, but it illustrates the balanced outlook with which he set about writing a poetry suited to his age and its tastes. If they wanted old stories he was prepared to provide them but always in a shapely and attractive form with no concessions to pedantry.

Theocritus invented the pastoral idyll which has had so long and so varied a career in European literature. He was born in Syracuse, and, before he left it for Alexandria and the eastern Mediterranean, he seems to have been fascinated by the songs of the Sicilian countryside. Long before him Stesichorus had felt their claims and taken themes from them for his own art, and, though in Theocritus' time the Sicilian peasants were already on the way to become a poverty-stricken proletariat, they still had their own traditional songs in which love played a lively part. Here was a recondite world which could be adapted to sophisticated tastes without any affectation or falseness, and in it Theocritus found a source for his most successful poetry. He knew enough of the Doric dialect of Sicily to write in a reasonable imitation of it, and, in transforming folk-songs into his delicate Idylls, he gave his contemporaries a poetry of escape from the city and a return to a more natural and far less complex existence. His shepherds are still occupied with their immemorial duties but they do not complain about hardships, which do not exist in so imaginary a world, and have plenty of time for song. Theocritus builds up a 'sweet, especial, rural scene', sets his shepherds in it, and makes them sing. Many of the Idylls are concerned with love, as no doubt their Sicilian prototypes were, and, though at times it may be painful, it is soon translated into lucent and delightful song. It infuses alike a singing-match between two shepherds and the gaiety of a harvest-home. Even when Theocritus takes up an ancient legend about Daphnis, who must have been a kind of year-god, he scales it down to a touching and not too disturbing pathos. These songs look perfectly simple, and we need not suspect that the shepherds who talk about them are disguised versions of Theocritus and his friends talking about their poetry. Once indeed Theocritus allows his own views on the long poem to be ascribed to a shepherd called Lycidas, but this is probably no more than a topical allusion brought in to titillate curiosity. The beauty of Theocritus' world is that it is complete and consistent and that we feel no need to look for ulterior meanings. Theocritus loved the country, as Callimachus may not have done, and knew it from his boyhood in Sicily and from the years which he spent in Cos. He was not unique in feeling its charm but in the Idyll he found for it a form which kept it unspoiled by brutal facts.

Theocritus must have seen that the pastoral Idyll had its limitations; for he explored other regions quite unrelated to it and found themes which brought out quite different powers in him. His masterpiece is perhaps Idyll 2, a tense, dramatic monologue, in which a woman conducts a magical rite to win back the lover who has left her. As she turns her magic wheel to regain him and melts a waxen image of him that he may waste with love for her, she tells her story and her misery. Theocritus enters with complete understanding into her anxious, brooding, ruthless spirit. She is dealing with dark powers of the night, with Hecate and with the Moon, and these are far more real than any grand gods. To them she describes her own terrible distress in sharp contrast with the silence of the wind and the sea. She both loves and hates her man, wishes him both back and broken. The first part of the poem is especially concerned with the magical rite, and the detailed account of it is punctuated by the recurring refrain

My magic wheel, draw the man I love to my house

and the second half tells the story in secret confidence to the Moon:

Mark, lady Moon, how this love came unto me.

Through the two halves there is a rising excitement which is quenched only when the rite is finished. In this poem Theocritus explores the underworld of Alexandria and finds himself splendidly at home in it. Totally dissimilar in tone but not in actuality is Idyll 15, which consists largely of a dialogue between two women who go to watch Queen Arsinoe as she celebrates the feast of Adonis. The tone of their talk is cheerful and gossipy, and the main episodes are of a delightfully trivial character – the leaving of the baby at home, horses from the cavalry-stables going to the races, the crush round the doors of the temple. Then a contrast comes with the hymn about Adonis, which is elaborate and highly decorated in the true Alexandrian manner. Theocritus marks the difference between the world of every day and that of religion, but it is the first that wins the honours.

Though in this poem Theocritus keeps his usual metre, his language is unashamedly conversational, and all the better for that reason. He is concerned, not with a myth or with shepherds' songs, but with a form of art which had some history behind it. The mime was as old as Epicharmus and played a part in the development of Attic comedy, but it had also its own life. In Sicily it presented scenes from every day and depicted typical actions in the lives of typical men and women. Sophron (c 470–400 BC), who was much admired by Plato, put new life into it, and was certainly known to Theocritus. But in Alexandria the mime was taken up and given some new turns by Herodas, who was more or less a contemporary of the Alexandrian poets. Eight mimes from him survive. They are all short, and all written in an iambic metre which deliberately moves at a halting pace to resemble ordinary talk. The subjects are taken from relatively low circles and are by no means lacking in dramatic interest. An old woman fails to persuade a young woman to give her affections to a young athlete. A nasty, unctuous pimp defends himself in court on a charge of trying to abduct a girl. A mother takes her son to a schoolmaster to be flogged. A woman and her maid carry offerings to the temple of Asclepius, and, while the mistress is brusque and impatient, the maid is lost in admiration at the statues. A woman, furious at the infidelity of her slave-paramour, orders him to be flogged, and then has him fetched back for branding, but is wheedled out of it by her maid. Two women talk together with an agreeable cynicism. A well-to-do lady introduces customers to her shoe-maker, who receives them with a nice mixture of servility and truculence. A farmer dreams that his goat has been torn to pieces by worshippers of Dionysus, and then wins the prize. This last is certainly a parable of Herodas' own work, but in general he depicts with a discerning realism the seamier side of Alexandria and derives a quiet humour from it. The Alexandrians matched their learned interest in the past with a lively curiosity about the present. This was not very exalted or inspiring, but it was at least human and amusing, and Herodas is within his limits quite a skilful artist, who chooses his words with care and often gives them an unexpected twist.

Of these Alexandrian poets Theocritus is without question the most accomplished and the most gifted. His command of sentiment, even of passion, his keen eye for natural things, his economy and restraint, his skill in adapting his manner to fresh themes, all deserve the renown which he has always enjoyed. Yet he too moves in a limited world. No doubt, like Callimachus, he would like to write impressively about the gods, but the Hymn on Adonis in Idyll 2 suggests that this was rather beyond his reach and, when either of them ventures into public affairs in praise of Ptolemy, we see how much was lost by the free Greek spirit when it yielded to an imitation of Egyptian theocracy. Callimachus may say:

> From Zeus come kings; nothing is more divine
> Than are the kings of Zeus,[8]

and Theocritus may begin a substantial poem:

> Of men let Ptolemy be named alike
> First, last, and midst, for he is best of men.[9]

We can hardly accuse the poets of insincerity, for they may well have meant what they said; but they cannot have felt it very deeply and were presumably moved to it because their own existence depended on that of absolute monarchy. The abundant praise showered on Ptolemy has little human content and illustrates how the old concern with public affairs has abdicated its responsibilities and surrendered to paternal care. It reflects the shrunken outlook which followed the death of Alexander and the decay of the old free institutions. Poets could not fail to be less adventurous, and, though they tried to compensate for this by a finer attention to the details of their technique, nothing could restore the spaciousness which they had lost and now ceased to desire. The change from Athens to Alexandria was a change from large to limited themes, which might indeed be presented in new and attractive forms but were none the less restricted by the poet's own taste, inspired by his own longings, and divorced alike from public affairs and from any questions about man's place in the universe or his relations with the gods. What kept the poets going was the example of the past, and from it they learned that literature should be treated with the utmost seriousness. But their circumstances forbade that they should write with the generous vision of their predecessors, and they had to find new sources of poetry in their own much narrower lives.

In addition to their longer poems both Callimachus and Theocritus wrote short elegiac epigrams on themes which did not call for any spacious handling but caught some vivid perception or moment or sentiment in a short compass. The elegiac epigram had originally been used mainly for inscriptions on tombs or for dedications in temples and had in its concentrated economy achieved noble and impressive results. But at some time before the flowering of Alexandrian literature it had been turned to new purposes. Plato in his youth seems to have led the way by writing short poems about love, but the love of which he spoke was not his own but ascribed to the same older generation as that about which he wrote his dialogues. Nor was love the only or the main theme of these poems. Some poets of limited but authentic gifts found a new delight and charm in the age-old sights of the countryside. Anyte of Tegea, who seems to have flourished about 300 BC, writes about a goat which boys have fitted with reins and drive around a temple, a shepherd who puts out gifts to Pan and the Nymphs because they have given him water, a statue of Hermes on the edge of an orchard by the sea-shore. At about the same date Addaeus tells of an old ox released from the plough and set free to graze in the deep grass, and Simmias of a partridge which used to decoy birds and is now dead. This slender, unambitious art seems to have established itself before Alexandria held the stage, but it did not pass unnoticed. It could be turned to many purposes, including the finer points of personal relations. Apollonius indeed seems to have avoided it, and his only known epigram is a sharp couplet in which he calls Callimachus 'an offscouring, a toy, a blockhead',[10] and perhaps he had cause for doing so. But Callimachus, who wrote a number of epigrams, sometimes used them for themes simpler than his usual kind and certainly more human and more revealing. His lines on his dead friend Heraclitus, 'whose nightingales are still living' has had a wide currency and is both touching and sincere, though perhaps less disturbing than the stabbing pathos of a couplet on a father burying his twelve-year-old son, 'his great hope'. Less effective are his poems on his own wayward loves and his moments of rancour and contempt, but even these gain something by being kept within narrow limits. Theocritus also uses the form sometimes to supplement his Idylls with miniatures of rural life, sometimes to provide imaginary epitaphs on poets whom he admires, but most successfully for purely personal matters as when he writes on the tomb of his friend Eusthenes, a physiognomer 'skilled to tell the character from the eye',[11] or for a dedication of a tripod by a choir-master, who was 'wise in all his ways'.[12] Such short pieces record moments keenly felt which might have gained very little if they had been expanded but in their neat brevity make their own effect.

The elegiac epigram was to survive for another eight hundred years and is certainly the most lively and most accomplished form of later Greek poetry. Just because it does not aim at very much but takes great trouble with its themes it is well suited to a world which found compensation for lost magnificence in the multifarious spectacles and sentiments of ordinary existence. But the heyday of Alexandrian poetry is the last chapter of Greek literature in the strict sense, if it is not already a postscript or an aftermath. The Greeks continued to write under their Hellenistic kings and then under Roman rule. They produced a noble historian in Polybius, distinguished philosophers in the tradition of Plato, orators versed in all the devices of argument and display, novelists who found romance in fantastic improbabilities, and satirists to whom nothing was sacred, and even in the fourth and fifth centuries AD poets who laboriously struggled to revive the epic. But this was another world. The strength of Greek literature in its great days was its intimate connection with a whole living society, its encompassing gods and its passionate sense of human worth. When the Greeks lost their independence, whether personal or local or national, something went out of them for ever. They kept their bright intelligence, their meticulous craftsmanship, their eager eye for beauty in persons or things, but they never recovered the fine confidence which enabled them to face the darkest issues with a courageous honesty and to enjoy the glorious gifts of the gods whenever, no matter how unexpectedly, they received them and knew that all was well.

NOTES

CHAPTER 2 HEROIC SONG

1 *Iliad* 9.189
2 ibid. 5.304; 12.449; 20.287
3 ibid. 3.158
4 *Odyssey* 10.113
5 *Iliad* 6.208
6 ibid. 21.101–7
7 ibid. 23.103–4
8 *Odyssey* 11.489–91
9 *Iliad* 6.429–30
10 *Odyssey* 11.198–203
11 *Iliad*. 6.357–8
12 *Odyssey* 8.579–80

CHAPTER 3 THE EMERGENCE OF PERSONALITY

1 Homeric Hymn 3.165–75
2 P.Friedländer and H.B.Hoffleit, *Epigrammata*, p. 54, no. 53.
3 First published by G.Büchner and C.F.Russo, Accademia Nazionale dei Lincei, *Rendiconti*, 1955, pp. 215 ff
4 P.Friedländer and H.B.Hoffleit, *Epigrammata*, p. 38, no. 35
5 ibid. p. 49, no. 46
6 ibid. p. 10, no. 2
7 ibid. p. 29, no. 25
8 Hesiod, *Theogony*, 26–8
9 Ibid. *Works and Days*, 288–91
10 ibid. 210–11
11 Archilochus, fragment 1
12 ibid. fragment 53
13 ibid. fragment 51.48
14 Pindar, *Pythian*, 2.54–6
15 Archilochus, fragment 94
16 Semonides, fragment 7.27–40, translated by Gilbert Highet
17 Callinus, fragment 3
18 ibid. fragment 1.18–21
19 Tyrtaeus, fragment 6.1–4
20 Solon, fragment 13
21 ibid. fragment 20
22 Mimnermus, fragment 1.1–3
23 *Iliad* 6.146
24 Theognis, 869–72
25 ibid. 425–8

CHAPTER 4 LYRIC SONG

1 Alcman, fragment 1.16–17
2 Stesichorus, fragment 192
3 Alcaeus, fragment 348
4 ibid. fragment 45.1–3
5 ibid. fragment 34.9–12
6 ibid. fragment 319
7 Sappho, fragment 16.1–4
8 ibid. fragment 1.21–4
9 ibid. fragment 114
10 ibid. fragment 136
11 ibid. fragment 130
12 ibid. fragment 132

13 ibid. fragments 49; 1.14; 2.89
14 Alcaeus, fragment 384
15 Ibycus, fragment 282.23–6
16 ibid. fragment 286
17 Anacreon, fragment 361
18 ibid. fragment 395.7–12
19 Scolia Attica, no. 7
20 Chor. adespot., fragment 1018
21 Simonides, fragment 567
22 Simonides, fragment 594
23 ibid. fragment 521
24 ibid. fragment 543
25 ibid. fragment 92
26 ibid. fragment 542.34–40

27 ibid. fragment 581
28 Bacchylides, 3.53–6
29 ibid. 5.151–4
30 ibid. 16.30–34
31 Pindar, *Olympian*, 1.1–6
32 ibid. *Pythian*, 1.86
33 ibid. *Nemean*, 8.32–4
34 ibid. *Olympian*, 6.55–6
35 ibid. *Pythian*, 4.82–5
36 ibid. *Nemean*, 10.67–72
37 ibid. *Pythian*, 1.1–12
38 ibid. *Olympian*, 1.52–3
39 ibid. *Olympian*, 2.71–4
40 ibid. *Pythian*, 8.95–7

CHAPTER 5   THE TRAGIC VISION

1 Heraclitus, fragment 119
2 Aeschylus, *Libation-bearers*, 900–2, translated by George Thomson
3 ibid. *Seven against Thebes*, 689–91
4 ibid. *Agamemnon*, 31–3, translated by George Thomson
5 ibid. 1327–9
6 ibid. 1388–92, translated by George Thomson
7 ibid. 958
8 Aeschylus, *Prometheus Bound*, 88–92
9 ibid. *Libation-bearers*, 755–7, translated by George Thomson.
10 *Oxyrhynchus Papyri*, 2161, col. ii, 6–11
11 Aeschylus, *Eumenides*, 996–1002, translated by George Thomson
12 Quoted by Plutarch, *De Profectibus in Virtute*, 7
13 Quoted by Athenaeus, 1.22a
14 Sophocles, *Women of Trachis*, 1278

15 Aristotle, *Poetics*, 1452 a 30
16 Sophocles, fragment 846
17 ibid. *Antigone*, 450–2
18 ibid. *King Oedipus*, 1071–2
19 ibid. *Electra*, 1224–6, translated by J. T. Sheppard
20 ibid. *Oedipus at Colonus*, 1627–8
21 ibid. *King Oedipus*, 738
22 ibid. *Women of Trachis*, 547–9
23 ibid. *Philoctetes*, 806
24 ibid. *Electra*, 1194
25 ibid. *Women of Trachis*, 920–2
26 ibid. *Oedipus at Colonus*, 607–13
27 ibid. 1242–49
28 Euripides, *Hippolytus*, 1441
29 ibid. *Heracles*, 1341–6, translated by Gilbert Murray.
30 ibid. *Trojan Women*, 884–8
31 ibid. *Suppliant Women*, 216–18
32 Aristotle, *Poetics*, 1453 a 30

CHAPTER 6   FROM MYTH TO SCIENCE

1 Xenophanes, fragment 24
2 Empedocles, fragment 112.4
3 Anaximenes, fragment 1
4 Heraclitus, fragment 60
5 ibid. fragment 52
6 ibid. fragment 62
7 Hecataeus, fragment 1

8 Herodotus, *Proem*.
9 ibid. 5.9.3
10 ibid. 3.80.1
11 ibid. 8.94.4
12 ibid. 2.121.5
13 ibid. 6.129.4
14 ibid. 8.41.2

15 ibid. 1.32.1
16 Anaximander, fragment 1
17 Heraclitus, fragment 94
18 Herodotus 1.8.1
19 ibid. 1.107.1
20 ibid. 7.213.1
21 ibid. 3.80.5
22 ibid.7.104.4
23 ibid. 3.52.5
24 ibid. 3.119.6
25 ibid. 7.162.1
26 ibid. 2.35.2
27 ibid. 1.136.2
28 ibid. 2.37.2
29 ibid. 8.3.1
30 ibid. 5.66.1
31 ibid. 6.131.2
32 Thucydides 1.1.1. All translations from Thucydides are by Rex Warner
33 ibid. 1.22.4
34 ibid. 1.22.4

35 Democritus, fragment 119
36 Thucydides 3.82.4
37 ibid. 1.138.3
38 ibid. 6.72.2
39 ibid. 7.86.5
40 ibid. 5.105.2
41 ibid. 2.64.5–6
42 ibid. 2.65.8
43 ibid. 1.23.6
44 ibid. 1.22.1
45 ibid. 1.70.9
46 ibid. 1.144.1
47 ibid. 2.40.1
48 ibid. 2.43.3
49 ibid. 4.86.6
50 ibid. 6.92.4
51 ibid. 7.77.7
52 ibid. 8.68.1
53 Plutarch, *Pericles* 8
54 Thucydides 4.14.3
55 ibid. 7.87.5–6

CHAPTER 7   THE ANTIDOTE OF COMEDY

1 Thucydides 8.73.3
2 Aristophanes, *Clouds*, 275–90
3 ibid. *Birds*, 244–9

4 ibid. *Knights*, 197–201, translated by B.B.Rogers
5 I Corinthians, 13.23

CHAPTER 8   THE DRAMA OF PHILOSOPHY

1 Protagoras, fragment 1
2 Gorgias, fragment 3
3 Protagoras, fragment 4
4 Plato, *Apology*, 42
5 ibid. *Phaedo*, 118 a
6 ibid. *Epist.* 314 c
7 Aristotle, fragment 73

8 Plato, *Georgias*, 492 d 2
9 ibid. 471 c 8
10 ibid. 527 e 5
11 Plato, *Phaedrus*, 274 e 6
12 ibid. *Laws*, 7.803 b 3
13 ibid. *Epist.* 5.332 a 8

CHAPTER 9   DEBATE AND DISPLAY

1 *Iliad*, 9.443
2 Tyrtaeus, fragment 8.8
3 Thucydides 1.138.3
4 Plutarch, *Themistocles*, 29
5 Eupolis, fragment 94, 6–8
6 See above p. 201
7 Aristotle, *Rhetoric*, 1402 a 17

8 Gorgias, fragment 6.15–16
9 Antiphon 3.2.10
10 ibid. 2.2.9
11 ibid. 5.8
12 Andocides, *On the Mysteries*, 63
13 ibid. 57
14 Andocides, fragment 45

15 ibid. *On the Mysteries*, 99
16 Lysias, *Against Eratosthenes*, 5
17 ibid. 7
18 Plato, *Phaedrus*, 279 a.
19 Dionysius, *On Style*, 23
20 Isocrates, *On the Antidosis*, 181
21 *On the Sublime*, 279 a
22 Demosthenes, *On the Crown*, 169
23 ibid. *Olynthiac*, 2.10, translated by Gilbert Murray

24 Ibid. *On the Crown*, 324
25 ibid. 262
26 ibid. 296
27 Aeschines, *On the False Embassy*, 16
28 ibid. 34
29 ibid. 79
30 Aeschines, *Against Ctesiphon*, 134
31 Hyperides, fragment 80
32 Lycurgus, *Against Leocrates*, 150

CHAPTER 10   THE SHRINKING HORIZON

1 Cleanthes, fragment 1.6–13, translated by M. Balkwill
2 Erinna, fragment 1.28–30
3 Callimachus, fragment 465
4 ibid. Hymn 5.107–15. Translated by T. F. Higham
   The word rendered by 'cat' is uncertain, and perhaps the right version is 'gray-tailed horse', but in that case it is not clear what the 'small creatures' are.

5 ibid. Hymn 5.74–5
6 ibid. 80
7 Theocritus 7.47–8
8 Callimachus, Hymn 1.79–80
9 Theocritus 17.1–2
10 Apollonius, fragment 13
11 Theocritus, epigram 11
12 ibid. 12

SUGGESTIONS FOR FURTHER

READING

OUT of the vast number of books and articles on Greek literature mention is made here only of a few which may be found useful, notably translations, mostly in prose, and critical studies. Nothing is said of books in languages other than English or on purely technical points of scholarship.

CHAPTER 1

H.J.Rose, *A Handbook of Greek Literature* (1937); Gilbert Murray, *Ancient Greek Literature*[3] (1907); C.M.Bowra, *Ancient Greek Literature* (1933); R.W.Livingstone, *The Greek Genius and its Meaning to Us*[2] (1915); W.Jaeger, *Paideia*, 3 vols (1939–44); F.R.Earp, *The Way of the Greeks* (1929); A.W.Gomme, *The Greek Attitude to Poetry and History* (1954). History: J.B.Bury, *History of Greece* (1951); N.G.L.Hammond, *History of Greece* (1959); Chester G.Starr, *The Origins of Greek Civilisation* (1961).

CHAPTER 2

Translations: E. V. Rieu, *Odyssey* (Penguin, 1946); *Iliad* (Penguin, 1950). Homeric question, analytical: G. Murray, *The Rise of the Greek Epic*[4] (1934); D.L.Page, *The Homeric Odyssey* (1955). 'Unitarian': A.Lang, *Homer and the Epic* (1893), *The World of Homer* (1910); J.A.Scott, *The Unity of Homer* (1921); J.T.Sheppard, *The Pattern of the Iliad* (1922); C.M.Bowra, *Tradition and Design in the Iliad* (1930). Formulaic structure: M.Parry, 'Studies in the Epic Technique of Oral Verse-making' in *Harvard Studies in Classical Philology*, xli (1930) and xliii (1932). Archaeological background: H.L.Lorimer, *Homer and the Monuments* (1950). Style and Technique: W.J.Woodhouse, *The Composition of Homer's Odyssey* (1930); S.E.Bassett, *The Poetry of Homer* (1938). Development to Homer: M.Nilsson, *Homer and Mycenae* (1933); T.B.L.Webster, *From Mycenae to Homer* (1958); C.H.Whitman, *Homer and the Heroic Tradition* (1958); C.S.Kirk, *The Songs of Homer* (1962). Historical background: D.L.Page, *History and the Homeric Iliad* (1959). Troy: W.Leaf, *Troy* (1912); C.W.Blegen,

272

Troy and the Trojans (1963). Ithaca: W.Leaf, Homer and History (1915); R.Rodd, Homer's Ithaca (1927). General: A.J.B.Wace, A Companion to Homer (1962).

CHAPTER 3

Translations: Evelyn White, Homeric Hymns, Hesiod (Loeb, 1914); early inscriptions, P.Friedländer and H.B.Hoffleit, Epigrammata (1948); Archilochus, Semonides, Callinus, Tyrtaeus, Solon, Mimnermus, Theognis: J. M. Edmonds, Elegy and Iambus I (Loeb, 1930).
Hesiod: A.R.Burn, The Age of Hesiod (1936); F.Solmsen, Hesiod and Aeschylus (1949). Elegists: C.M.Bowra, Early Greek Elegists (1938). Solon: I.M.Linforth, Solon the Athenian (1919); K.Freeman, The Work and Life of Solon (1926). Theognis: E.Harrison, Studies in Theognis (1902); D. Young, Borrowings and self-adaptations in Theognis (1964); T.W.Allen, Theognis (1934).

CHAPTER 4

Translations: J.M.Edmonds, Lyra Graeca, I-III (Loeb, 1922–7, with somewhat fanciful text); R. Lattimore, Pindar (1959); R. Fagles, Bacchylides (1961).
General: C.M.Bowra, Greek Lyric Poetry² (1961); A.E.Burn, The Lyric Age of Greece (1960). Sappho and Alcaeus: D.L.Page, Sappho and Alcaeus (1955). Pindar: L. R. Farnell, The Works of Pindar, I (1930); G.Norwood, Pindar (1945); J.H.Finley, Pindar and Aeschylus (1955); C.M.Bowra, Pindar (1964).

CHAPTER 5

Translations (verse): D.Grene and R.Lattimore (editors), The Complete Greek Tragedies (1959).
General: A. E. Haigh, Tragic Drama of the Greeks (1896); G. Norwood, Greek Tragedy (1920); H.D.F.Kitto, Greek Tragedy (1939); A.W.Pickard-Cambridge, revised by T.B.L.Webster, Dithyramb, Tragedy, and Comedy² (1962).
Theatre, production: R.C.Flickinger, The Greek Theater and its Drama² (1936); M.Bieber, History of the Greek and Roman Theater² (1961); A.W.Pickard-Cambridge, The Theatre of Dionysus in Athens (1946), The Dramatic Festivals of Athens (1953); P.Arnott, Greek Scenic Conventions (1962).
Aeschylus: H.W.Smyth, Aeschylus (1924); G.Murray, Aeschylus (1940); W.B.Stanford, Aeschylus in his Style (1942); F. R. Earp, The Style of Aeschylus (1948); G. Thomson, Aeschylus and Athens² (1948); E.T.Owen, The Harmony of Aeschylus (1952).
Sophocles: T.B.L.Webster, Introduction to Sophocles (1936); C.M.Bowra, Sophoclean Tragedy; F.E.Earp, The Style of Sophocles (1944); C.H.Whitman, Sophocles (1951); R.F.Goheen, The Imagery of Sophocles' Antigone (1951); A.J.A.Waldock, Sophocles the Dramatist (1951): J.S.Opstelten, Sophocles and

Greek Pessimism (1952); V.Ehrenberg, *Sophocles and Pericles* (1954); H.D.F. Kitto, *Sophocles, Dramatist and Philosopher* (1958).
Euripides: G. Murray, *Euripides and his Age* (1913); G.M.A.Grube, *The Drama of Euripides* (1941); R.P.Winnington-Ingram, *Euripides and Dionysus* (1948); L.H.Greenwood, *Aspects of Euripidean Tragedy* (1953); G.Zuntz, *The Political Plays of Euripides* (1955).
General: John Jones, *On Aristotle and Greek Tragedy* (1962).

CHAPTER 6

Translations: A.de Sélincourt, *Herodotus, the Histories* (Penguin, 1954); R. Warner, *Thucydides, History of the Peloponnesian War* (Penguin, 1954).
General: J.B.Bury, *The Ancient Greek Historians* (1909); L. Pearson, *The Early Ionian Historians* (1939).
Herodotus: J.Wells, *Studies in Herodotus* (1923); T.R.Glover, *Herodotus* (1924); W.Spiegelberg, *The Credibility of Herodotus' Description of Egypt* (1927); J.A.K. Thomson, *The Art of the Logos* (1933); J.E.Powell, *The History of Herodotus* (1939); J.L.Myres, *Herodotus, Father of History* (1955).
Thucydides: F.M.Cornford, *Thucydides Mythistoricus* (1907); G.F.Abbott, *Thucydides: a Study in Political Reality* (1925); B.W.Henderson, *The Great War between Athens and Sparta* (1927); C. N. Cochrane, *Thucydides and the Science of History* (1929); J.H.Finley, *Thucydides* (1942); G.B.Grundy, *Thucydides and the History of his Age,*[2] 2 vols (1948); F.E.Adcock, *Thucydides and his History* (1963).

CHAPTER 7

Translation (verse): B.B.Rogers, *The Comedies of Aristophanes,*[2] 6 vols (1910–19).
General: F.M.Cornford, *The Origin of Attic Comedy* (1914).
Aristophanes: G. Murray, *Aristophanes* (1933); V.Ehrenberg, *The People of Aristophanes*[2] (1951); C.H.Whitman, *Aristophanes and the Comic Hero* (1964).
Menander: T.B.L.Webster, *Studies in Menander* (1950).

CHAPTER 8

Translation: B.Jowett, *The Dialogues of Plato*, revised ed. 4 vols (1953).
General: J. Burnet, *Early Greek Philosophy*[2] (1908), *Greek Philosophy: Thales to Plato* (1914); W. Jaeger, *The Theology of the Early Greek Philosophers* (1947); W.K.C.Guthrie, *A History of Greek Philosophy*, I (1962).
Plato: A.E.Taylor, *Plato* (1933); P.Shorey, *What Plato Said* (1933); W.F.R. Hardie, *A Study in Plato* (1936); F.Solmsen, *Plato's Theology* (1942); H.W.B. Joseph, *Knowledge and the Good in Plato's Republic* (1948); W.D.Ross, *Plato's Theory of Ideas* (1951); R.B.Levinson, *In Defense of Plato* (1953); J. Gould, *Plato's Ethics* (1955); I.M.Crombie, *An Examination of Plato's Doctrines*, 2 vols (1962–3).

CHAPTER 9

Translations: Antiphon, Andocides: K.J.Maidment, *Minor Attic Orators*, I (Loeb, 1941); Lysias: W.R.M.Lamb, *Lysias* (Loeb, 1930); Isocrates: G.Norlin, *Isocrates*, I (Loeb, 1928), II (1929), L.VanHook, *Isocrates*, III (Loeb, 1945). Aeschines: C.D.Adams, *The Speeches of Aeschines* (Loeb, 1919); Demosthenes; A.W.Pickard-Cambridge, *The Public Orations of Demosthenes*, 2 vols (1912). General: R.C.Jebb, *The Attic Orators*² (1893); J.F.Dobson, *The Greek Orators* (1919); A.W.Pickard-Cambridge, *Demosthenes and the Last Days of Greek Freedom* (1914); W.Jaeger, *Demosthenes: the Origin and Growth of his Policy* (1938).

CHAPTER 10

Translations: R.S.Seaton, *Apollonius Rhodius* (Loeb, 1912); A.W.Mair, *Callimachus* (Loeb, 1921); C. Trypanis, *Callimachus; fragments* (Loeb, 1958); A.S.F.Gow, *Theocritus*, I (1950); W.Headlam and A.D.Knox, *Herodas* (1922). General: J.W.Mackail, *Select Epigrams from the Greek Anthology* (1911); A.Couat, *Alexandrian Poetry* (1931); A.Körte, *Hellenistic Poetry* (1929); F.A. Wright, *A History of Later Greek Literature* (1932).

INDEX

Index

Index